FOREIGN NATIVE

Also by RW Johnson

African Perspectives (ed. with Christopher Allen) (1970)
How Long Will South Africa Survive? (1977)
The Long March of the French Left (1981)
Shootdown: The Verdict on KAL 007 (1983)
The Politics of Recession (1985)
Heroes and Villains: Selected Essays (1990)
*Launching Democracy in South Africa: The First
Open Election, April 1994*
(ed. with Lawrence Schlemmer) (1996)
Ironic Victory: Liberalism in Post-Liberation South Africa
(ed. with David Welsh) (1998)
South Africa: The First Man, the Last Nation (2004)
*South Africa's Brave New World: The Beloved Country since
the End of Apartheid* (2010)
*The African University? The Critical Case of South Africa and
the Tragedy at the UKZN* (2012)
Look Back in Laughter: Oxford's Post-War Golden Age (2015)
How Long Will South Africa Survive? The Crisis Continues
(first edition 2015; second edition 2017)
Fighting for the Dream (2019)

FOREIGN NATIVE

An African Journey

RW JOHNSON

Jonathan Ball Publishers

Johannesburg · Cape Town · London

Published in South Africa in 2020 by
JONATHAN BALL PUBLISHERS
A division of Media24 (Pty) Ltd
PO Box 33977
Jeppestown
2043

ISBN 978-1-86842-771-0
ebook ISBN 978-1-86842-772-7

Every effort has been made to trace the copyright holders and to obtain
their permission for the use of copyright material. The publishers
apologise for any errors or omissions and would be grateful to be
notified of any corrections that should be incorporated in future
editions of this book.

www.jonathanball.co.za
Twitter: www.twitter.com/JonathanBallPub
Facebook: www.facebook.com/JonathanBallPublishers

Cover by publicide
Design and typesetting by Catherine Coetzer
Set in Adobe Garamond Pro

Printed by **novus print**, a division of Novus Holdings

For Irina

CONTENTS

Preface

A number of people have played a key part in the genesis of this book. Back in 2015, thanks in large part to encouragement and help from two former Oxford students, John Winckler and Timothy May, I wrote and published a memoir of my time in Oxford – *Look Back in Laughter: Oxford's Post-War Golden Age* (London: Threshold Press, 2015). This proved quite successful and I wondered whether my South African publisher, Jonathan Ball, might be interested in bringing out a South African edition. Jonathan read the book and liked it, but felt that Oxford was too far away from the usually more parochial concerns of South African readers. However, he and Jonathan Ball's publishing director, Jeremy Boraine, suggested that it might be a good idea to carry the story forward and write about my time in Africa.

As with the book on Oxford, I have to caution the reader that this is not an autobiography. I do not regard my personal life as being of any general interest. What is far more interesting about almost all lives is the people and events one encountered on one's journey through, so to speak. My old Oxford tutor, Thomas Hodgkin, used to say that the main point of life – any life, but certainly his – was to observe history. But often in order to understand history one has to do it in the way that Richard Cobb – *l'incroyable Cobb*, as the French used to call him – illuminated French history by writing about many characters who may have seemed obscure or marginal but whose lives nonetheless reflected key aspects of the times they lived through. In South Africa the greatest exponent of the Cobb method has been Charles van Onselen. I would not compare myself with him but I have, nonetheless, tried to follow the same method, often writing about characters who are not household names but whose lives have deepened my own understanding and appreciation of the history we all lived through together. The reader will have to judge whether this is a good idea or not.

I should explain the book's title. Jeremy Lawrence, in his biography of his father, Harry Lawrence, a notable figure in the liberal tradition in South Africa, explained how his father held a 'surgery' every Saturday for residents of his working-class constituency, Salt River, in Cape Town. Anyone with a problem came along to seek Harry's help, and because he was known as a liberal, there was always a large queue of Africans at his door. They could not vote but Harry did his best for them. Many were black South Africans having difficulties with the apartheid pass laws which tried to restrict the number of blacks allowed into the cities. This was problem enough, Jeremy Lawrence writes, but it was quite eclipsed by the even larger number of black migrants from all the countries surrounding South Africa who had come in search of work. They had entered the country illegally and had no papers, so their problems were legion. This, in a perfect example of apartheid double-speak, was referred to as 'the problem of the foreign natives'. I have always felt that the 'foreign natives' include me, for I was born in England, came out to South Africa as a child, have both British and South African passports, and have spent my life coming and going between the two countries, spending roughly half my life in each of them. So although I came back to live in South Africa and love the country, I have always felt – and been made to feel – that I only sort of belong here. That is okay with me: I am happy as a foreign native.

Once again, as with the Oxford book, Timothy May performed the sterling service of editing my writing very closely. Everyone always needs to be edited and I was more than lucky to have Tim. To Jonathan Ball and Jeremy Boraine I owe the idea for the book but I am also indebted, for their comments on the draft, to both John Winckler and Belinda Walker. My wife, Irina, as always, read every word and was often my toughest critic. I am extremely grateful to her and the dedication of the book to her is but poor recompense. As usual, of course, I must accept entire responsibility for the work. This book is indeed rather like my life in that all the mistakes are mine, not anybody else's.

RW Johnson
Cape Town
January 2020

CHAPTER ONE

Northlands

'Maah boy, you gonna have to lurn Afrikaans, maah boy.'

I heard this refrain many times at this strange new school. It seemed like just one more threatening aspect of my new environment. A week earlier – this was May 1957 – I had been in St Anselm's, a Catholic school in Birkenhead, England. That had, on any reckoning, been bad enough. The Christian Brothers were brutal, wielding huge leather straps with whalebone centres against those in their charge. But this new South African school – Northlands Boys' High in Durban – was populated with boys a good head taller than anything I was used to. Everyone was very tanned – it was a beach culture. It was, allegedly, winter and thus the rugby season but I, with my lily-white skin, kept getting sunburnt while playing and the rugby pitch was so hard that it took a hammer to drive a nail into it. Getting tackled on that was like being tackled on concrete.

It all felt completely wrong. In addition, I had a strong Merseyside accent, which was mercilessly mocked, and my bright red hair led to the persecution that redheads have to treat as normal. On Merseyside I had not stuck out so much. From my earliest days I had been told that redheads had violent tempers. Everyone wanted to test this hypothesis by trying every provocation imaginable. It was vital to maintain an icy calm whatever the circumstances. I got a lot of practice at that.

I knew I faced at least two years of this. My father had served 18 years as an engineer on oil tankers. During the war he had twice been torpedoed and had spent a lot of time in open boats on the Atlantic. He longed for a shore job that would enable him to see more of his family. When President Nasser closed the Suez Canal, all oil tankers had to go round the Cape of Good Hope instead. So Mobil Oil decided that they needed a dry dock and reprovisioning base in Durban and asked my father to go out to be its marine superintendent. The long dreamt-of shore job at last.

So the family – then with three children but soon with six – moved to Durban. Ultimately, I had two sisters and three brothers. Bedrooms had to be shared and there were always crying babies. This made schoolwork or even just reading pretty problematic. Meal times were also somewhat hectic. My mother would say to guests: 'There's plenty for everyone but you've got to be quick.'

My father had been appointed for two years in the first instance. I found Africa so uncongenial that I kept a chart of 730 squares – two years' worth of days – and ticked them off morosely, the same response as a prison inmate.

But there were compensations. Northlands was a new state school and there was a teacher shortage, so a number of retired teachers and some real bottom-of-the-barrel rejects from Britain had been recruited. So the boys were thoroughly in charge – with hilarious results. It was an all-white school in those high apartheid days. Racism and homophobia were the norm. Corporal punishment was far less frequent than it had been in the Dotheboys Hall I had left behind, where the Christian Brothers had beaten me on at least every second day.

At first, I found it hard to believe. During lessons, boys just drifted around the classroom, chatting as they pleased. At St Anselm's such behaviour would have brought severe beatings. Our Northlands form master, a man well over 70, called Daffy Jones, had no control. Boys often left the classroom for a smoke or simply departed for the wonderful beaches we could see from our classroom window.

Sometimes boys from other classrooms sauntered in, such as the notorious Van Gelder, whose bare-faced cheek was legendary. When Daffy saw Van Gelder sitting grinning in the back row, he would give a cry of rage and charge down the aisle, shouting, 'Out! Out!' Van Gelder would give a happy whoop and would easily elude Daffy, dodging behind desks and grinning broadly as he pleaded, 'But sir, why are you mad with me? I only came here to ask your advice on an academic matter.' Since everyone knew that Van Gelder had never given any consideration to academic matters if he could possibly avoid it, this would further enrage Daffy. Class members would emit cries of tally-ho and shout encouragement to Daffy or his quarry. This raucous pantomime would conclude only when Van Gelder slipped out of the door.

Truancy, an ever-present fact of life, gave a heightened significance to the class register. In our class a rotund and rubicund Jewish boy, Dennis Rubin, would keep the register for Daffy, and Daffy leaned heavily upon him. But as soon as Dennis began to sing out names, the fun would begin. Dennis would, for example, call out the name Peter Jackson. Someone would say that Jackson had gone out for a smoke. Someone else would say, 'Actually, he's gone out for a wank.' Animated discussion of these possibilities would follow. Daffy's agitation would grow and Dennis's face would become more and more suffused with red as he manfully tried to choke back his laughter. Someone would then interject, 'Sir, Rubin's laughing.' Daffy would spin round to look, causing Dennis to have a coughing fit.

By this time another boy would be on his feet: 'Please sir, may I fuck your daughter?' Daffy would jump up, 'My God, boy, what did you say?' The boy would reply: 'Please sir, may I get a drink of water?' A dialogue would ensue in which every other line would be an obscene impertinence, causing Daffy to start up with outrage, only to slump back down when it was corrected to a rhyming statement of pure banality. Dennis would shake, red-faced with helpless but repressed laughter. Boys would then interject, 'Sir, Rubin's collapsing,' or 'Sir, Rubin is going to burst,' causing Daffy to glance angrily at Rubin. Dennis would pull himself together with a visibly heroic effort, grimly keeping his mouth shut for fear of laughing. And so it would go on.

Northlands was built on the slopes that run from the ridge of Umhlanga Rocks, with terraced playing fields stretching down towards the Indian Ocean. Those were the days of buzz-bikes – motorbikes with an engine of 50 cc that could do 80–90 kph. Anyone from the age of 14 upwards could own one. My parents could never afford such things for me but scores of Northlands boys rode them. So the boldest of the truants would arrive at school, sign the register, and then set off for the beach, shooting down successive terraces and finally out through the grounds of the junior school below. It was a striking sight.

Many truants belonged to the Pirates, an elite life-savers club. In our class we had one Pirate, Paul Connolly, a languorous and impossibly tanned boy. Paul was a nice guy but his appearance in class was episodic at best. Other boys would point out to Paul that being a life-saver was not a career. This made no impact. Paul was already lost in a world of beach, sun and girls that, to him, seemed like immortality.

The Pirate king was Alan Dunbar, a burly, blond sixth-former and by far the toughest boy in the school. All the First XV were scared of Dunbar, as were some teachers. Dunbar would arrive on a buzz-bike, sign the register, and then saddle up his bike with his blonde and scantily dressed girlfriend. I remember the school's deputy principal staring out while Dunbar and girlfriend saddled up and then careened down the terraced slopes. Interjections began. 'Sir, Dunbar is bunking off,' and 'Sir, do you think Dunbar is screwing that girl?' The teacher blanched and turned away: 'I don't need to know about all that.' He was clearly as scared of Dunbar as the rest of us.

Truancy was generally ignored but one day a new young teacher gave out the results of a test and awarded Izzy Levitan a zero. Izzy, a tough rugby ace but a mild-mannered and friendly boy, rose quickly. 'Sir, you can't give me nought, sir.' The teacher pointed out that Izzy had played truant and never written the test, so he would have to get nought. 'Sir, if my elder brother sees a nought on my record, he is going to larrup me. Just give me 20. Twenty still fails, sir.' During the ensuing altercation Izzy advanced towards the teacher's desk, pulling out a large pair of dressmaker's scissors from his pocket and shouted 'Twenty!' as he plunged them into the teacher's desk, where they stood, quivering. 'All right, 20,' said the white-faced young teacher. Izzy was his mild-mannered self again in an instant. It was not entirely surprising to learn later that Izzy had become an Israeli paratrooper.

Once the register had been signed, all the class registers would be collected by an African called Sam. Sam was at least 50 but all such male Zulu servants were called 'kaffir boys'. Oddly, this was not unkindly meant, though everyone knew that 'kaffir' was not a word to be used to an African's face. Despite this complete and unselfconscious racism, the boys would josh Sam in friendly fashion. They liked him and he them. Coming from a liberal-minded English family, I found such manifestations of racism monstrous, but my protestations were dismissed with scorn.

It took a while to understand. The word 'kaffir' was used as a general derogatory adjective. A cross-batted swipe in cricket was called a 'kaffir shot', someone who dropped a rugby pass would be 'playing like a kaffir', and so on. Like most schoolboys, my fellow pupils were sexually obsessed, but while they would be eager to look down the dress of a girl from the neighbouring girls' school, they would stare in asexual boredom at the sight of the rural black women who came bare-breasted into Durban from Zululand.

But Durban whites in general – echoed by their children – really disliked Indians ('coolies'). Zulus, I was told, were straight up-and-down people but Indians were all crooks. From this, I gradually decoded, the whites saw the Indian as competitors – who were coming up fast. Moreover, this was only eight years after the Zulu riots against the Indians, in which 142 people were killed and more than a thousand injured. Whites tended to take a grim satisfaction in the fact that their own dislike of Indians was more than matched by the Zulus. What was most disturbing, for both black and white, was the speed with which Indians were changing from being sugar cane cutters into small shopkeepers and then into increasingly affluent middle-class folk – attracting jealousy and resentment as they did so.

I can remember only one incident of really bad schoolboy behaviour towards a person of colour. I was part of the cricket team on its way to an away match. The bus began its journey by driving at a crawl through the crowded Indian market area of Durban. One of the boys leaning out the window suddenly said, 'Look at her!' It was an old Indian lady, riding in a rickshaw with her purchases all around her. The boy had brought a watermelon with him to eat and had already cut it in half. This he hurled out of the window at her, catching her full in the face. I remember her slowly pulling pieces of slushy watermelon out of her eyes, looking too stunned to emit a sound as the bus drew away. Several boys cheered. I felt as if I had been electrocuted. This, I thought, must have been the way young Nazis laughed as they tormented Jews. I went to sit on my own at the back of the bus. My team-mates' laughter at the incident told me how completely on my own I was. Nobody in that team would have done anything similar to an African man or woman. Indians were different.

I soon had a sharp lesson about race. Short of money as always, I got a Christmas job at the Durban post office, sorting parcels. My bosses were Afrikaners and unmistakeably National Party (NP) supporters, but there was also a gang of Zulu workers who carried the heavy sacks about. During tea breaks the Afrikaners would tease Elias, one of the older Zulus, pulling his leg in a good-natured fashion. It was often extremely funny and one day I joined in and made some teasing remark to Elias. Straight after the break a Mr Steenkamp came to see me. 'Look here,' he said, 'you can't make such remarks to Elias. He is a Zulu man and you are just a boy. You need to show him respect, a Zulu man expects that. If not, he's likely to hit you and then we'll have a racial incident on our hands.' Utterly humiliated, I accepted the rebuke. Clearly, Steenkamp, apartheid supporter though he was, had a much better understanding of black people than I did, and, despite his unsympathetic exterior, he was demanding respect for them. I was mortified and thoroughly put in my place.

What actually fascinated me most about race was the way the whole thing had got into people's heads (black and white) so that they easily invented new restrictions and complied with them. Going home from school I often stopped for a cold drink at a little shop. One day I saw that a great hole had been knocked in its front wall: the shopkeeper was building separate entrances for white and non-white, an absurdity that not even Verwoerd had thought to make law. Both black and white immediately and uncomplainingly adapted their behaviour to the new double-entrance nonsense. Apartheid was not just the law, it was in people's brains, it was in the air.

Trudging home during the Emergency of 1960, I was accosted by a motorist. 'I found this young kaffir with African National Congress (ANC) leaflets in his possession, so I'm taking him to the police station,' he said. 'Can you direct me?' On the car's back seat sat an African boy of about 16, crying bitterly, clearly terrified – the police were sure to beat the hell out of him. I unhesitatingly gave the driver directions that would land him up miles from a police station. And then worried that this had not been clever. The man would surely get angry as he realised he was lost but would find the police station in the end. It might then go really badly for the boy.

. . .

Opposite us lived Mr and Mrs Dobby, immigrants from Yorkshire who had enthusiastically embraced being part of the master class. I was, though, more interested in the two strikingly beautiful coloured girls who walked past our house every day on their way to work. They lived nearby and occasionally their father – a white man – would issue forth, but he never said hello. In the years we lived there I saw his wife just twice, stepping out onto their verandah, her face covered by a mask of white cream. She was clearly hiding in the house, and plastering her face with cream was her attempt to 'pass for white'.

Harry Dobby cursed these 'bloody coloureds, who shouldn't be living in a white area'. He had, he said, 'a good mind to tell the police and get them evicted'. My father, who had advised us to stay clear of local politics, nonetheless told Harry that if he ever did such a thing, he, Stanley Johnson, would never speak to him again: the coloured family were doing no one any harm. My father had been outstanding at every sport, had played soccer for Liverpool, was over six feet tall, and was a very strong man, so this warning was enough to shut Harry Dobby up. Still, the drama of the situation haunted me. I would shyly greet the two daughters every morning but could never forget the notion of their mother hiding in her own house and the sheer awfulness of that white cream. What sort of conversations did that family have? The beautiful daughters smiled back at me but never spoke. The policy was clearly to be invisible and inaudible.

Meanwhile, at school, maths was a problem. The game in maths lessons was to distract our teacher, known as Old Man Askew, into reminiscences of his greatest day in 1917 when he had marched, under the command of Lord Allenby ('he treated me like a father'), to take Jerusalem. This resonated in our class, which was one third Jewish. (Other boys often called our class 'the synagogue'. The Gentile majority in our class indignantly resisted this out of tribal loyalty and defended their Jewish classmates.) Soon in any Askew lesson one would hear, 'Sir, please sir, can't you tell us more about Lord Allenby, please sir.' And often he did. Maths went out of the window.

Old Man Askew had a habit of standing at the back of the class and shielding his eyes with his hand as he stared at the blackboard in front. Silently, all the boys would start shielding their eyes in imitation, until, finally, Askew would realise he was being mocked and charge at one of the offenders. The boys would protest that the brilliantly bright light was forcing them to shield their eyes ('Sir, when I don't do it my eyes hurt and I start to cry'). Outside, indeed, the sun routinely burned fiercely down across the vast panoply of Durban Bay. In all my school years the classroom lights were never once switched on.

Boys in the desks at the back could get away with most. Peter Duffield, who sat there, managed to smoke a whole cigarette in Askew's class, lifting the lid of his desk so that he could blow smoke into it. The whole class revelled in the experiment. At the very end Askew sniffed and said, 'Boys, I can smell smoke.' He was hurriedly told that this was 'an optical illusion'. Luckily, he didn't see the several snuffed-out cigarette ends under Duffield's desk. Duffield, whose father was a racing commentator, had cleaned up on a 5–1 bet on his cigarette exploit and now embarked on the tougher proposition of exploding a firework in a maths class.

So one day Peter lit a firecracker and threw it into his desk as Askew, up at the blackboard, sawed on for the umpteenth time about Pythagoras. Peter then folded his arms and stared with a beatific grin at Pythagoras. The cracker exploded with a great roar, magnified by the enclosed space within the empty desk. Askew visibly jumped and stared wildly around. Duffield continued to stare with happy fascination at the square on the hypotenuse, but blue smoke began to billow up through the inkwell in his desk. Duffield attempted to wave it away with one hand while still staring fixedly at the board. This did not deter Askew, who descended on him like an avenging angel. Duffield was sent to stand outside the room until, at the end of the class, Askew would take him to the Head to be flogged.

Whereupon a boy rose to say, 'Sir, you can't blame Duffield. He comes from a broken home.' (None of us had the least idea of Duffield's home circumstances.) Another, apparently in tears, added, 'Sir, you know how jockeys have little whips for their horses? That's the way Duffield has been whipped for years, sir.' Soon, interjections came thick and fast.

'Sir, you wouldn't want to have Duffield flogged if you knew the whole story.'

'Sir, Duffield really looks up to you, sir. He's always talking about Lord Allenby.'

'Sir, Duffield hero-worships you and Lord Allenby.'

'Sir, when Duffield's dad gets drunk, he beats Duffield with the leg of a chair.'

'Sir, Duffield sees you as his father figure, sir.'

'Sir, Duffield's mother is a prostitute.'

'Sir, and now she's getting older she finds it harder to get clients, sir.'

'Sir, when she can't find any clients, she takes it out on Duffield.'

'Sir, she hits him with the same chair leg.'

'Sir, Rubin's gone all purple.' (As usual Rubin was making heroic, though unsuccessful, efforts to stifle his laughter, lifting his desk lid to hide his face. The rest of the class were too brazen to do more than smile.)

'Sir, Duffield was crying today when he came to school.'

'Sir, Rubin is having a heart attack.'

'Sir, surely you could let Duffield off? He sees you as his true father.'

'Sir, remember Lord Allenby, sir. He was like a father to you.'

'Sir, Rubin's having a stroke.'

At which point the lesson ended. Askew opened the door and

enveloped Duffield in a large fatherly hug, affectionately saying, 'My boy.' Duffield accepted this as naturally as he could – no doubt assisted by the winding-up gestures made by class members. Having duly been let off, Duffield returned to his desk and lit up a Chesterfield in pure satisfaction. He seemed instinctively to understand that the rest of the class had got up to some devilry but never bothered to enquire what it was and no one bothered to tell him. Rubin continued to giggle helplessly.

At first, I thought these pantomime scenes happened only in our class, but towards the end of one school day I was sent with a message to the sixth form class above ours. A teacher was trying to keep order but everyone was ready to go. One boy I knew, called Gavin Stewart, had put on his satchel and was heading for the door when the teacher stopped him, saying there were still ten minutes to go. Immediately his classmates began, 'Sir, you have to be careful with that boy, sir, he's a boy genius.' 'Yes, sir, his name is Justin Hargreaves and he is the inventor of cold steam.' And so on. It was just the same as in my class.

. . .

I had only been at Northlands for a week when a huge boy – at 14 he was already six foot two – came up to me in class and began to tease me, though in a not unfriendly way. This was Colin Reardon. We soon became fast friends. He introduced me to his cousins in the same year, Brian and Winston Reardon. At that point Northlands had some 20 classes – four in each year – and there was a Reardon in every single class.

The preceding generation of Reardons – a poor family of Irish descent – had all become builders and mainly they had prospered. By my day, a number of Reardons had already been through Northlands. They had all been leading sportsmen and academically at least adequate but they had also been incorrigible rebels, so the school had resolved that never again could a Reardon be a prefect. Colin, Brian and Winston now lived under this mark of Cain. Naturally sympathising with them against this quasi-ethnic injustice, I became a sort of honorary Reardon.

In one respect only, Northlands was outstanding – athletics. The world 100 yards record was then 9.3 seconds. Our school record was an astonishing 9.6, held by a boy with the wonderful name of Bobbie Klobbie. Roger Bannister had broken the four-minute mile only a few years before: our school mile record was 4 minutes 12 seconds. So it went on. Brian Reardon ran the Under-17 110 yards high hurdles in an astonishing 13.4 seconds and would have been an Olympic athlete but for South Africa's expulsion from the Olympic movement over apartheid.

As always in South Africa, rugby was important. The Christian Brothers had been rugby fanatics and back in England I had been a fairly successful lock forward. The key was motivation. When we were to play a major Protestant institution like Birkenhead School, the Brothers would say, 'You have to remember that not long ago, people like that were burning people like us at the stake.' If we played away, they would add, 'This is a Protestant school, so don't leave any valuables in the changing room.' We would issue forth and murder the opposition, who never knew what had hit them. At Northlands we would play against Hoërskool Port Natal and their large bronzed Afrikaners would absolutely murder us. I realised that, once again, it was a holy war – they were refighting the Anglo-Boer War – and this time I was on the wrong side.

Bobbie Klobbie was pressed into service as a rugby winger, producing one of the most remarkable scenes I ever witnessed on a rugby pitch. Our First XV was pressing hard towards the try line when the other side made an interception and their winger was suddenly away, with almost the whole length of the pitch to run and a huge head-start. Our captain shouted, 'Get him, Bobbie!' and Bobbie streaked after him. Ordinarily, no one could have caught their winger, but Bobbie came up behind him like a jet fighter behind an ox-cart. Bobbie never liked tackling so he just leaned down in full stride and flipped up the ankle of the flying winger. The boy did a spectacular involuntary cartwheel and swallowed his tongue. He had to be rushed to hospital and the other school filed legal charges against Northlands.

Our most imposing teacher was 'Paddy' Power, a large red-faced Englishman. Paddy's mind was never far from drink. If his eye lit upon John Mackay in the front desk he would declare, 'Mackay. Yes, a good man, Mackay. And Mackay's whisky is not bad stuff either.' Similarly, when he demanded the answer to a question he would bellow, 'Don't be vague, ask for Haig,' a famous whisky tagline of the time. When we read *Lorna Doone* he dwelt with appreciation on the description of John Ridd's schooldays in which, during breaks, Ridd's teachers would adjourn upstairs, there to partake of 'foreign cordials'. 'That's the very thing!' he would bellow. He would frequently return to the theme of foreign cordials.

Power's drinking companions were Mr Cressey, who taught arithmetic, and Mr Carrick, who taught geography. Cressey had a large moustache and talked in an exaggerated drawl full of RAF slang: 'Be careful with that window, boy. Christ, I told you not to prang it. What a ghastly prang. You know what you chaps are? You're a complete shower. An absolute bloody shower.' And so on.

The big issue with Power, Cressey and Carrick was Monday morning, when they were hung-over and in a foul mood. Cressey suffered from delirium tremens ('DTs') and on some Mondays would enter the classroom clutching his head with one hand while he flapped his other hand at us, snarling 'Free period, free period.' We would observe total silence but Cressey would nonetheless charge down the aisles every now and again, yelling and lashing out indiscriminately. One could only guess at what was going on in his inebriated imagination.

In later years Colin Reardon told me he had met our old headmaster, Percy Hardaker, who revealed that on many Monday mornings his first job was to go down to the brothels of Point Road near the docks. There he would find Power, Cressey and Carrick, shove them under the shower to sober them up and then drive them back to school where he would push them into our classrooms. This was what we, as 14- and 15-year-olds, had already pretty much surmised.

Northlands was thus great fun and educationally pretty hopeless. It was perfectly clear that most of our teachers could not prepare us for exams. There was only one thing to do – teach ourselves. We designated boys who were seen as top in each subject. Those a bit behind them would consult this class leader on how to do his subject, and once this was explained they in turn would pass on their knowledge to still weaker class members. This necessitated a great deal of chatting and consultation in class but it worked well. There is nothing better for internalising material than having to explain it clearly to someone else.

. . .

My younger brother, Philip, had befriended a young Afrikaner, Renier Schoeman, in the class below me, and Renier often came home with him. At 13 he was already an Afrikaner Nationalist ideologue and a great admirer of Prime Minister Verwoerd. I, a young liberal, argued fiercely with Renier. Once, arriving home on a boiling afternoon, I collapsed on my bed and slept. I awoke to find Renier making a note of 'subversive' books in my bookcase, presumably for report to the security police. One day I told Renier that we were moving towards a police state, with letters opened and telephones tapped. He vigorously denied this. I said, 'Fine, I'll wait for you to get home and then I'll phone you and say, hey Renier, we have all the dynamite ready, we just need you to come up with the percussion caps and we are in business to do some serious sabotage' – for the idea of sabotage was then being mooted on the left. Renier blanched: 'No, you mustn't, I mean I won't be home – I will put the phone down – how can you be so irresponsible?' 'If you are right,' I said, 'and the phones are not tapped, you have nothing to worry about.' But the prospect so frightened Renier that he wouldn't go home until I promised I would make no such call.

Renier's father, a policeman, was a dear old Afrikaner with a little spade beard. Renier also had an elder brother called Boetie (brother) who was a wild man. This was an acknowledged role. Everyone at school would say that Van Gelder, for example, was 'a wild man', which meant he might do absolutely anything. Looking back, this was part and parcel of being a frontier society: wild men had always existed in such places – Davy Crockett, Wild Bill Hickok, Doc Holliday, Billy the Kid, and so on. Natal in the 1950s was not far removed from that. Another 'frontier' aspect of life was that rabies was a constant theme in the press, and when we went on rugby tours of Zululand we would indeed see rabid dogs, stiff-legged and terrifying, in the streets of Empangeni, Mtubatuba and Gingindlovu. The only thing to do was to shoot such animals; most whites had guns and did just that. I remember reading of a rabid lion in Empangeni: he was doubtless shot like the rest. In such a society there was space for wild men.

Even for a wild man, Boetie Schoeman was pretty wild. He was an elemental force, always full of aggression, and never obeyed the rules. Once I was in his pick-up truck when another driver ploughed gently into the back of us in West Street, Durban's main thoroughfare. Boetie just said 'Aw fuck,' turned off his engine and got out to examine the damage. The driver behind had wound down his window and was staring at the damage too. Boetie inspected the dent, sauntered on down to the offending driver – with the light already green and cars hooting for us to move – and delivered a huge uppercut, leaving the man unconscious and slumped over his wheel, his horn blaring horribly. Boetie drove off, saying something very rude in Afrikaans. I pointed out that assaulting the driver meant that Boetie could hardly claim damages for the accident. 'Fuck that,' he said. 'It's like the Lexington (cigarette) ad: After action – satisfaction.'

One result of my arguments with Renier (and with similarly minded boys in my own class) was that one day I drew a graph on the blackboard showing that if, in 1960, 3 million whites were bossing 10 million blacks, by 1990 5 million whites would have to boss 40 million blacks, with the figures getting ever steeper thereafter. Majority rule, I argued, was a demographic certainty: the only sensible thing was to prepare for it. My opponents declared that this was a treasonous statement and anyway nonsense. Anything but white rule was simply unimaginable. For me, the oddity was that the situation was already clear to a 16-year-old schoolboy like me, yet neither the ruling party nor its official opposition were able to acknowledge such facts for another 25 years. The key word was 'unimaginable'. The facts were clear enough: it was simply a failure of imagination.

...

After two years my father's term of duty ended and the family returned to Merseyside for a few months, which meant that I was placed back at the mercy of the Christian Brothers. It was even worse than I remembered – an almost totalitarian atmosphere with frequent flogging. Many of the boys had become delinquents in reaction and shoplifted on the way home. Happily, my father was confirmed in his Durban job for a further period, and to my great relief I returned to Northlands. No more counting the days away: I was far happier in Durban.

But the worst thing at Northlands was Cadets (military training) on Friday afternoons: all of us, dressed in army khaki, were endlessly marched around the playing fields. The prefects and sportsmen held officer rank and took great pleasure in ordering us all about. Once a year military 'trainers' would arrive from the army at Natal Command. These were terrifying men, determined to show you how tough the military life could be. Some boys were picked up off the ground by their ears.

Others were made to run round the track for 400 metres carrying heavy rifles over their head under the burning Durban sun. They referred to us as 'you bleddy rooineks' (English rednecks) and gave blood-curdling speeches about how you had to be ready to 'fight the kaffirs'.

Colin Reardon and I both hated Cadets, an antipathy increased by our general rebelliousness against the prefect class. As always, a poll of fifth formers was taken about who should be prefects. Brian Reardon's name came top, with Colin's not far behind. As Reardons, they were ruled out of consideration. We were outraged. I was warned that unless I changed my attitude, I too would not be a prefect. I quickly said that I didn't want to be one anyway. This direct rejection of the governing code of behaviour was seen as a threat to school authority and Colin and I were often in trouble. Principled opposition was taken far more seriously than any amount of real bad behaviour.

Every morning, assembly was held in the school hall. Frequently Colin and I would be in trouble for bunking Cadets and so the headmaster would conclude by saying that we must report to his study after assembly – which meant being flogged. There was at that time a boy in a lower class with the surname of Hitler. Unsurprisingly, he was also a miscreant. Accordingly, the Head's address on Monday mornings would often conclude with 'After prayers I want to see the following in my study: Colin Reardon, Johnson – and Hitler'. No matter how often this happened, the school assembly would erupt into giggles and occasional shouts of 'Sieg Heil!' The three of us were always flogged.

At Cadets, I had suffered the indignity of progressive demotion from corporal (fourth form) to lance corporal (fifth form) to private (sixth form), which meant I was ordered about by boys two years younger than myself. This was punishment for my open wish not to be a prefect. The whole thing was a colossal waste of time and horribly uncomfortable in the Durban heat. We noted that those boys who bunked Cadets by escaping through a hole in the school hedge were always caught, but that one boy who was a Jehovah's Witness simply walked out of the school front gate every Friday, excused on religious grounds. Colin and I decided that we too would walk out of the front gate and, if asked, would simply say, 'We're excused.'

This worked like a charm for a while. However, the Head, Percy Hardaker, was passionately in favour of Cadets and would appear on the parade ground – a short, fat Bunteresque figure – as our Commandant. One day, while changing into his khaki uniform in his study, Percy looked out and saw Colin and me walking out. The result was another Monday morning summons (along with Hitler) to be flogged. We also got a lecture about our bare-faced cheek in just walking out.

Colin thought we had better go to Cadets next week. I said, 'Hell no!' and on Friday I just walked out of the front gate again. The result was another Monday morning summons (with Hitler but *sans* Colin) to be flogged. Percy was apoplectic: how could I simply repeat my offence, straight after getting six the previous Monday? I said that my objections to Cadets were political and were just as valid as religious principles. I loathed Cadets because it was, quite manifestly, a preparation to fight against our black fellow countrymen and to keep them in a permanent state of oppression. This was immoral, and should it come to fighting, I would take the other side.

I suggested a compromise: I would miss Cadets every Friday but would obediently report to Percy every Monday for another six. But, of course, in Percy's eyes I was subverting the whole system, saying I was happy to accept the worst he could do provided I could have my way. He exploded with rage and said I would be expelled from the school if I missed Cadets again. I was cornered. South African law might find me guilty of treason for saying I would fight on the other side. After consultation with Colin, I attended Cadets in the main thereafter, slipping out only on odd occasions. If Percy saw me do so, he kept quiet about it, so maybe I got my compromise in the end.

...

Strife and violence were in the air. 1960 brought the murder of nine policemen in the Cato Manor settlement behind the University of Natal, the Sharpeville massacre and the state of emergency. My elder sister was already at the university and when Cato Manor erupted my father drove up there to pick her up. Accompanying him, I saw Saracen armoured vehicles standing on campus as a huge crowd of angry Africans poured up the hill towards them. 1960 also saw the disastrous independence of the Belgian Congo, which immediately erupted into massacres of both whites and blacks, the rape of nuns and other horrors. This made a lasting mark on the consciousness of white South Africa, epitomising what it most feared about majority rule. One friend, then a schoolgirl in Northern Rhodesia, later told me how she had seen the luxury cars – Mercedes, big Peugeots and the like – driven over the border to Ndola airport by whites fleeing the Congo. The cars were left lined up outside the airport, the keys in their ignitions, a gift to whoever wanted them – an eloquent statement about the anger and desperation of the refugees.

Before long, one heard of boys one had known at school becoming mercenaries in the Congo. One of these was Boetie Schoeman, who later became a bush guide and big-game hunter. Boetie had a favourite routine when he saw a snake. He would rush forward, grab the snake by the tail, whirl it round his head till it was thoroughly giddy, and then kill it with ease. Sometimes he was not quick enough and the snake would bite him. This would seriously annoy Boetie. He would kill the snake and then inject himself with snake serum: his arms were pockmarked with snakebites and needle marks. Returning from such a trip, Boetie got into a fight in a Joburg pub, knocking down a far bigger man who then announced that, being a policeman, he was still the winner. So Boetie shot him dead. This produced a long jail sentence during which he was extremely badly treated by warders determined to avenge the dead policeman. Boetie seemed to suffer from mental illness when he came out of jail. It was a sort of sign. South Africa was becoming less of a frontier society. There was no room for a 'wild man' any more.

When we finally finished at Northlands, Colin, Brian and I walked home together, immensely glad to be done with school. Yet my feelings were tinged with warmth. I was glad to be an honorary Reardon. Northlands had allowed me to escape from the clutches of the Christian Brothers and had taught me to work on my own, a valuable lesson for the future. I had laughed almost every single day at school, so how could I say that I had been unhappy there? There had been much that was silly or disgraceful but it had been a release. Despite all the racism, the Cadets and the drunken teachers, it had been a journey into laughter and into freedom.

CHAPTER TWO

On Campus

Thence to university. In 1961, the University of Natal in Durban was a small but pleasant institution, largely created by the vice chancellor, Ernie Malherbe, Jan Smuts's wartime head of military intelligence.[1] Later, when I was on the Student Representative Council (SRC), I got to know him. A small, tough Afrikaner with a distinguished academic record, he was a firm liberal critic of apartheid. The government regarded such independent-minded Afrikaners as virtual traitors. Naturally, the radicals on the SRC (of whom I was one) fought with him but you couldn't help respecting him. He once told me how, during the war, men who were now leading cabinet members had been signalling to German U-boats off the coast. He had wanted to have them thrown into detention camps but the canny Smuts stayed his arm, warning against making political martyrs out of their opponents.

Until a few years before, the campus had towered over a vast black squatter camp, Cato Manor, but that had been bulldozed and the inhabitants forcibly moved away. Now all was greenery and upper-class white housing (though the squatter settlement was later re-established and is bigger than ever today). The university sat on a steep hill with a fountain and a pond on top and lush gardens falling away as the hill

---

1   See EG Malherbe, *Never a Dull Moment* (Timmins Publishers, 1981).

descended. The campus was lined with palm trees and a statue of King George V emphasised its colonial origins. Often, I would gaze over the incomparably beautiful vegetation and Durban's magnificent harbour below and feel that it was rather like the Harry Belafonte song, 'Island in the Sun'. When it was dark you would hear the magical sounds of the Durban night – the crickets, the cicadas and fruit bats, almost drowned out by the roar of hundreds of bullfrogs.

Amid Durban's effortless physical beauty, culturally speaking not much happened. Even the best schools behaved as if their main purpose was sport, with academics an afterthought. Often in the most magnificent homes you would find not a book in the house and the pictures on the wall were frequently tasteless. Later, reading some of Clive James's barbed comments on his native Australia, I was strongly reminded of Durban.

Apartheid was the main problem in South Africa but the University of Natal had an additional problem: there were not enough Jews. Both Johannesburg and Cape Town had large Jewish communities, whose cultured and highly intelligent products were prominent at the English-speaking universities there, both as students and academics. Moreover, those communities contributed generously to those institutions, giving them facilities and endowments far beyond what Durban could afford.

Durban's proud boast was that it was the confluence of three cultures – English, Indian and Zulu – but what exactly had that mixture produced? For the cupboard was pretty bare. The only notable writer from Durban was Roy Campbell and he been a very awkward customer and had supported the Fascists in Spain. Of course, Alan Paton lived in Natal and was a great figure. But that was it. Even today, if you google 'Durban poets' what flashes up on the screen is 'Do you mean Durban *port*?'

Even at school we had heard that 'alternative' people (the word then was 'beatniks') congregated at university and we were very eager to find such people. I was doing a BA degree in Latin, English, history and political science (it is odd to recall that I could then read Latin as rapidly as English) and most of the alternative types were to be found in such subjects. Among the first I met were Phil Joffe and Mike Kirkwood. Phil was a devotee of *Mad* magazine, decorating his life with quips from Alfred E Neuman. If you sat next to Phil in a seminar you could not but notice that his file was covered with a montage from newspaper headlines reading:

The sEx LIFE *of the LanD* CRAB

Phil himself was a dark, compact Jewish bodybuilder, endlessly involved in Mr Universe competitions on Durban's North Beach. This he tried to combine with a life of determined intellectualism on campus. His insights often seemed to be aimed more at navel- rather than head-level. Early on Phil told me that he had 'worked out' that the all-purpose reply to everything was 'Fuck off'. If somebody asked you for a lift, or a date or what time it was you could, in every case, reply, 'Fuck off', and be perfectly understood. Phil, struck by the wondrous simplicity of the thing, had business cards printed with 'Fuck off' in copperplate script. Whenever he was accosted, he would say, 'Hi, here is my card.' Or he might approach girls in the library and when he failed to get a date would say, 'Well anyway, here is my card.' And so on.

Phil was later to become a senior academic in the English department. As he became too old for bodybuilding heroics, he graduated to performing get-fit classes on breakfast TV. As you staggered out of bed there would be Phil, powerfully attired in leotard and T-shirt, putting through their paces a whole squad of Lycra-clad beauties moving to a disco beat. In theory, the girls were very sexy, but they all wore fixed smiles as they went through their calisthenics, which somehow robbed them of any allure.

The University of Natal had a large speech and drama department, thronged by hundreds of students and ruled in queenly fashion by Professor Elizabeth Sneddon. This seemed absurd: it was as if theatre was a major South African industry, like mining. Sadly, now as then, South African theatre struggles to survive at all even on a diet of copied foreign plays and musicals (usually rock 'tributes' in which locals mime famous groups). Shakespeare plays are put on exclusively at educational institutions where those plays are set books. Phil, who was always most interested in English literature, was also a student of speech and drama.

One day, Professor Sneddon was teaching her class about the importance of gesture, giving speeches in a sort of elocution voice and then illustrating them with histrionic gestures. She insistently urged her students, 'You must project, project.' It was all way over the top, something she got away with because deference was paid to her as a *grande dame*. After a great deal of this flummery she picked Phil out at random.

'Now, Mr Joffe, I am going to enact a scene with you. I shall utter no words, relying merely on gesture. You must to respond to me purely in gesture. You must utter no word.'

She then floated in front of Phil with a flirtatious swagger and sway (though she was already approaching 60). She dropped a handkerchief at his feet and then turned, making appealing eyes at both Phil and the handkerchief. He was clearly expected to pick up the handkerchief and graciously hand it back. Phil looked hard at her and then at the handkerchief and then gave her a V-sign and turned his back. Sneddon deigned not to notice him and went grandly on her way, despite the students' horrified giggles.

Mike Kirkwood was very different: tall, dark and generally reckoned to look rather like Jack Palance. He habitually wore a sort of cowboy outfit – jeans and a suede jacket with long fringes. Mike had a sort of brooding presence, wrote good poetry, and had an original mind. He had such a Hemingwayish image that he was quite routinely regarded as a great writer of the future. He was no slouch at either rugby or cricket, but his fellow players would relate with awe how, even after a rugged game on a hot Durban day, he would change back into his clothes with no intervening shower.

Like Mike and me, Mog (Edmund) Morris wrote for the student newspaper. His contributions were somewhat eccentric and Mike cautioned me that Mog was 'very right wing'. How did that happen, I asked, for it was assumed that all intellectuals were liberals. His family came down from Kenya, said Mike.

This was explanation enough. Embittered whites who had sickened of African nationalism in Tanzania or Kenya routinely trickled down south, often telling angry tales of the corruption and ineptitude which had overtaken these countries. Such immigrants were often very racist. For liberals they were a predictable curse.

Many things about Mike were *sui generis*. I used to give him lifts on a motor scooter I had acquired. This meant letting myself into his house – no one ever answered the door – and making my way to Mike's bedroom. This was a sparsely furnished room with Lucky Strike packets nailed up right round the picture rail. Mike, once woken, would ask, 'Do you think you can see a shoe and some socks down your end of the bed?' A search of the bed would reveal no sheets but several empty Coke bottles and beer cans, plus the missing shoe and socks and various other items. Mike would stride downstairs without washing or breakfast, shouting a goodbye to his mother. Sometimes a strangled cry came back, but I never actually saw Mrs Kirkwood. Mike's father was a doctor and a considerable drinker. One would see him playing Lotto alone down at the beachfront late at night, somewhat the worse for wear. Mike showed him great affection and was wonderfully unembarrassed by this. We all admired his easy naturalness.

One of Mike's year was Barbara Schuddeboom (later Trapido), a willowy blonde. Barbara passed as sophisticated in our fairly unsophisticated world and she and her family were all Liberal Party supporters. Being a Liberal meant being in favour of universal suffrage and complete racial equality, an option only favoured by a handful of whites – indeed, the government routinely denounced Liberals as virtual communists. At school in 1959 I had been thrilled when Helen Suzman and ten other MPs defected from the United Party (UP) to form the Progressive Party, favouring a non-racial but qualified franchise. Even supporting the Progs had then drawn considerable criticism but here at university there were, remarkably, full-blown Liberals ...

The most famous local Liberal was Alan Paton, the writer, but he was not regarded as fully respectable. The newspapers repeatedly condemned Liberals as stupid and dangerous, and their letter columns said much worse than that. Liberals were *kaffirboeties* – unhealthily close friends with Africans. The clinching question was always 'Would you like your sister to marry a *kaffir*?' (My family actually answered this question: one of my brothers married a black woman, my elder sister partnered with a black man, and my son also married a black woman.)

Although Paton was the most famous writer in South Africa, no newspaper ever asked him to write an article for them in those days. Only irresponsible or downright wicked people, after all, could be openly against white supremacy. But Paton never once bothered to reply to this torrent of criticism and denunciation. His calm disregard for personal abuse was so striking that it added considerably to the respect many of us felt for him.

One fellow student, Cathy Challis, had been a member of the Liberal Party in Pietermaritzburg and knew many of its leading personalities. This carried considerable authority, for Maritzburg was seen as more cultured than Durban. Indeed, many Natal people talked about 'the capital', meaning not Pretoria but Maritzburg, the provincial capital. For Natal regarded itself as a separate world. Later, Rowley Arenstein told me that when he arrived in Durban in 1939 to become the

Communist Party organiser, he was frequently asked, 'So you've come from Joburg. And how are things going in South Africa?'

Maritzburg – later brilliantly satirised as Piemburg in Tom Sharpe's *Riotous Assembly* – certainly saw itself as somewhat superior. One was constantly told that 'the best English in the world is spoken in Pietermaritzburg' though, confusingly, the same claim was sometimes made for Cape Town. For all I know the same claim was made at one time or another for Melbourne, Toronto or Aberystwyth.

Cathy Challis was soon to morph (so to speak) into being Mrs Cathy Morphet. Indeed, no one was quite sure of Cathy's maiden name. In those days a friend called Dave Hayden ran the university jazz club and since it was understood that there was a link between progressive jazz and progressive politics, many of us would gravitate daily to the music room, where Dave held sway. Without fail he would start with Dave Brubeck's 'Take Five', regarding it as the most perfect piece of music ever written. It is indeed hypnotic and is the largest selling jazz single of all time.[2] In later years Cathy moved to the USA where she became Cathy Brubeck, the wife of Dave's eldest son, Darius. She and Darius then migrated back to Durban, establishing the Centre for Jazz and Popular Music, which was how I came to meet Darius and, later, Dave himself. Naturally, there was a lot more of 'Take Five',[3] a tune that has thus had a strange role both in Durban and in my life. I asked Cathy not long ago how many times she'd been married and she replied, 'Oh, I don't know. I stopped counting.'

It was an age of motorbikes and scooters – most students could not afford cars. When I later got to know Tom Sharpe, I learnt how, when he had worked as a photographer (and Liberal Party member) in

---

2 Wikipedia.

3 However, it should be noted that the song was actually written by Paul Desmond, the wonderful saxophonist in the Dave Brubeck Quartet.

Maritzburg, he frequently drove his motorbike down to Durban with Albert Luthuli, the ANC leader, on the pillion.[4]

Another prominent Liberal was Walter Felgate, a stocky, hirsute man of 30 or so who was doing an anthropology degree. He had a severe manner and seldom smiled but was clearly independent-minded and intelligent. He would arrive every morning at the university wearing shorts and on a huge motorbike, on the back of which sat Fatima Meer, wife of Ismail Meer, a well-known lawyer and confidant of Nelson Mandela. Oddly, perhaps, no one ever questioned the clear defiance of apartheid that such an arrangement represented.

Fatima was an angry woman, her face often knotted with bitterness. But she looked almost entirely to Walter, who spoke with great emphasis and articulacy: talking with him meant being the recipient of successive pronunciamentos. One tended to nod agreement – and Fatima certainly did, usually without speaking herself.

Fatima seemed to go everywhere with Walter. Whenever Walter was delivering a political harangue, which was often, Fatima would sit next to him, adding supporting remarks. In later years I wondered whether Walter and Fatima had actually been having an affair. It would have been illegal under the Immorality Act, but even in those high apartheid days such things were not unknown. After all, Fatima, an exceptionally difficult woman, had soon separated from her husband, who was in turn conducting an affair with the (white) communist journalist Ruth First. Moreover, Walter's stern image did not prevent him from having relationships with a number of women. Indeed, Walter once held forth to Mike and me on the plight of the African family under apartheid: rural men leaving for work on the mines would leave their families behind and then have other relationships, and perhaps other children, with

---

4   There may be evidence of this in Tom's wonderful collection of photographs at the Tom Sharpe Foundation at the University of Barcelona.

women nearer their place of work. Mike listened sympathetically but then laughed, 'Well, maybe it's not so bad, Walter. After all, that exactly describes how you choose to live your own life.' This left Walter seriously unamused.

Walter was doing his thesis on the Tsonga people, on the Natal-Mozambique border, Frequently, on his return from the border, Walter would hold forth with great vehemence about how the whole Tsonga economy and society were based on growing and selling their crop of dagga (marijuana). One had to take this fact very seriously, he warned, and not be decoyed into empty moralism: for the Tsonga dagga was a matter of life and death. At the end of one such peroration Mike, who found such earnestness a soft target, commented, 'But Walter, that's what all druggies say about their habit.'

Mike was attracted by Walter's sharp logical mind and his larger worldly experience, so they spent much time together. The drawback, Mike later told me, was that the various schemes that Walter hatched invariably handed most of the hard work to Mike and most of the benefits to Walter. Walter once persuaded Mike to go with him down the South Coast, where he kept a small boat. They would fish for clams, sell them to the local hotels, and thus finance their sojourn down there. Mike happily agreed and off they set on Walter's motorbike. Upon arrival at their destination, Walter explained that they would steer the boat out beyond the breakers and Mike would then dive over the side bearing a heavy stone whose weight would carry him to the bottom. In his other hand he would hold a length of rubber tubing that Walter had brought with him, carefully keeping his thumb over the end to prevent water getting in. Walter would sit in the boat, holding the other end of the tube in the air, so that when Mike needed to breathe, he would simply put the tube into his mouth and suck in more air.

Mike dived in and the stone took him to the bottom. Standing on the sand, he could see almost nothing – certainly no clams – for the light down there was very poor. He wandered around, still seeing nothing and then, needing more air, inserted the tube into his mouth and sucked hard. To his horror he found himself inhaling extremely noxious fumes. Spluttering and gasping, he beat his way back to the surface and enquired what the hell Walter had put into the tube. It emerged that, before leaving the university, Walter had simply darted into one of the laboratories, where he had 'liberated' a length of tubing previously used for chemical experiments. The most recent experiment had evidently involved the production of hydrogen sulphide (rotten egg) fumes, which were what Mike had inhaled. Walter, insisting that Mike was making a mountain out of a molehill, rinsed the tube out with sea water and pronounced it ready for a further dive.

Mike was dubious – the tube still smelt awful – but went over the side, wandering around again in the clam-less murk. After a minute something barged powerfully into his back, almost knocking him over. Jamming the tube end into his mouth, he saw that he had been nudged by a large shark, which was now circling him. Panicked, he shot to the surface and clambered into the boat, yelling, 'Bloody hell, Walter, there's a shark down there!' Walter was unimpressed: 'Of course there are sharks, Mike. This is their habitat. Don't make such a fuss. All you have to do is advance towards the shark shouting. They hate noise. If that fails, punch it on the nose. That'll stop it.' Mike replied that, on the contrary, he would sit in the boat while Walter went down to shout at, or punch, the sharks. Despite his confidence in his shark-repulsion techniques, Walter declined to do this and the expedition came to a summary end.

. . .

Towards the end of my first year it was announced that there was to be a general meeting of the student body to discuss a hotly contested question of the segregation or integration of white students with their black peers in the Non-European section of the university, or UNNE.

I decided to attend. The SRC, which was decidedly on the liberal side, had clearly hoped to tip the balance by inviting the president and vice president of the National Union of South African Students (Nusas) to address the meeting – and everyone knew that was an extremely liberal organisation. Its president was the small but charismatic Adrian Leftwich, an already fabled character, his deputy an African from UNNE, Thami Mhlambiso. Leftwich, who had a somewhat incongruous crew cut, began by explaining his appearance. He and Thami had been driving down from Johannesburg when they were intercepted by the security police. They had denounced Adrian as a *kaffirboetie* and forcibly shaved his head, warning that if he didn't desist, worse would follow. He recounted this episode as if it were a funny story and then spoke in general terms of how Nusas had opposed the Separate Universities Act (officially the Extension of University Education Act, which segregated tertiary education) and remained adamantly opposed to it. He spoke with a charm and power that I have seldom seen equalled.

When Thami got up to speak there was a hush: I doubt if many there had ever been addressed by an African before. He began by glancing at Adrian's close-cropped hair, exclaiming, 'Well, Adrian, you're a real *kaffir* now.' This brought the house down, no doubt partly due to the release of tension. Thami then spoke quite beautifully in a highly articulate English. He stressed that as Nusas officers he and Adrian were strictly forbidden to intervene in the affairs of any individual campus, though, of course, their very presence could only help the integrationists.

It emerged that the SRC had formally taken position for the integrationist side. The chief integrationist was a tanned, grim-faced young man with a mop of blond hair, Peter Mansfield. He spoke with great passion but it was soon clear that the campus conservatives, led by the engineers and the sportsmen, were ranged against him.

Then came a succession of engineers and sportsmen, all arguing that they only wanted to avoid controversy and 'keep politics off the campus' – by preserving segregation. This established the pattern for the evening. Each time, Mansfield rose to reply to a rising chorus of boos. His courage was magnificent, particularly when one realised that he lived in one of the residences that were hotbeds of those hostile to him. I was captivated by the drama of the thing and at one stage rose to speak in Mansfield's favour. It gradually became clear that the conservatives looked to one man, Tommy Bedford, who sat two-thirds of the way back in the hall. Tommy was by far the best rugby player on campus – he was to captain the university, the province and later the Springboks. His prestige was correspondingly enormous. People anxiously glanced towards him to see which side he took. Tommy never spoke but he was clearly not an integrationist. Voting was by a show of hands, and people just noticed which way Tommy voted. The conclusion was never in doubt.

The next day the entire SRC resigned, saying they could not conscientiously preside over re-segregation. The result was that all 13 places on the SRC came up for election. Like most students, I paid minimal attention. But then Peter Mansfield, who had recalled my speech in his support, asked me to stand for the SRC. I was thunderstruck, having had no inkling of such an ambition. But I admired Mansfield too much to say no. In the event both Peter and I were elected.

Being on the SRC meant that I soon found myself deeply immersed in the politics of Nusas too, attending a Nusas congress at the University of the Witswatersrand (Wits) in Johannesburg. The new Nusas president, Jonty Driver, pointed out to us that there was a continuous history of trouble and protest at black schools and suggested that we set up a research project to enquire into the question. He asked if I would run it. It would take a year of my life and be very poorly paid though it was an intriguing possibility. But a combination of family and personal circumstances made it impossible, so Jonty threw the question open to the floor. It so happened that Peter Mansfield and I had been somewhat irritated by the antics of one of the Maritzburg delegates, Harry Wilson, a flamboyant liberal given to over-the-top rhetoric. In a trice Harry was on his feet saying he couldn't care what damage it did to his academic or personal career (the idea clearly being to show me up), he would happily give up his time to run the research project. He was strongly applauded. I later reflected that had I done the project I would have been in a position of some expertise when the Soweto riots broke out in 1976, and my life might have taken a different turn. Harry Wilson turned out to be a police spy, whose masters doubtless wanted to have control over such a sensitive project. His 'research' never came to anything.

...

The University of Natal stood well behind Wits and the University of Cape Town (UCT) in the pecking order of South African universities, but I loved it. Three academics there made a deep impression on me. Ray Sands, the professor of English, was witty, perceptive and gay. My schoolboy homophobia simply dissolved in the face of his lightly borne sophistication. Jane Notcutt cut me down to size when I wrote an essay on Shakespeare full of the 'grand' phrases ('the Bard of Avon', 'the Immortal Bard', etc) that my schoolteachers had encouraged. Ms Notcutt red-pencilled the lot: 'For God's sake avoid such rubbish, say what you mean and mean what you say. Be direct and to the point. It's hard enough to tell the absolute truth. Aim only at that, nothing more.' This had a permanent effect on all I have written since.

My history professor, Jeffrey Horton, gave outstanding lectures on 18th-century Britain. It was an education in itself to see a man so transported by immersion in a subject he loved – a vision of what an academic life might be. He was very kind to me, and when I entered for the Rhodes Scholarship, he gently guided me towards Magdalen, his own old college. I never regretted that choice.

I have thought much since then about how academics influence the young.[5] The most important thing is simply example. If you are lucky you meet at least a handful of people whose life and example have a lasting impact on you.

Several of my generation became writers – and not always the ones you'd expected. Tom Sharpe, who had spent Christmas 1960 in jail, was deported from South Africa in 1961 on charges of sedition over an anti-apartheid play he had written. He became an enormously successful writer of comic novels. Barbara Schuddeboom also enjoyed success as the novelist Barbara Trapido. Jonty Driver wrote biographies, novels and poetry. Mog Morris, who dropped out of university, emigrated to the USA where in 1980 he won the Pulitzer Prize for *The Rise of Theodore Roosevelt*, the first volume of a trilogy. He was then invited to be Ronald Reagan's biographer and spent much time in the Reagan White House, even attending cabinet meetings. The result was classic over-reach – Mog had been a beatnik, after all – in which the book (*Dutch: A Memoir of Ronald Reagan*) was presented as the work of an imaginary author, who by chance was also called Edmund Morris and who was a fictional friend of Reagan. Mog said he used this device because he had decided that nobody could understand Reagan, who in some ways was not a real person at all. This enraged the critics, though since Mog had been paid $3 million to write the book he may not have cared very much.

The University of Natal (Durban) was a small campus and the university had little money, so things were all done on a shoestring. But the lecturers worked hard and some of them were very good. I look back on it with considerable affection. Later it got much bigger and was then ruined under the administration of William Makgoba. The

---

5   See Johnson, *Look Back in Laughter*, especially pp 89–136.

(crazy) attempt was made to make Zulu a language of administration and instruction, despite the entire lack of academic books in Zulu. Many leading academics were driven out and it was generally believed that both phone conversations and emails were being monitored. All normal academic norms were disrespected, ludicrous appointments were made, and many of the best students fled. Ultimately, the university was left with a debt of R2 billion. The African students who now form the majority have inherited an institution that is merely a shell of what it once was. One of my later students in Oxford, Peter Godwin (who wrote several memorable books on Zimbabwe), used to say of growing up in Rhodesia: 'I come from a country which no longer exists.' That is how I feel about my alma mater. It did good things for me but it no longer exists.

CHAPTER THREE

A Step to the Left

The Sharpeville massacre of 21 March 1960 was a watershed for my generation. The shooting, which cost 69 lives, seemed a brutal affirmation of the ugliest side of apartheid. It immediately posed the question of whether peaceful opposition to apartheid was even possible. Those who launched Umkhonto we Sizwe (the Spear of the Nation, or MK), the armed wing of the Communist Party, which soon acquired ANC backing, tended to argue that their own resort to violence was a strategic necessity. But the truth for most of us was far more elemental – a desire to hit back at the apartheid regime just as hard as it had hit the demonstrators at Sharpeville. It was driven by moral outrage far more than by any real assessment of practical possibilities. This was to be a fatal weakness.

Meanwhile, through my sister Francesca I had met Ronnie Kasrils and his girlfriend, Eleanor Anderson. Ronnie was a communist, though not well educated: until then all the radicals I had known had been intellectuals. Ronnie's Marxism was fairly rough-cut but he was keen to share it in a surprisingly open and genial way. This was an early clue that Ronnie's sense of discretion was dangerously weak, for the South Africa of 1961 was no place in which to cheerfully admit to Marxist views. He was really a Joburg boy – there were stories (though I never saw it myself) about him riding motorbikes down to Durban with dagga hidden behind the headlight. He seemed mainly concerned with wooing Eleanor, who worked at a bookshop in central Durban. Ronnie worked at the Lever Brothers advertising agency, Lintas, where he had met a young man of bohemian charm called Barry Higgs. Barry had a facility with words – he was a skilful copywriter – and had ambitions to be a poet. His poetry was, however, a strange mix of the Marxism he had picked up from Ronnie and Spike Milligan humour. His version of 'The Red Flag' began:

> The people's flag is deepest pink.
> It's not as red as some folks think.

I also remember a poem that began, not very promisingly,

> Bourgeois, bourgeois, bourgeois louse
> You just like sitting
> In your bourgeois house.

Such poems would, after a radical start, soon descend into fantasy, and Barry, on reading them, would collapse into shouts of laughter. He was immensely engaging and we soon became fast friends. From the outset Barry had a yen for a younger assistant in the bookshop, Sybilla Haesloop. I remember strolling over there with Ronnie and Barry, and Barry reaching into his jacket pocket and presenting her with a recently caught fish, its silver scales still gleaming. What girl with a sense of humour would not be charmed? Barry's company brought many such surreal moments. Eleanor, for her part, would brightly enquire about which books I was reading for my various courses. The next time we met she would reach into her basket and there under a cloth would be the volumes in question, all of which she would give to me. I was somewhat overcome by this generosity, feelings that were somewhat lessened when Eleanor cheerfully replied, 'Don't be silly. I shoplifted them. Property is theft.'

This apparently happened a lot. Thereafter, though feeling rather prim, I refrained from listing the books I needed.

Barry had a well-developed taste for local wine. I blush to remember the dreadful stuff we drank – huge great gallon jars of Lieberstein, a sweet white wine, and an equally cheap red Muscadel. Barry and I often sat out on verandahs in the warm Durban evenings with a bottle of one of these noxious brews. After a drink or two our conversation always turned to the possibility of hitting back at the regime with acts of sabotage. It was, we decided, quite easy: you could start cane fires or attack garages and set fire to the petrol pumps. All of our schemes stopped short of taking on either the South African police or army and in general never got beyond the fantasy stage.

Barry had sublet a room from a young lecturer, Stan Trapido, in a house owned by the professor of psychology, Ronald Albino. Albino and his wife, Veronica, lived on the ground floor, Stan on the first floor, and Barry in an attic with a balcony. One evening there we killed off a large jar of Lieberstein. Barry, rather than descend to the bathroom, took the short cut of peeing over the balcony into the garden below. We soon heard the heavy tread of Stan Trapido coming up the stairs. Stan, looking stressed, said that Professor Albino had just complained. He and his wife had gone to bed on this warm Durban night with the French windows open, only to be spattered with urine blown in through the open doors by the night breeze. Barry explained that it wasn't urine: he had merely shaken the dregs of the Lieberstein (he displayed the empty bottle) over the balcony. Stan, much relieved, retired to tell the Albinos. A minute later we heard Stan's funereal tread again. He re-appeared at the door, more stressed than ever: 'Professor Albino says he knows the difference between white wine and pee.'

Barry and I might fantasise but by the middle of 1961 it was obvious that Ronnie was involved in something serious. We discussed it in whispers. Ronnie had become increasingly furtive and was clearly

involved in some kind of mission. Moreover, he was recruiting a gang
– he would sometimes boast to us of what splendid fellows he had
recruited, particularly extolling the virtues of one Bruno Mtolo, 'a really
good comrade'. (Many years later Ronnie lamented to me that he had
not recruited Barry and myself.) But Ronnie's judgement was not good.
Bruno became a notorious police informer and his evidence helped send
Mandela and his comrades to jail on Robben Island. He was later
assassinated by MK.

In mid-October I was at a drinks party at Ronald Albino's house
when we heard a loud 'crump', plainly a muffled explosion. I was standing
near Barbara Schuddeboom and Stan Trapido. Stan went white: 'It's
Ronnie,' he said, echoing my own surmise. Stan had a history in the
Congress of Democrats (a communist front organisation), which had
already attracted interest from the security police, and the last thing he
needed was proximity to a sabotage campaign. The explosion had indeed
been Ronnie's attempt to blow up the offices of the National Party
newspaper *Die Nataller*. Within minutes the security police burst into
our party, taking careful note of everyone there, for we were all viewed
as suspects. MK took credit for the blast.

A week later, I had begun to walk towards the campus bus stop
when I saw Ronnie ahead of me, dropping a trail of leaflets as he walked.
I stooped and scanned one. It was an MK call to armed action, expressed
in the most incendiary terms. I shuddered, knowing that possession of
such a leaflet would guarantee a long jail sentence. Scooping them up,
I handed them to Ronnie. 'For chrissake Ronnie, be more careful,' I said.
'Don't you realise how lucky you were that I was behind you? Anybody
else might have gone straight to the police.' Ronnie brightened: 'You've
got to admit they're bloody good leaflets, don't you think?' He was quite
irrepressible. It was another lesson in how bad Ronnie's security was.
Meanwhile I was left to reflect that I knew a key secret that I would
rather not have known: if I was detained, the police would beat the truth

out of me, in which case I would go to jail too. But this was just Ronnie's way; he often ignored security with a cheerful insouciance. I always saw Ronnie as a sincere but naive revolutionary romantic. But, to be fair to him, we were all lax about security; we were too used to living open lives.

· · ·

In 1962 there was a parliamentary by-election in Musgrave, in Durban. I hoped to see the Progressive Party do well; of its 11 MPs, only one, Helen Suzman, now remained, but she provided a ray of hope, a one-woman opposition to apartheid. I canvassed for the Prog candidate, Ray Swart, and also met Helen Suzman. But, to our horror, the United Party candidate increased the UP majority in the seat. Clearly, the Progs were buckling under the sheer weight of *swart gevaar* (black peril) propaganda. It was going to be a long haul. It was not until 1974 that Helen Suzman ceased to be the sole Prog MP.

I was much taken up by SRC affairs when one day Mike Kirkwood came to see me. He had moved into a little room at the back of 79A Essenwood Road, the home of Rowley Arenstein, a communist lawyer who took all the area's political cases against the state. He was listed, banned and under house arrest but continued to be a thorn in the side of the authorities. Two years before a group describing itself as the Ku Klux Klan (KKK) had attacked Rowley's house but been beaten back by a large group of ANC activists. The American civil rights struggle was then at its height, with continuous publicity about freedom marchers and the KKK. Naturally, our local white supremacists identified with the latter.

Mike had got to know the Arenstein family – Rowley, his wife, Jackie, and their two young daughters, Jenny, nine, and Bess, eleven. After the earlier attack the Arensteins had moved to a ground-floor apartment for security's sake, but the KKK was again making continual anonymous phone calls, threatening to burn down the Arenstein home. This had credibility; the Cape Town house of a banned communist had recently been firebombed. The horrible irony was that Rowley and his family could not move, for both Rowley and Jackie were under house arrest, so they had to be at home from 6 pm every evening until 6 am.

Mike explained that most of the ANC activists who had protected Rowley from the KKK on the previous occasion were now in jail or in exile. So people were desperately needed to stand guard outside the Arenstein apartment to try to fend off the KKK. Mike wanted me to volunteer. I was far from keen, for any involvement with the Arensteins almost certainly spelt trouble. Among Durban's sober citizens the very mention of the Arenstein name brought a sharp intake of breath. Rowley was right at the top of the security police hit list. Every time Nelson Mandela and Walter Sisulu came to Durban they always visited Rowley's apartment. It was a veritable hive of sedition. But for me the clincher was the unbearable idea of two little girls being victims of a firebombing. So I agreed.

I soon met the Arensteins. Rowley was an almost Talmudic figure, spare, bespectacled and goateed. In his sitting room were arrayed all 57 volumes of Lenin's *Collected Works* and he loved nothing better than endlessly rereading them. In any discussion on any topic Rowley would soon lift his hand and say, 'Ah, but what does Lenin say?' – before answering his own question at considerable length. This always settled the argument. Even if you didn't agree, no one wanted Rowley to begin another peroration, and, naturally, in Rowley's eyes, Lenin could never be wrong about anything. Mike, Barry (who had also moved into a room behind the Arensteins) and I often joked that even if you asked Rowley what time lunch was, he would respond, 'Ah, but what does Lenin say?'

Jackie Arenstein, formerly a daredevil communist journalist, was then in her forties, short, raven-haired and strikingly attractive. No matter how often the security police burst into her home she never lost her self-possession or showed the slightest sign of fear: she was a tigress. She had grown up in a well-to-do Jewish home but her father had strongly disapproved of the education of women and had other social views to match. Jackie had rebelled, left home, and married Rowley, probably her family's least favourite man in Durban. But Jackie was strange: she had a most un-Marxist interest in existentialism and frequently wondered aloud what Albert Camus had meant when he said this or that. Perhaps not accidentally, this was an area where Rowley could supply no answers. I too was interested in Camus, Sartre and the rest of the *Temps modernes* crowd, so Jackie and I had some good though rather unlikely conversations about existentialism while she slaved away in the kitchen.

Although Jackie herself never uttered a word on the matter, others spoke of an intense romantic relationship between her and Tom Sharpe. When I later got to know Tom there was certainly no doubt of his devotion to Jackie, though he spoke warningly of the time when a number of Mpondo chiefs had taken up residence in the Arenstein household. (Rowley had represented them during the Mpondo rebellion.) Jackie had cooked and slaved for them but, Tom said, she also quietly confided to him: 'They're all very good chaps but come the revolution they'll be among the first ones we'll have to get rid of.' One could not but wonder if her encounter with Tom (a Liberal) had not begun her gradual disaffection from Rowley's Marxist certainties.

The apartment right next to the Arensteins was tenanted by Laura Hitchens, a single parent without previous political convictions who had thrown in her lot with the Arensteins out of simple good-heartedness. This was crucial: Laura was neither banned nor under house arrest but one of her sitting-room windows opened only a few feet away from the front windows of the Arenstein sitting room. When both windows were open it was easy to converse with Jackie or Rowley despite the orders forbidding any such contact. Barry, Mike and I would treat Laura's flat as a virtual second home, thus allowing us safe contact with the Arensteins.

Indeed, we were often in the Arenstein household until 6 pm and even later because in the event of a security police raid – and these were frequent occurrences – there was usually time to slip through the window back into Laura's apartment, there to confront the police. Jackie made pots of tea all day long, so we often congregated in the Arenstein kitchen to drink them, with Jackie cheerfully musing about Camus. Sometimes the police would burst straight into Laura's sitting room, while one of us was still illegally with the Arensteins next door. You then had to bolt into the garden or into the servants' quarters so that at least you would not be breaking the house arrest rules when the police moved from Laura's flat to spot-check the Arensteins next door. There were some close shaves and sweaty moments.

The servants' quarters were occupied by, respectively, Mike, Barry and Melville Fletcher. Melville, like Rowley, was a devoted communist with a Lenin goatee. A former activist who had organised sugar plantation workers, Melville knew and hated the great 'sugar barons', as they were known. He was an extremely good-hearted man, though he became irascible at Barry's relentless teasing and *Goon Show* humour. At first he would sit, stroking his abundant moustache and commenting, 'This poor man has had no proper education' or 'Strange that he should think such childish nonsense funny'. Barry would grin ear to ear and continue his teasing until Melville would explode out of his chair with great shouts of wrath, pursuing Barry – emitting wild shouts of laughter – all round the Arenstein ménage.

Melville too was banned and under house arrest, but every time he went in search of a job the security police would inform the would-be employer that since Melville was a listed communist, any employer who took him on would fall under suspicion too. This guaranteed that Melville remained unemployed and thus penniless. Rowley, a self-employed lawyer, was in a stronger position.[6]

Mike and I helped Melville to pen a letter to John Vorster, the then minister of justice and the regime's tough guy in charge of bannings, listings and the security police. In it Melville outlined his situation: it was due to the actions of the minister that he was under house arrest and thus confined to his room. But it was also due to Melville's being listed, and the security police's pressure on employers, that he was unable to obtain a job. Thus, he was unable to pay the rent for his room and yet he was legally forced to reside there. The letter then concluded: 'I realise that, unlike me, Minister Vorster, you are not a socialist. Nonetheless, you will surely agree with me that the only solution to this conundrum is for you to nationalise my room.' No reply was received.

Barry enjoyed mixing with the many communists among the Natal Indian Congress (NIC), particularly Billy Nair (who ended up doing 20 years on Robben Island with Mandela). Billy came from humble origins – his parents had immigrated from India and his father was illiterate. Barry, coming from an uneducated background himself, was naturally attracted to other autodidacts, which was why he liked Melville too. What particularly engaged him was Melville's determination to keep up appearances. Once a week Melville would comb his beard and whiskers, put on a tie and an old-fashioned double-breasted blazer, and then march out to a cafe. There he would order afternoon tea and genteelly sip his tea with his little finger crooked, and greet each passer-by with a gracious smile. This was Melville's way of showing that, whatever his troubles, he still belonged in polite society. On Melville's

---

6   In 1966 Rowley was imprisoned under the Suppression of Communism Act. He was struck off the roll and could not practise as an attorney when he was released in 1970. So he became a legal clerk in a friend's office and continued to handle political trials. The government then prohibited him from entering any attorney's office. Only in 1994 was Rowley readmitted as an attorney. He faced old age in a state of penury.

return to the insalubrious world of 79A Essenwood Road Barry would greet him with exaggerated politeness, offer him tea with his little finger crooked, and generally give a satirical imitation of Melville's tea-room jaunt. This always ended with an enraged Melville chasing Barry back to his room amid Barry's delighted peals of laughter.

The serious thing was, of course, the KKK. Barry, Mike and I would often take their anonymous phone calls. We would pass the phone quickly to one another, affecting different voices as we replied, as if to suggest that there was a large gang of defenders gathered at the Arensteins. We then had to run straight back to Laura's because the security police would suddenly arrive, rather implying that they had made the call or, at the least, had listened in to it.

We knew the KKK would not attack by day when Essenwood Road was full of middle-class shoppers. But every night two of us would stand nervously on guard outside 79A until dawn. We counted on the notion that the mere sight of us would show the attackers that they had to get past us before they could reach the Arenstein home. We appealed to left-wingers in Durban to rally round, but night after night would find just Barry, Mike and me, together with Costa Gazidis, a dashing young doctor of Greek extraction. We were desperately short-handed and appealed in vain to Ronnie, who was often seen striding purposefully near 79A. Ronnie was adamantly unavailable. He was busy blowing up electricity pylons and setting sugar-cane fires as part of the MK sabotage campaign (security was, again, laughable) and this was regarded as more important than protecting the Arensteins.

Barry was largely unemployed and invariably hard up. But Jackie always provided delicious meals and Barry paid no rent to the Arensteins, so he had free board and lodging. During the day he would hammer out poems on a small portable typewriter. Indeed, this machine played a key part in Barry's economy. Occasionally it would be noted that Barry was wearing a hangdog air and it would emerge that he had had to pawn his beloved typewriter. Jackie and Laura would then cluck away in motherly fashion, saying how sad it was that, Barry, a writer after all, should lack his typewriter. The two women would then somehow scrape together enough money for Barry to redeem his typewriter at the pawn shop. He generally seemed to make enough profit on the transaction to come home not only with his typewriter but also a half-gallon of wine. With this he would make merry until he was again forced to pawn his typewriter and the whole cycle would repeat itself.

Once Barry took off for South West Africa (Namibia), there to work on the diamond diggings. This involved a ten-day hitch-hike through the Kalahari. It was horribly hot during the day, he said, but freezing at night. Lacking money for accommodation, he just slept on the sand. How did you manage that, I asked. Barry laughed. Every day before sunset he would buy a cheap bottle of brandy and then drink all of it, sending himself off into a blissful coma, with his night-time body warmth guaranteed by the brandy. Barry didn't last long in South West before drinking his way back across the Kalahari in similar fashion.

For months, our little band kept guard on the Arenstein home. I often found it difficult to stay awake during lectures the next day, and exam revision became really hard. Moreover, my parents could not afford my university fees, so I worked all weekends and vacations in local bookshops. One way and another I was busy 24 hours a day. When, in later years, many activists reminisced about their role in the struggle, I often reflected on how few of us there really were.

Just behind 79A stood a synagogue, and one day, acting on a tip-off, Barry and I climbed up onto its roof. Sure enough, we found it littered with empty lager cans and cigarette stubs. Clearly, it was being used (by the security police or the KKK) to keep the Arenstein residence under surveillance. This must have required the connivance of the synagogue authorities. Feeling sick at heart, we told Rowley but said no more to anyone: we felt it was Jewish community business.

Only years later did Rowley tell me how he had had another major worry at that time. Unbeknown to us, Ronnie was actually Jackie's nephew, and so she and Rowley felt a family duty towards him. (The fact that Ronnie was refusing to protect Jackie and her children was generously overlooked.) Ronnie, for his part, needed transport for his nocturnal exploits involving dynamite and derring-do, so he prevailed on Rowley to lend him his battered old car. This was extremely risky, for the car might lead the police back to Rowley. More than once Rowley found percussion caps scattered on the car's back seat the next morning, almost giving him a heart attack: such evidence could have sent him to jail for many years. But Jackie and Rowley were disciplined activists. They showed no sign of resentment at Ronnie's refusal to protect them. They knew Ronnie was under discipline too – and that was enough.

Rowley had originally been sent down to Durban as a Communist Party organiser in 1939. His recruits came chiefly from the Indian community – some of the leading lights of the NIC as well as Indian workers. Rowley was told to gather what information he could about British war plans – Durban was the main Royal Navy base in southern Africa. A number of Indian waiters in the Durban beachfront hotels were Party members and they happily relayed the naval officers' conversations they overheard. Given the Nazi-Soviet pact, some of that information was probably relayed to the Nazis.

The police already kept a tight watch on Rowley. Not long after Germany attacked the Soviet Union in June 1941 the police approached him and asked why he had done no campaigning for a while down the Natal South Coast. Rowley asked why they wanted to know. They were, it emerged, greatly concerned at the anti-war propaganda spread by the communists in the first two years of the war: some African or Indian Party members might still be affected by the spirit of the Nazi-Soviet pact sufficiently to help the German U-boats then swarming off the Natal coast. But only communists had credibility among such folk, so the police offered to lend Rowley a car to go campaigning down there in support of the war effort. This he declined, but he duly went down south to explain that the Nazi attack on the Soviet Union had turned the old imperialist war into a Great Patriotic War, which they should all support.

In 1950 the Communist Party of South Africa was forced to dissolve itself when the government passed the Suppression of Communism Act. Rowley had become habituated to a situation in which the Party leadership was in Johannesburg or Cape Town and the Party in Durban was treated as a mere addendum, so when in 1953 he heard that some elements in Joburg wanted to relaunch the Party underground – as the South African Communist Party (SACP) – he was dubious. Having made his way to Joburg, he was taken aback to find that the initiative was little more than a putsch by a small group of self-chosen 'leaders'. There had been no democratic vote on the issue by Party branches. So although Jackie and Rowley continued to regard themselves as communists, they never joined the SACP.

Rowley's differences with the SACP were ideological too. When the Afrikaner Nationalists took power in 1948, many within the Party had greeted this as a new onset of fascism. Many Party militants were ex-servicemen and were bitterly conscious of the fact that some Nats had sided with Hitler during the war, but of course it was useful in propaganda terms too to insist that the Nats were Nazis. Rowley argued that this was a fundamental misanalysis: the Nats were racist and reactionary but not fascist. DF Malan, their leader, had taken a strong line against the pro-Nazis in his ranks and had squashed them. Moreover, Rowley pointed out, when Hitler took power in Germany, all notions of law and order were immediately abandoned and the round-up of Jews, communists and social democrats into concentration camps began right away. In South Africa, on the other hand, despite the fact that many of the Party leaders were Jews, nobody had been imprisoned, there were no concentration camps and activists like Rowley were still happily organising. The Nats were extremely legalistic and even 'respectable': they would doubtless suppress the Party in time, though by passing a Bill through Parliament with the usual three readings, debates and amendments.

This difference was crucial, Rowley argued, for it meant that a legal space existed for continued trade union activity, the heart of the matter for any communist. Rowley was an expert at this game. If a black trade union was forbidden, he would set up a Bantu Friendship Association, which effectively took its place. By the time the government had realised what was happening, Rowley would have changed the name to the Bantu Brotherhood Association and then it would take the government another nine to twelve months to act against that, by which time it would have yet another name. And so on it went, with Rowley always ahead of the authorities. He was careful always to stay within the letter of the law. Although personally banned and under house arrest, he broke those orders as much as he dared. He was, for example, banned from attending meetings, defined as three persons or more. He played an active role on trade union committees, but whenever the police raided, they would always find Rowley alone in the bathroom. He thought and acted quickly and had nerves of steel.

By the late 1950s Rowley realised that various elements within the SACP were beginning to think in terms of guerrilla warfare. The subject led to grave disagreements within the Party. The chairman, Jack Simons, would have nothing to do with it, but the leading lights of the Johannesburg Party – Michael Harmel, Lionel (Rusty) Bernstein, Joe Slovo and Joe's wife, Ruth First – all favoured armed action. Both Slovo and First, but especially Ruth, were following the war in Algeria with great attention and saw key parallels there. The Algerian communists had taken the view that the most progressive future lay in afforcing the powerful French Communist Party and they had therefore argued against a struggle for independence. But the nationalist Front de Libération Nationale (FLN) had simply gone ahead in 1954 and launched its armed struggle. The result was that the communists quickly lost all support as radical opinion polarised around the FLN.

Slovo and First were mortally afraid that something similar might happen in South Africa. When the Pan Africanist Congress (PAC) had led the campaign against the pass laws and triggered Sharpeville, it seemed that their worst fears might be realised: by outflanking the ANC (with which the SACP was allied) on the left, the PAC might overtake it. It was thus essential that the SACP regain the radical initiative by launching guerrilla action. This idea was informally sold to the Party's Central Committee, which included the rising young star of the ANC, Nelson Mandela. He was made head of MK, which prepared to launch the armed struggle. Thus, MK was entirely the creation of a particular SACP faction, but it was hoped that Mandela's leadership would gradually draw the ANC in too. The then ANC leader, Albert Luthuli, was a strong Christian and completely opposed to the use of violence, but it was hoped that the launching of MK would see Mandela effect a leadership coup against Luthuli.

Rowley was horrified when he heard this. Such action, he argued, would play into the regime's hands. Its police and army were hugely superior in military terms and South Africa's terrain was unsuitable for guerrilla warfare. All that would happen was that the regime would feel it had been freed from all legal restraints and would smash not only MK but the ANC, the PAC and the trade unions as well. The struggle for African rights would be set back years, even decades. Accordingly, as he later related to me, when Rowley heard that the SACP had secretly sent Walter Sisulu to Natal to canvass support for the armed struggle, he evaded the police and attended the secret meeting, held on a farm north of Durban.

Poor Sisulu must have hated Rowley that evening, for he

immediately wanted to know what democratic authority there was for the abandonment of non-violence. There had been no SACP or ANC conference resolution nor even discussion about it. Nor had there been a resolution by the ANC National Executive Committee or the Party's Central Committee. So how could such a fundamental change be made? Sisulu had no answer to this. What made it worse was the strong presence in the Party and the Congress movement generally of the NIC. For leading Indians, no matter how radical, were generally faithful to the Gandhian tradition – indeed, Gandhi's farm lay close to where they were meeting that night. So even Congress stalwarts like Ismail Meer and JN Singh were against any turn to violence.

Sisulu was reduced to maintaining that, despite the lack of any proper mandate and despite the hideous practical reasons against armed struggle, it was nonetheless the morally right thing to do. Rowley just laughed at this: how could it be morally right to get people killed for no real purpose? How could it be right to take action that guaranteed the suppression of black trade unions? How could it be right to desert the moral high ground of non-violence when you knew the militarily superior regime would be bound to win and thus be able to justify its own violence?

The unsayable truth was that the key reasons for armed struggle were that it would enable the SACP and ANC to keep the initiative over the PAC, and would enable Mandela effectively to carry out a leadership putsch against Luthuli. According to Rowley, Ruth First seemed almost to hate Luthuli, calling him 'a stupid old man', an 'Uncle Tom', and so on. But if Mandela led the armed struggle, he would seize the radical initiative and leave Luthuli, the apostle of non-violence, behind. At the end of this process, the armed-struggle faction would have effectively seized power within both the SACP and the ANC. Mandela would become the effective leader of the ANC, and since Mandela was already on the SACP Central Committee and thus under Party discipline, the

SACP would control or at least strongly influence the ANC. All of which was to come to pass, though Sisulu could hardly explain that. Indeed, he himself may have only half-understood the truth, though it was he who had recruited Mandela to the SACP.

Rowley was able to win a clear majority at this meeting, to Sisulu's great embarrassment, but of course that did not prevent the emergence of MK and the turn to violence. It was with growing desperation that Rowley then watched every part of his predictions come true – the ANC and PAC banned, MK routed, the security police using torture because violence was now allowed, black trade unions suppressed, and those who escaped fleeing into exile. The whole anti-apartheid movement was set back by a generation. All of this Rowley later related to Mike, Barry and me, and his influence was decisive: none of us joined the armed struggle, which otherwise we probably would have done.

I have never ceased to feel grateful for that. As the years went by one knew many people whose lives were ruined to no purpose by their involvement in that struggle, MK achieved almost nothing militarily. Most of its foot soldiers were easily caught, imprisoned for long periods, often tortured, and frequently ended up working for the security police. Those who remained in exile sometimes got used as cannon fodder in wars they had never wanted to fight. The MK guerrillas who sought to get the ANC to pay attention to their woes were rewarded with prison, torture and sometimes death. When the struggle was over most of them were spat out and left to live out their lives in grinding poverty or as criminals, while their old leaders flourished and got rich.

It was typical of Rowley that when Harold Strachan – the first white man to go to jail for sabotage – sought his help, he did not hesitate to give it, just as he was always ready to defend PAC activists. Harold had had a hard time in jail and had been approached by a *Rand Daily Mail* journalist, Benjamin Pogrund, who suggested that Harold should spill the beans about prison conditions, for no one really knew what went on in jail. Rowley advised Harold that it would be an excellent idea to expose the grim truth about life in prison, but also extremely risky: the law specifically forbade anyone from telling untruths about jail conditions – and this law would be bound to be used against Harold, no matter how truthful his newspaper articles. As soon as the first article appeared, Rowley predicted, the police would serve a gagging order on Harold and thus prevent any of his other articles from being punished. But, to do that, they would have to find Harold to serve him with the order. So Harold and Pogrund must write all the articles in advance and then Harold should disappear so that the police could not find him.

Rowley asked Pogrund how he would write up the articles. Pogrund said he would interview Harold at length, using a tape recorder, and would then write that up. In that case, advised Rowley, it was essential that all the tapes be destroyed before the first article appeared. Otherwise the police would seize the tapes and, inevitably, there would be at least some small differences between the tapes and what appeared in the articles. These would then be used to 'prove' that Harold had not told the truth. So this too was agreed.

Harold and Pogrund proceeded as planned and a series of articles was written. Harold then disappeared. The first article appeared, creating a major sensation. The police went wild, raiding the house or flat of every known radical in search of him. He was nowhere to be found. With each successive article, the police tried desperately to find Harold. The articles made a splash around the world and were raised in debate at the United Nations (UN). Harold then re-emerged; he had simply taken himself off to Mfolozi Game Reserve, reasoning that no one looked for anyone in a game reserve. The police pounced on him but it was too late to stop full publication.

However, the police managed to convict Harold and send him back to jail again. Both Harold and Rowley claimed that this was because Pogrund had not destroyed the tapes after all, though Pogrund denies this. Suffice it to say that the first duty of a journalist in a matter such as this is to protect his source, but Harold in fact paid a very high price for telling the truth, while Pogrund made his name with the scoop. To be fair, it should be added that Pogrund was a doughty anti-apartheid activist, several times tried, once jailed, and later forced into exile himself.

CHAPTER FOUR

Strange Encounters

I got used to the routine whereby I would roll up at Laura Hitchens's flat, play a few games of Scrabble with Laura, Mike, Barry and Costa, saunter over to see Jackie and Rowley, and then, around midnight, take up guard duty at the Arensteins' front gate. All the evening's jokes would then be forgotten and we stood around until about 5 am, getting scared every time we saw a car's headlights approaching. It was particularly tense if there had been more KKK phone calls that day. If nothing had happened by 5 am, we thought it safe to creep inside and flop onto Laura's sofas. A few hours later I would head off to the university.

There were many subplots. Bess and Jenny were both pretty young girls whose space had been invaded by this group of large men. We never talked about the KKK or firebombs while the girls were around; they understood their situation well enough. Moreover, strangers had always wandered through the Arenstein home. The Mpondo chiefs who had come to ask for Rowley's help during the 1960 Mpondo rebellion had really settled in. Jackie was astonished by their enthusiasm for washing – the Arenstein bathroom was in continuous use all day long – and also for her cooking. Bess and Jenny had treated that visitation as normal too, though one could guarantee that this hadn't happened to any other white girls in Durban, let alone the nice young Jewish boys and girls they met at gatherings of the Habonim youth movement.

Then there were Laura's parties. These were fun, but tense – they were often raided by the security police, partly attracted by the Arensteins' proximity, partly because black students used to attend them. The police were visibly angry, perhaps even disgusted, if they found white girls dancing with black men, but this was not illegal so there was nothing they could do. (It was always black men – I never saw a black girl at these parties.) But it was illegal to have any liquor about, so we had to be careful about that – not easy when most of the partygoers were engaged in getting drunk. In addition, of course, there was the question of the pass laws. The police suspected any blacks they found there after dark and some of the UNNE students were already on their list of political suspects.

I was nervous for another reason. My younger brother, Philip, had taken to socialising at a residence for black nurses and was courting one of them, Edna Moshesh. This risked heavy punishment under the Immorality Act and was a source of great worry to my parents – Phil had brought Edna home to meet them. This was extremely unusual – to put it mildly – in the South Africa of 1962, but my parents treated Edna as they would have any other girl. I worried that Phil and Edna would fetch up at one of Laura's parties, adding another level of danger, but they never did. The Arensteins never attended any of the parties – it would have been too dangerous and, anyway, Rowley was less interested in parties than in the Party.

Rowley's disapproval of the armed struggle completed his alienation from the SACP. He was independent-minded and smarter than most, but there was also a definite regional tinge to it, as there is to most things in South Africa. In the eyes of the SACP leadership, Durban was a dependent satrapy and a backwater. The unspoken but always present assumption was that Zulus were the most 'backward' Africans and that emissaries sent down there had a tendency to 'go native'. The Party bosses in Johannesburg who had sent Ronnie to Durban may have done so because, once Rowley had gone rogue, they wanted a completely reliable apparatchik down there, which Ronnie certainly was.

However, Rowley was still a Marxist-Leninist and what now came to his rescue was the Sino-Soviet split. The whole SACP leadership had been recruited as good Stalinists: taking the side of the Soviet Union was second nature for them. They had supported Soviet intervention in Hungary in 1956, and when the Sino-Soviet split occurred in 1960 the SACP soon backed the Soviet side. In any case, the Soviet bloc was providing the SACP with the arms, money and training needed for the armed struggle, and this patronage was decisive.

So, naturally, Rowley took the Chinese side. He would quote each of Mao's latest blasts against Khrushchev with approval. We were disposed to believe what Rowley told us but this was something of a stretch. For example, Rowley cited how Mao had condemned Khrushchev for 'adventurism' for placing Soviet missiles in Cuba, but then, when Khrushchev was forced to remove them under American pressure, Mao denounced him for 'capitulationism'. We protested that this meant that Khrushchev could hardly win whatever he did. Rowley would counter that the SACP was exactly the same: its resort to armed struggle was adventurist but the result would be complete defeat and it would then relinquish the battlefield entirely to the Afrikaner Nats. Rowley was unconcerned by the contradiction between supporting ultra-militant Maoism and opposing armed struggle.

Barry, Mike and I all respected Rowley. His courage was exemplary, and even in the most frightening moments he kept a cool head. We were all influenced by him, though usually finding his Maoism a subject for humour. Copies of the *Peking Review* (this was long before Peking became Beijing) lay littered around his house, though they were hastily tidied away if the security police appeared. Quite how Rowley got hold of such banned material was not disclosed. Mike, Barry and I would loyally pore over copies of the *Review*. The language was so ideologically dense as to be unreadable but we were much taken by Mao's turn of phrase, particularly his description of Khrushchev as 'the running dog of American imperialism'. We liked that. A small black dachshund often ran in and out of Laura's and the Arensteins', and we got into the habit of calling it 'the running dog'. Melville had a phobia about dogs and would protest, 'Keep that filthy beast away from me,' causing Barry to try to lead him all the more in Melville's direction.

Melville's room was extremely small, more of a box really, with just room in it for a bed and a chair. Melville, when returning from one of his tea-room soirées, had a habit, as he closed the door of the room, of twisting and falling onto the bed so that he came to rest lying on his back with his hands folded behind his head. Barry, fascinated by this, would get Melville to demonstrate how he did this in a single smooth motion. It was so smooth as to be soundless, save for the strong protest of the bedsprings. When Melville went to his room, Barry, with a delighted grin on his face, would cock his ear, waiting for the sound of those springs.

One evening, while Melville was out, Barry got me to come to Melville's room where we both tried to copy Melville's backward-falling movement. Barry pointed out that as you came to rest you inevitably stared straight at the back of the door, which had a coat hook on it. Barry quickly gathered up the dachshund and an old khaki rucksack. Hanging the rucksack on the door hook, he placed the dachshund in it. It just sat there calmly, with its long nose pointing out of the bag. Barry gleefully pointed out that when Melville came back and fell onto his bed, he would have the surreal experience of being eyeball-to-eyeball with the dog he loathed. And so it was. Melville came back, nodded good night, and retired to his room. We heard the door shut, the sound of the bedsprings – and then a huge yell of rage as Melville saw the hated dog staring back at him. Melville came racing out, bent on revenge, but Barry ran before him, in peals of laughter.

. . .

One night, arriving for a Laura party with a carload of UNNE students, we saw a young constable patrolling the street outside, hardly accidentally. One of the Africans in the car, Asher Ntanga, said, 'Leave him to me.' He burst out of the car and began an extraordinary pantomime act, rolling his eyes, calling the policeman *baas* and showing his pass. It seemed so over the top that it was difficult not to laugh but the policeman accepted it as normal. While he was talking to Asher, the rest of the car's passengers, disembarking 30 metres behind, crept into Laura's. Asher was always up for escapades of this kind.

Costa Gazidis was a considerable party animal. A darkly handsome young man, Costa attracted quite a variety of women, one of them Laura herself. Costa and she formed a natural couple but, as the other men all knew, Costa was never able to resist if another attractive woman hove into view. At one of Laura's parties Laura herself had disappeared, the lights had been dimmed, and Costa was smooching another girl, when Laura reappeared from her bedroom, took in the scene in a glance, and cried, 'Oh, Costa!' with such a pitch of anguish and reproach that to this day it rings in my ears.

The default activity before we went on guard was Scrabble. Both Mike and Barry were good players, but Melville, though he was a literate man who tried hard, was weak. It annoyed him to lose to Barry – and Melville could swear fluently in Zulu and Norwegian as well as in English and Afrikaans. One evening, after a chat with Rowley, I re-entered Laura's flat by her window and found the Scrabble game in full swing when suddenly there was a shout of triumph from both Barry and Mike. Melville, rather hopelessly, had put down DOG on a double-letter score. Barry had then put down all seven of his letters to transform this into RUNNINGDOG. He was immediately awarded the game.

One night, Barry and I were on guard around 3.30 am when we saw a car turn the corner and sidle towards us. As it drew level with the gate Barry said, 'Jesus, it's them!' Sure enough we could see four figures in the car with nylons over their heads – a ghastly sight. The men saw us and suddenly accelerated away. We stood rooted to the spot, unsure what to do next. A minute later the car came back around the block. As it got closer Barry said, 'Christ, they've got guns!' And sure enough there were two stick-shaped objects protruding out of the front and back windows. As the car drew level with us it again began to accelerate away but simultaneously there was a volley of shots and we heard the bullets whine past us. We couldn't work out whether they had aimed at us or over our heads just to scare us. Either way, our presence at the gate had thwarted them and they had let us know their displeasure.

Triumphant, if shaken, Barry and I retired to the Arenstein kitchen. The whole household had heard the shots so we were joined by Rowley (in pyjamas), Jackie looking very fetching in a dressing gown and Mike in T-shirt and shorts. We eagerly reported the event while Rowley expatiated on its probable meaning and Jackie served us all tea. We were all enjoying ourselves when four security policemen burst into the room and their leader said, 'Well, well, and what an interesting little illegal gathering we have here.' I saw Rowley turn ashen. As well he might, for we were all obviously breaking banning and house arrest orders. This could mean jail time for all of us. The police were clearly delighted at having netted Barry, Mike and me. We had to give our names, addresses and occupations and were then told to leave, which we did with our tails between our legs. It was an obvious disaster caused by careless overconfidence. We suspected, of course, that the policemen were the same men who had shot at us, and that they had simply taken off their masks and returned to discover who had foiled the planned attack.

This inaugurated a miserable period of being woken abruptly at 5 am for early-morning interrogations. I was up late revising for exams at the time but would be shaken awake and taken down to the security police headquarters. None of the office doors, I noticed, had any names or numbers on them, which rather increased the feeling that I had come to a secret place where anything at all might happen. As I waited to be questioned the door was left open, and I could see the boisterous locker-room activity next door as one large, bull-like policeman, evidently in a bad temper, punched the lockers shut, one after the other. One policeman said, 'That's Tiny. I really don't want to have to let him loose on you.' It was an obvious ploy but scary nonetheless.

I played the naive liberal and earnestly expounded the case for universal suffrage to an obviously scornful Sergeant Visser. I explained, truthfully enough, that I had felt compelled to help protect the two little Arenstein girls from the threat of firebombing. The police assumed that only communists would be found consorting with the Arensteins, yet on the university campus I was a well-known liberal. So, which was I, communist or liberal? I dreaded this line of questioning, for I knew that if word got out on the campus that I was consorting with communists, I would be pretty nearly lynched by the right-wingers.

Yet Sergeant Visser and his colleagues did not pursue this line of questioning very far. The overpowering theme of government propaganda was that liberalism and communism were much the same thing, and I daresay Visser and company regarded this as pretty well self-evident. These interrogation sessions would end with Visser telling me that the police had noticed that people like me, who were studying political science and who counted many Jews among their friends, were always the most dangerous. I waited for something more threatening, but the interrogation that had begun so fiercely would then rather peter out and I would make my way home, rattled but relieved. At one point one of my interrogators demanded point-blank to know why I had so many Jewish friends. I answered, truthfully, that they were often the most interesting and intelligent people I knew. This produced knowing looks and scowls.

Mike and Barry were simultaneously pulled in for interrogation sessions of their own, but none of us were arrested or detained. We guardedly discussed the situation. The police had caught us red-handed, so why were we still at liberty? The answer seemed obvious: the police were leaving us free in the hope that we would lead them to further new names and contacts. Which meant we must be under close surveillance. We were all very jumpy, for the police were busily detaining numerous suspects in their attempt to track down MK activists and also the (ex-Liberal) African Resistance Movement (ARM), which was blowing up pylons at the same time. Word drifted out of various forms of torture being used to break detainees down.

Our jumpiness was increased by several incidents. Peter Mansfield and I had decided that the SRC should bring out a special pamphlet on 21 March to commemorate the anniversary of Sharpeville. We held several whispered meetings to draft the pamphlet and typed it onto Roneo (copier) sheets, ready for several hundred copies to be reproduced. We were so worried about police surveillance that we held several of our meetings in the middle of a rugby pitch at twilight. But, all the same, on 20 March the police raided the SRC office, carrying off our Roneo sheets and other papers. One policeman, who was carrying away our Roneo machine, made a remark that betrayed that they knew about our meetings on the rugby pitch. We decided that they must have had directional microphones.

Meanwhile Mike and I had joined a Marxist study group, together with Ronnie and Graham Pechey, a young lecturer in English literature. Graham, though self-effacing, was sophisticated, clever and well-read both in literature and in Marxism. Mike and I had both read rather less of the Marxist classics, while Ronnie seemed to have read least of all. Despite this, Ronnie always took the lead – no doubt because his ill-disguised role in MK meant he was our political senior, so to speak. The result was awful, as time after time Ronnie tried to guide us through the fundamentals of the dialectic with the air of a conjuror showing his party tricks to children, while the rest of us tried to shift the conversation onto a higher plane. We never succeeded. But at a certain point Ronnie just vanished. He had gone underground: the police were on to him at last. We quickly curtailed further meetings, scared not only of surveillance but also of the possibility that under interrogation Ronnie might talk about the group.

Soon after this, alarming phone calls began at home. The caller would ask, 'Can you get Ronnie to the phone?' If I said 'Ronnie who?' the voice would say, 'Ronnie Kasrils. Be a good chap, Bill.' I would say that Ronnie didn't live there. The hope was clearly that before I could catch myself, I would say, 'OK, I'll call him.' Then one day a post office engineer arrived to mend the phone. I told him that nothing was wrong with the phone and watched him, which made him nervous. After a while he left, without finding a fault. This pantomime was repeated several times until, arriving home one day, I heard my mother say that the engineer had returned and this time had mended the fault. That is, the line was now bugged. I was careful thereafter about what I said on the phone, but only later did I learn that phone microphones are permanently on, picking up everything said in the room.

Worse was in store. Barry and I went up to Wits University in Joburg for a Nusas congress. On the evening before the congress we dined with some student friends, including Spike de Keller from Cape Town, whose easy charm and humour won us all over. Early next morning we learnt he had been snatched by the security police on suspicion of terrorism. We were utterly shocked and indignantly protested his innocence, but the Nusas leadership quietly tipped us off that Spike was probably guilty as charged.

More shocking still was the news that Adrian Leftwich had been detained on similar charges. Adrian had always spoken passionately about his (and Nusas's) complete rejection of violence, so we were even more confident of his innocence. But reports soon drifted out that Adrian too had been blowing up electricity pylons for the ARM. Worse still, no sooner had Adrian been detained than he voluntarily told the security police everything he knew, thus incriminating all his comrades.

We felt betrayed – Adrian had been a hero in our eyes. Especially painful was that when the government had brought in 90 days' detention without trial, the UCT psychology department had decided to conduct trial solitary detentions under observation to see what their effects would be. Adrian volunteered to be a guinea pig but had had to be extricated from the experiment after less than 48 hours, for he was quite unable to bear the isolation. It beggared belief that he had nonetheless pressed ahead with his ARM activities, which were almost bound to result in his detention.

Politically, this made liberals like Peter Mansfield and me walking wounded – and my advocacy of racial integration had already made me a marked man in the eyes of the campus conservatives. When the SRC elections came round again, I asked Tommy Bedford (an architecture student) to design and draw my election posters, as he had done before. Tommy accepted the commission with an ironic laugh: he would doubtless be voting against me, along with the rest of the rugby club.

On election eve I was working late on the student newspaper, only leaving the office around midnight. As I mounted my scooter, my eye was caught by the row of palm trees lining the campus. All the election posters (including my own) had been pulled down. In their place were large, professionally made posters announcing, 'Johnson is a Communist', 'Throw Johnson Off the SRC', 'Down with Communism', and so on. This was doubtless the work of the security police; it was implausible that students could have done such a thorough and expensive job. The posters had clearly been put up with the aid of a ladder; they were placed about three metres up on each tree, too high to reach from the ground.

It was a lucky break for me. The people who had torn down the old posters and put up these new ones had probably waited till 10.30 or 11 pm before sneaking onto the campus. They could have had no idea that I was still there, doubtless the last person on the campus that night. The intention was obviously for the new posters to hit students in the eye as they arrived the next morning, quite likely swaying some voters. No one would have reckoned with the fact that by standing on the saddle of my scooter, I could just reach up high enough to pull the posters down. It was a difficult job done in poor light, but after an hour it was done. Next day I was narrowly re-elected to the SRC.

Mike, Barry and I realised that we were operating on borrowed time. The police clearly had us under surveillance. Sooner or later they would detain us and then squeeze us like lemons to see what we knew. It was at this point that two things happened.

First, Barry told me that Mike was now shacked up with Maggie Strachan, the attractive young wife of Harold Strachan. Barry was troubled. 'I don't know Harold, but he's a comrade. He was brave and went to jail for the struggle. It's just not right for Mike to be sleeping with his wife.' Well aware that Mike would take very ill any intervention in his private life, Barry nonetheless went to state his concerns. He got a flea in his ear. In fact, Barry had hit on a much larger problem. As more and more people disappeared into jail, many explicitly told their wives that they did not expect them to remain celibate throughout that time, and those partners who vowed fidelity did not always keep those vows. When Dave Kitson got 20 years for his leading role in MK, his wife, Norma, with his full encouragement, divorced him and married someone else, who, in turn, she divorced when Dave eventually came out so that she could reunite with Dave.

Second, Barry himself disappeared for a while. His worried girlfriend, Sybilla, came to ask me to go round to Barry's flat to see if he was there. I realised that she was scared that Barry might be detained and the security police might be watching his flat, arresting whoever called there.

Annoyed but resigned, I agreed to go. Barry was there in his usual jolly state: an old girlfriend had materialised and Barry had spent an enjoyable week with her. He was deeply amused that, by coming in Sybilla's place, I had saved him from an awkward scene.

By this time my final exams had hove into view. I would have liked to continue with postgraduate work but knew my parents couldn't afford to keep me at university. There were six children to educate, after all, and I was the first family member to gain a degree. So I decided to enter for the Natal Rhodes Scholarship. A long round of interviews ensued. Finally, I was summoned to an interview with the whole selection panel in Pietermaritzburg. I was tense throughout: if the security police detained me this would doubtless scupper any chance of the scholarship.

I had meanwhile made a new student friend, Rob Amato. When Rob first appeared on campus, he told us that his father had gone bust in Johannesburg and had now retreated to East London, where he had set up Transkei Oil Products – Top Oil. Rob was, at 19, running Top's Durban office and had decided to do a degree at the same time. He was clever and funny, spoke French, and was far more sophisticated than most. Apart from his many talents he had an extraordinary vitality and a huge laugh. He and I were virtually inseparable for a year or two. We showed one another what we wrote, discussed everything, and laughed immoderately.

Rob's family was exotic. His father, Ben, a Sephardic Jew from the island of Rhodes, had sought his fortune first in Belgium and then in the Belgian Congo, where he prospered. When Hitler came to power in Germany. Ben returned to Rhodes and told his fellow Jews, 'You're crazy if you stay here. Hitler means to kill the Jews, not just in Germany but throughout Europe.' Go where, they asked? 'As far away from Europe as possible,' Ben told them. He recommended the Belgian Congo. So, many of them followed Ben back to Léopoldville (today's Kinshasa). Of those who remained behind, every man, woman and child was

slaughtered by the Nazis. Rhodes is a small island and there was nowhere
to hide.

Ben Amato ultimately became a tycoon in Johannesburg, owning
16 textile factories at his peak. But every time he bought, he borrowed
to the hilt to expand yet further, creating an unsteady pyramid. This, as
so often, ended in tears, the collapse of the Amato empire, bankruptcy
and a welter of headlines about crooked Jewish businessmen. Rob, who
anyway found his Jewishness a burden, was humiliated before his school
peers.

Yet Rob was proud of his buccaneering and endlessly resourceful
father. His black workers once launched an explosive wildcat strike,
catching Ben unawares. He decided it would be better to have trade
unions to negotiate with – at least he would know what his workers were
thinking. The law made this difficult but, nothing daunted, Ben set up
a workers' sports club run by an elected committee – with whom he
then negotiated about wage levels. Despite his dreadful fall, Rob's father
was the great paternal engine of the family, offstage but still utterly
dominating.

Rob liked visiting my large, unruly and untidy family, though his
own home life could not have been more different. Despite his stories
of his father fighting back from penury, Rob seemed always to have
money. It wasn't just his car: he often insisted on paying in restaurants,
ordered wine and cigars, and generally lived as he wanted. His mother,
a lady of notably graceful mien, doted on him. He was, so to speak, her
only consolation, since her daughter had emigrated and she and Ben
Amato hadn't been a functioning couple for a long time. Everyone seemed
relieved about that, including Rob. With his huge self-confidence, his
many talents and zest for life, Rob filled that space and, indeed, any
room. Other students sometimes complained that Rob's personality was
too overwhelming, but Rob in turn felt he was the victim of a far more
overwhelming personality – his father's.

Mrs Amato was always delighted to welcome me to her flat. It was somehow assumed that she would provide lunch or dinner (and she was a notable cook), depending on when we rolled up. When we ate, she would bring in the food and then wait on table, hugely gratified if Rob liked what she'd cooked. This embarrassed me, though Rob took it for granted. So accustomed was Rob to this princely fare that he would sometimes turn it away, displaying a connoisseur's fastidiousness. He once swept some delicious veal cutlets into the bin uneaten. 'It's so difficult to know with veal. Why take a chance?' Mrs Amato smiled, apparently proud that her son had made such a good call. He seemed born to command.

Rob claimed that Top Oil's competitors – Lever Brothers, pre-eminently – staged price wars to coincide with his university exams. I thought Rob a little too prone to see himself at the centre of events but was more impressed by this extra dimension, this *monde d'affaires*, of which he seemed to be master. 'This groundnut oil is fabulous stuff,' he would say. 'You can use it for cooking, for heating, to make soap or paint. Even the husks of the nuts get eaten by pigs. Nothing's wasted.' His father pared costs to the bone and kept prices low, and Rob pushed the oil into every little Indian corner shop he could find.

Sometimes we'd drive round together in Rob's car with crates of the stuff rattling in the boot, discussing Scott Fitzgerald or the iniquities of apartheid, until we reached a new little shop Rob had found. As he stepped out of the car the world of letters would disappear and Rob would become the hard-driving salesman. After a while he would hurl himself back into the car, cursing Lever Brothers or sighing about what hard deals Indian shopkeepers drove.

The business seemed to work, and I'd notice rows of Top Oil containers on the shelves of obscure cafes where I'd stopped for a Coke. Not that it ever seemed enough. The business always seemed to be on top of Rob. Some days he'd show up on campus wearing a smart suit and cursing about how many letters he'd already had to dictate that morning. At 19, I didn't know any other 19-year-olds like that. True, I too mixed study and work, but I was a wage slave, paid a pittance, whereas Rob, with his secretary, office and car, was a boss.

His father remained the hidden presence to which Rob's life was forfeit. I never met Ben. He was down in East London, hundreds of miles away, and to me he might as well have been on the moon. But Rob had continuous, intense phone conversations with him and felt him breathing down his neck all the time. 'My dad is a force of nature, a dynamo. He works all hours of the day and can't understand anyone who doesn't. I admire him immensely but he's always demanding more. I love him and I can't stand it.' His father considered Rob's studies to be a childish hobby: he was impatiently waiting for Rob to stop wasting his time at the university so that he could devote himself to Top Oil full time. Sometimes Rob would sound so oppressed by his father that I would ask, 'Why do you do it? Why not just be a student? You're only 19.' Rob would look anguished. 'You don't understand. My father's a great man who's been ruined. He has to rebuild and he's put his whole life into it. I owe him everything, I have no choice. And there's the whole Jewish thing, the son helping the father, being his reincarnation. I'm the only son. There's no escape.'

When I faced the final interview with the Rhodes Scholarship board in Pietermaritzburg, Rob said he had Top Oil business in Maritzburg so he would drive me up. It's a drive that has always fascinated me. As you climb up steeply from the subtropical coast, the highway cuts through rocky cliffs and outcrops but even more dramatic is the speed with which the vegetation changes. That exotic coastal belt of palms, frangipanis and strelitzias fades after only a few miles into woodland greenery. Not long after that the trees fade away and you're on a harsh upland populated by millions of aloes and other cactus-like plants. Anyone who lived in Natal (today KwaZulu-Natal) would have used that road a thousand times over but you could never cease to be impressed by it. And so it was that day as I sat tensely next to Rob, wearing a suit and tie in the broiling summer heat, thinking of the interview ahead. He talked and chatted amiably and dropped me off in central Maritzburg.

In the late afternoon Rob picked me up again. I was, in every way, deeply uncomfortable but he was cheery. I took off my jacket and tie, throwing them on the back seat.

'How'd it go?' he asked.

'Terrible. A complete disaster. I got into a fight with the chairman of the board.'

'Judge Harcourt?'

'Yes. He asked what I thought of Eric Louw's presentation of South Africa's case at the UN. I said he was wasting his time with silly legal arguments because apartheid was a political and human rights problem. You can imagine what he, as a judge, thought of the phrase "silly legal arguments".'

Rob gave one of his huge laughs. 'Christ, I'd love to have seen that. Were you trying to annoy him?'

'No, I just didn't think.'

'Even better,' Rob exclaimed, delighted.

'Then he asked me why I hadn't taken out South African citizenship and I said I'd wanted to until I found that I'd then have to serve in the army. He said, so what's wrong with that? I said, the army will only be used to repress the blacks and in that fight I'm really on the other side. He went dilly. It turns out his son, of whom he's very proud, is an army captain.'

'It sounds wonderful. A triumph! Anything else?'

'Oh yes, it got worse. He said you may not approve of our native policy but you have to remember the law is the same for everyone whatever their colour. I said that was quite hard to believe. If you read about a black man who'd raped a white woman, he was usually sentenced to death. Harcourt interrupted and said quite happily that he'd had to give out quite a few such sentences. So I asked how many times had the same applied to a white man who'd raped a black woman? I had never heard of a death sentence in such a case. Harcourt couldn't deny this but he went extremely red in the face and looked like he was going to explode.'

Rob began to laugh again, a great big laugh that more than filled the car. I found I was smiling too. By this time, we were out of Maritzburg, zooming along the straight, flat road into the stretch near Camperdown with great switchback inclines and declines. Ahead, the Valley of a Thousand Hills, dotted with innumerable Zulu huts, was beginning to loom about us. Even in summer in Natal the light dies quickly and outside the sun was nearly setting.

'It was just here that I wrote a car off not long ago,' said Rob happily. 'I felt so tired that I just relaxed, went to sleep at the wheel and ploughed off into the bush. The car did a double somersault. I was so relaxed in my sleep that I didn't get a scratch. I walked away without even a bruise but the car was a complete wreck.' He said this with a certain pride and seemed to feel that his decision to sleep had been entirely justified by the result. All's well that ends well.

'Seems to me you had a good afternoon,' he said. 'You should feel proud. You did well.'

'How do you mean? I screwed up completely.'

'You said what you really believed. You showed you didn't care about the result. That's screwing up magnificently, with style. It's like a toreador deciding to lose to the bull rather than win by cheating. Or, rather, you decided you would ride the bull out of the arena instead of killing it. Hemingway would have approved.'

Rob began to sing the Toreador Song from *Carmen* in a rather fine tenor, smiling happily. 'You'll see,' he said. 'You won't regret today. It's been a good day.'

Suddenly I felt he might be right. A wave of relaxation and contentment washed over me as Rob's relentless good cheer and sheer affectionate warmth buoyed me up. Outside it was getting dark, but inside the car we were in a little compartment, almost a cocoon, of our own, where there was optimism and laughter, where all was right with the world. I knew now that everything would be okay. Despite all the anxious months looking ahead to this day, despite the fact that I had no idea what I'd do if I didn't get the Rhodes Scholarship, I suddenly felt no worries. I could handle the disappointment; I could handle whatever came. Real friendship is a wonderful thing and Rob had made me feel so secure in his that I just stretched out and watched the aloes flash by in the dusk, feeling a wonderful sense of ease.

Rob dropped me at home and drove off. I fell exhausted onto my bed, sleeping happily and heavily. I was woken by a phone call. It was Judge Harcourt saying I had won the scholarship. It really had been a good day.

All manner of excitements followed. My mother, to whom my university career was always something of a mystery, looked pleased and asked me again which subjects I was studying. The phone rang a lot. But, looking back, what I remember most fondly was that drive back from Maritzburg, a journey begun in despair but ending in laughter and serenity. Not many journeys in life are so magically beneficent. We travel hard roads, long miles and steep inclines: a lot of life is uphill. Only very occasionally can one travel so well as I did that day. One need not travel in hope, I realised. Far more depends on optimism and on the pure – because unearned – gift of friendship. My luck that day lay not just in the scholarship but in Rob's enormous talent for affection. It is the same with all the rest of life, with all those long, hard roads. The real question is not how long, how hard or even which way; it's whether you are as lucky as I was that day with your companions en route.

CHAPTER FIVE

Grahamstown 1964

I had won the Rhodes Scholarship in December 1963 and the Oxford term only started in October 1964, so I had nine months on my hands. This was just as well, for my parents could not afford the sea or air fare to get me to Oxford – my father suggested hitch-hiking through Africa as an 'adventure' (even in those days it would have meant traversing several war zones). Luckily, Jeffrey Horton, my history professor, got me three jobs in short succession, all of them highly memorable.

First, I worked as a research assistant at Killie Campbell's magnificent house in Durban. Killie was a scion of the famous sugar-baron Campbells. Every morning and afternoon there would be tea in Killie's study, and anyone working in the library was welcome to attend. Since I was there more continuously than anyone else, I got to know Killie quite well. As a girl, she told me, she had been taken on holiday to England every year and there she spent almost all her time going round second-hand bookshops. This became her great love. She had never been seriously tempted to marry and had early on decided that her life's work would be to assemble a great library about Africa. Every year she would return from England with chests full of books – she had plenty of money and did not need to ration herself. She had bought this huge and magnificent house, designed by Cecil Rhodes's architect, Sir Herbert Baker, and filled it with books and priceless manuscripts.

Killie was strongly opposed to apartheid and the National Party government and was a member of the Black Sash movement, an organisation of white liberal women. She had strong family loyalties to Jan Smuts's United Party and at election time would dispatch her chauffeurs to drive UP voters to the polls (a task that, they told me, they hated because the UP was quite reactionary on race). I doubt whether she ever considered joining the more liberal Progressive Party, although her views were more liberal than those of most UP supporters. This would sometimes put her in an ironic position. She told me with great enjoyment of how the minister of native affairs, Mr De Wet Nel, had visited Durban and how she had joined the crowd of Black Sash members demonstrating against him as he arrived. But, of course, any visiting dignitary was bound to call at Killie's house, so her chauffeur had to race back from the airport in order for her to be able to graciously welcome into her home the man she had just been demonstrating against.

Killie loved having authors and researchers come to use her library. Of these there were many, for her library was one of the finest in the world on southern African matters. While I was there the two writers most frequently present were Charles Binns and Donald Morris. Killie was fascinated by the rivalry between them. Binns had brought out his book *The Last Zulu King: The Life and Death of Cetshwayo* the previous year but was hard at work on another, *The Warrior People*. Morris overtook him completely the next year with *The Washing of the Spears: The Rise and Fall of the Zulu Nation*, his epic and highly readable best-seller.

Morris was a genial, charming man but one day he turned me almost to stone as we were having tea with Killie. He told her that he would love to write more books but, heck, he had another job too – he worked for the US embassy, indeed, for the Central Intelligence Agency (CIA). I was astonished that he should admit this. For a brief moment I wondered if he knew of my own leftish background and was sending me a warning signal. But then I remembered that Mandela had been arrested near Pietermaritzburg in May 1962, allegedly on a CIA tip-off.[7] Perhaps I was sitting opposite Mandela's betrayer?

The thing that really worried Killie – already in her late sixties – was what would become of her house and library when she died. She often lamented the situation to me. She had wanted to leave it to the Zulu people (she was an honorary Zulu chief) but said that it would then not be properly maintained and looked after. She had considered giving it to the City of Durban but when she had invited city councillors to the house, she had heard some of them talking excitedly of how they could turn it into an entertainment palace with slot machines. Why not leave it to the University of Natal, I asked. She said she had tried but the vice chancellor, Ernie Malherbe, had refused it.

I sought an interview with Malherbe and asked why he would turn down such a priceless house and collection – heavens, Killie even had pieces of Marie Antoinette's furniture. Malherbe said gruffly that I did not understand: a house and library like that would cost a great deal in maintenance and librarians' salaries. The university simply could not afford that. I went back to Killie and told her. 'You mean if I left them a sum of money to pay for all that then it would be all right?' she asked. I said yes, I thought so. 'Then that's what I'll do,' said Killie. I went back to Malherbe and he accepted the offer. Killie died long ago. How well the university has looked after her bequest is an open question.

My second job was as a research assistant to Gwendolen Carter, a professor from Northwestern University in Evanston, Illinois. Gwen, a polio victim, had both her legs in irons and walked with great difficulty but she was enormously strong and determined. Her mission was to

---

7   This rumour was confirmed many years later by Donald Rickard, who had been working at the US embassy in Pretoria at that time. Rickard said the general US opinion at that time was that Mandela was 'the most dangerous communist' outside the Soviet Union. Mandela always denied that he was a communist but he was in fact on the Party's Central Committee. See BBC News, 'Nelson Mandela: CIA tip-off led to 1962 Durban arrest', 15 May 2016.

build the world's greatest library of Africana at Northwestern, and she had come out to South Africa with the aim of taking back as much material as she could. Gwen was a force of nature – dynamic, always cheerful and relentlessly entrepreneurial. Durban was a sleepy city and few of its academics did much research, but for Gwen research was the name of the game. She also had an open chequebook. She hoovered up whatever seemed interesting – and she was particularly interested in the politics and history of the ANC and the Communist Party.

I remember driving out with Gwen to the old Gandhi house on the Phoenix Settlement in Inanda, where the Mahatma had had a farm and also a printing press from which he produced his newspaper, *Indian Opinion*. Gwen went into the house to speak to a Mrs Gandhi, one of the Mahatma's descendants, while I waited in the car. Next to the house was a large shed, which housed the press but which was also piled to the ceiling with old copies of *Indian Opinion* and a large number of documents of all sorts. These had been simply dumped there for years. Gwen and Mrs Gandhi finally came out of the house looking pleased and I realised a deal had been done. 'Okay,' said Gwen, 'we'll take this.' What exactly would we take, I asked? 'The lot.' We hauled away many lorry-loads of documents.

This sort of thing upset many local historians, who said these materials should have remained in South Africa and this was a sort of dollar imperialism. I was sceptical of such critics. After all, those documents had been sitting in that shed for 50 years and no local historians had bothered to look at them. Moreover, they were deteriorating in the humid Durban climate, a prey to rats, moths and cockroaches. It was surely better that they be conserved, properly sorted and catalogued in a modern air-conditioned library, even if it was in distant Illinois.

In fact, Inanda filled up in the 1980s and 1990s with a huge African squatter camp. For a while the Indian community hung on, but their shops came to resemble forts, with each encased in multiple sets of iron bars, electric fencing, and so on. Nothing worked: the shops were still ransacked. In the end the Africans physically drove the Indians out, and during the rioting Gandhi's house was attacked and his old press destroyed. Had Gwen not removed those documents, they too would have perished.

This turned out to be Gwen's first and last trip to South Africa. She openly sympathised with the ANC, and the security police had noted her repeated trips to visit old ANC cadres and listed communists. So once she left the country, they banned her from ever re-entering it. (Mandela thought her attendance at his trial was probably the last straw for the security police.) From Northwestern she maintained her correspondence with Mangosuthu Buthelezi, Steve Biko, Kwame Nkrumah and other notable Africans. Sadly, she died, aged 84, in February 1991, just too soon to see the new South Africa.

My third job was with Winnie Maxwell, the renowned professor of history at Rhodes University in Grahamstown (today's Makhanda). My junior lecturer's salary would, providentially, pay my air fare to Oxford and even repay a little of my debt to the University of Natal. It was awkward, though: I was only 20, younger than many of those whom I had to teach.

Grahamstown was an academic toytown with endless churches and pubs in a claustrophobically small community. The locals, who all knew one another, loved it. I, knowing no one, was extremely lonely. Winnie Maxwell made things no easier: she was tough, demanding and called everyone 'laddie'. A domineering figure, she cultivated several hard-to-swallow eccentricities, the chief of which was her habit of adjusting her voluminous underclothes in mid-conversation. One moment she would be discussing the Great Reform Bill of 1832; the next she would, without warning, fling her dress over her head, revealing an amazing collection of knickers, suspenders, pantaloons, girdles and petticoats to which she would then proceed to make adjustments before pulling her dress back down and continuing her discussion of the events of 1832. None of the members of her department ever quite accommodated themselves to this routine.

The friends I made at Rhodes were all members of the Liberal Party. They were an interesting bunch. Terence Beard, a tall, bearded political scientist who already had a banning order, was an Oxford graduate who loved the ironies of British life. He told me how he'd met Sir Hugh Foot (the later Lord Caradon), who had remarked to him that South Africa seemed to be a police state: 'And I should know. When I was Governor of Cyprus I ran one.'

Terence shared a flat with an English lecturer, Eric Harber, who was a highly individualist mix of Catholicism, drollery and literary sensibility. Eric frequently made distinctions that others would not have attempted. Once, for example, he described one of his students to me as 'bright, but stupidly bright, if you know what I mean'. Occasionally I was invited to dinner at their flat. Eric would be entrusted with making a stew while Terence, from the sitting room, roared with laughter as he called out items from the newspaper that caught his fancy. As Eric and I worked in the kitchen Terence warned us of his strong dislike of herbs and spices of any sort. Eric would happily promise to put no such ingredients into the stew but would then, with equal cheerfulness, make liberal use of them, muttering, 'Terence will never notice.' Sure enough, Terence would eat the deeply spiced stew with gusto, pronouncing it absolutely delicious.

Clem Goodfellow was a tall, pipe-smoking Cool Hand Luke character. Winnie Maxwell had been deeply impressed by his abilities (he had degrees from both Oxford and Cambridge) and attracted him to the history department by dangling the prospect of a senior lectureship. However, whereas Winnie dominated all other department members with ease, she had met her match in Clem. When she made *ex cathedra* announcements about Historical Truth – which she expected everyone to accept as gospel – Clem would suck on his pipe, treat her views as merely an interesting opinion, and subject them to rational analysis in a way to which Winnie was wholly unused. The prospect of a senior lectureship for Clem soon faded away, although his academic merits were beyond dispute.

Clem loved Grahamstown and his many friends there and had no wish to leave – but his career was now blocked. Somewhat idly, he then applied for a senior lectureship at what is today the National University of Lesotho in Roma. He had no wish to go to Roma but thought a good offer from there might give him a bargaining counter with Winnie. Roma quickly offered him the job. Taken aback, Clem held out for a full professorship. Roma quickly obliged. Clem added that he would also need to be head of department. Roma agreed again. At which point Clem went to see Winnie, hoping this would clinch her semi-promise of a senior lectureship. Winnie simply replied, 'I hope you'll be happy in your new job.' Clem found that, effectively, he had resigned. He had fatally underestimated the extent to which Winnie had made the Rhodes history department her castle, which she was prepared to defend against all comers. She had decided that making Clem her deputy would mean allowing a possible challenger inside the castle walls. This could not happen.

Daantjie (pronounced 'Dine-key') Oosthuizen, the professor of philosophy, was a soft-spoken and humane man. It took great guts for an Afrikaner like Daantjie to be a Liberal Party member, but Daantjie never referred to his resulting difficulties. Whenever some new political outrage occurred, we would all be convened in Daantjie's study to discuss what to do. Terence, who was banned and thus legally forbidden to attend meetings, would furtively slip in and, later, out. For Daantjie, with his calm and saintly air, was our natural leader. His chief lieutenant was Cedric Evans, a forcefully logical presence. Eric Harber disliked the rationalist pretensions of the philosophers, and on leaving the meeting would chuckle knowingly, 'You see what these logic-choppers are doing?

They're so absurdly sure they know, while the rest of us are just blundering about with faith and feelings. So they've taken Cedric Evans and rearranged his mind so he is now a philosophical Frankenstein. I've warned Daantjie what would happen and now it is happening: Cedric is using the same philosophical clap-trap to criticise them.' Such lines would be delivered with an air of complete certainty, for Eric seemed to rely on some inner mystical core, inaccessible to the rest of us.

Formerly a scientist, Norman Bromberger had become a history lecturer, utterly gripped by his new subject while still knowing little of it. Students would relate with awe how Norman gave them essay topics that he knew nothing about. A week later, they would find him asleep in his chair with several days' growth of beard and empty whisky bottles on the floor, relics of a series of all-night sessions as Norman read himself up to date. He would then demonstrate a complete and sophisticated mastery of all the areas covered by their essays. Norman was effectively putting himself through several history degrees at once while simultaneously teaching them.

I was put on the spot when Gwen Carter steamed into Grahamstown. Winnie welcomed her, but I could not mention my previous work for Gwen: Winnie might see that as a derogation from the absolute loyalty she demanded. Gwen soon acquired a complete set of the records of the Bunga, the council of Transkei chiefs. These were lying around in an obscure office and were being used for toilet paper. Gwen scooped them up for ten US dollars, thus greatly annoying Winnie, who spoke bitterly of how she had too much teaching to do the research she would have liked. True, Winnie taught a lot, but she did get long vacations and those Bunga records had been lying around for years, undiscovered. Had Gwen not snatched them they would literally have gone down the toilet.

A chief Grahamstown delight was *Grocott's Mail*. Grocott's was the sort of old-fashioned general store on the High Street that features in cowboy films ('Gonna ride my hoss inta town and hitch it to the rail outside the general store,' etc). From time immemorial – actually, from 1870 – the shop published *Grocott's Mail*, a large-format broadsheet of about six pages. Every issue was a treat, for it attempted to cover both local and world news. The main headline might be 'Grahamstown Girls' Choir Wins 2nd Place in Eisteddfod' but at the foot of the page would be items like 'Khrushchev Threatens New Berlin Crisis'. This would continue in surreal fashion with items about sheep trials or cake competitions jostling for space with a forthcoming British election or an assassination attempt on De Gaulle. Better still, at the back of the store you could see a man wearing sleeve garters and a green eyeshade, the spitting image of the small-town newspaper editor in Mark Twain's America. This was, apparently, Mr Grocott.

Many tales were told about *Grocott's Mail*. One concerned Alan Dick, whose uproarious reign as editor of the student newspaper in Pietermaritzburg was still the stuff of legend. Mr Grocott, wishing to take his family on holiday to Europe, had chanced upon Dick. Grahamstown soon awoke to a new newspaper. The first sign was when Cliff Richard and the Shadows – then enjoying a local musical notoriety equalled only by Elvis Presley – drove in cavalcade through Grahamstown, greeted by enormous, cheering crowds. Dick, whose own tastes ran more to progressive jazz, did not approve, so the next day's *Grocott's Mail* had no headline or photos of this earth-shattering event. At the foot of the page lay a tiny item of just two sentences: '"Cliff" Richard and the "Shadows" passed through Grahamstown yesterday. 'Tis believed they were minstrels.'

However, nothing rivalled the paper's coverage of the Organization of African Unity (OAU) conference in Addis Ababa. These conferences, routinely aiming fiery rhetoric at South Africa, always riled the white population to a state of indignant fury. On this occasion, the OAU resolved that all African states should contribute one per cent of their budgets to a fighting fund to help secure the armed liberation of South

Africa. This produced paroxysms of rage among many whites, but *Grocott's Mail* ran with the headline 'Only One Per Cent!' – berating African states for their meanness. Many South Africans had fought the fascists in North Africa, the paper argued, so other Africans should take an equally vigorous attitude towards the liberation of South Africa from the same curse of fascism. For one glorious day *Grocott's Mail* was the most radical paper in South Africa, indeed probably in all Africa.

The reaction was thunderous. Farmers drove in 60 kilometres to cancel their subscriptions, and the gentlefolk of Grahamstown made their views known in anything but gentle ways. Mr Grocott was summoned back from his European holiday and Alan Dick sent on his way. Soon the ancient calm descended on Grocott's once more as the man in the green eyeshade toiled away, producing the old enchanting mix of toytown news and echoes of the wider world.

...

Yet the tension in the town was electric. The security police kept the Liberals under observation and waited to pounce. The sabotage campaigns by MK and the ARM had caught the police unprepared so they pulled in anyone who might be remotely suspicious. This made me anxious: I was of no importance politically but I knew too many of the wrong people and had been caught red-handed at Rowley's. That would be quite enough for the security police to see what they could squeeze out of me.

The nearby Transkei Bantustan had just received its 'independence', and the Grahamstown Liberals did their best to help its opposition Democratic Party, led by Knowledge Guzana, which, quite rightly, denounced this collaboration with apartheid. I once accompanied Eric Harber on a madcap expedition to Guzana's home near Umtata (now Mthatha), shadowed from the outset by the security police. After playing hide and seek with the police, we settled down in Guzana's little house to help him write his speech for the opening of the Transkei parliament, for Knowledge, a schoolteacher, had no idea of how a parliament worked or what such an occasion required. He was a charming, friendly man, keen to avail himself of any help we could give. I took him through a speech I had roughed out, explaining parliamentary conventions as I went. Eric spoke about non-racialism and universal suffrage in a unitary South Africa and how Knowledge's efforts fitted into that.

The security police were bound to arrive at Knowledge's house soon and it was vital that we should not be there when they did. But while they were not prepared to allow Liberals to subvert the government's Bantustan policy, they were far more concerned that some Liberals might be involved in the ARM. One day, I discovered that Terence Beard had been detained by the police in the early morning. I sneaked across to Daantjie's rooms, where I learnt that Norman Bromberger, Cedric Evans and Peter Rodda, an English lecturer, had also been detained. This led us to fear for Eric, Clem, Daantjie and, indeed, myself.

Many of the studies in our wing of the Arts building were now locked, their occupants detained. A near neighbour was the Afrikaans writer André Brink, who was understood to sympathise with our views. Brink always wore the polo-neck sweater that then denoted an Angry Young Man. (The original Angry Young Man had been Colin Wilson, with his book *The Outsider*, published in 1956. There had been many photos of him posing on Hampstead Heath in polo-necked dissidence.) Everything about Brink radiated a sense of intellectual dissent and a certain self-importance. He was famous as one of the Sestigers – the angry young Afrikaners of the literary world. On difficult occasions such as this, Brink would drop by and say of course he was with us but 'given my position' he could obviously not be seen with us. It was never clear to me what distinction he was drawing, for Daantjie, of course, was with us up to his neck and was ostracised by most other Afrikaners as a result.

Brink seemed greatly taken with the idea of being a brave dissident while not actually being willing to pay the price of being one.

After a week, Terence was released. Better still, he had seen Norman Bromberger in jail. Norman had decided that solitary detention was a heaven-sent opportunity to get fit, so he was doing lots of press-ups, stretching exercises and jogging. We had dreaded the possibility of torture and were hugely relieved. For John Harris, an ARM activist, had just placed a bomb in Johannesburg Park Station, killing one person and maiming 23 others. The security police had reacted with fury; torture was becoming the new normal.

We were kept on our toes by the professor of fine art, a Lancastrian called Brian Bradshaw. These were crazy days and Bradshaw had clearly imbibed deeply of the zeitgeist and become an open fascist, bitterly opposing all Liberals and leftists. He had formed a movement with a jagged streak of lightning as its symbol and had drawn up a fascist manifesto that he pinned to the university notice boards. He was in the habit of issuing violent orders to his followers, a group of leather-jacketed youths who were quite willing to beat up all those who opposed him. Each new outrage by Bradshaw would be discussed in Daantjie's room – naturally Bradshaw enjoyed the protection of the security police, and the university authorities were too scared to intervene.

But even with the dangerous Bradshaw there had occasionally to be a truce in no-man's-land to settle a key point. The Liberal most willing to do this was Cedric Evans: his belief in his philosophical principles was so strong that he wore them like armour and was thus willing to face anyone. Thus, one might rarely glimpse, amid faculty members sipping tea in the senior common room, the amazing sight of Cedric in close conversation with Bradshaw. The faculty loathed Bradshaw but thought the Liberals suicidally brave and gave them a wide berth. On one occasion, a member of this timorous majority, a certain Jones, saw Cedric and Bradshaw in conversation and jovially approached them, saying, 'Well, I see the lion is lying down with the lamb.' Cedric turned, smiled, and asked, 'And which of us is the lion, and which the lamb?' Jones, put on the spot, fled. Even Terence, whose banning order meant he could not enter the senior common room, enjoyed that.

...

The early 1960s were a very frightening time in South Africa, especially in the country's four English-speaking universities, the main centres of liberal and leftist thought and, as such, in the crosshairs of the security police. The minister of justice, responsible for the police, was the redoubtable John Vorster, the strongman of the regime, who exuded a ruthless determination to crush dissent by whatever means required. One day, coming out of Grocott's, I collided head-on with him. He was in Grahamstown for some important trials – the Eastern Cape Provincial Division sat there. Vorster was extremely unamused. Behind him, on the street and on top of the buildings opposite, I saw armed men suddenly loom up – clearly Vorster's bodyguards, ready to take out any threat to the minister. I mumbled my apologies, reflecting that had the police bothered to question me, thus discovering my connections with the likes of Rowley and Ronnie, they would doubtless have detained me on the spot.

My chief worry was that the security police found it difficult to credit that there were two rival sabotage movements, MK and the ARM. They were accordingly searching for possible links between the two – and I realised that I would be an almost perfect candidate, given my friend-ships with the Grahamstown Liberals and my links to ANC and communist sympathisers in Durban. Every interrogation of detainees soon established a roster of their friends and contacts and my name would crop up on all too many of those lists. So my own detention was purely a matter of time. Given that by October I had to be in Oxford to take up my Rhodes Scholarship, the question was whether I could leave the country in time to escape detention. But the security police, who were doubtless monitoring my movements, would not let me leave the country if they wanted to interrogate me, which suggested they would pounce by late September. Apart from a general anxiety about detention, I was worried that it might prevent me from getting to Oxford. Moreover, it might create a deal of trouble with the Rhodes selection committee. For all I knew, they might revoke my scholarship.

In this rather anxious mood, I left Grahamstown for Port Elizabeth and boarded a Union-Castle liner en route for Durban. The next morning, a Sunday, we docked in East London. I was wondering how I would get through this interminable day when I saw tied up opposite the Mobil tanker on which I knew my father was currently sailing. I set off round the docks to board the tanker. My father was delighted and sat me down with a cold beer. We chatted away for some time when he suddenly exclaimed, 'Oh yes, by the way, congratulations!' I was puzzled and my face must have shown it. 'It's your 21st birthday!' my father said. And so it was. I had entirely forgotten: my mind was too full of other cares. But we had a splendid day.

Back in Durban, I became almost unbearably tense as the day of my departure loomed, waiting for the security police to pounce. The day came, I boarded the aircraft, and as we took off I felt a great weight drop from my shoulders. After I got to Oxford, I received a letter from my mother relating that the security police had come to detain me ten days after I had left. They furiously demanded how I had managed to leave without applying for an exit visa. But I had not needed a visa; as a British citizen I could simply walk onto the plane and go. The police had expected my visa application to act as a tripwire – an elementary mistake. The day they came for me they also detained Mike Kirkwood and Barry Higgs – and Barry was badly tortured. Hearing of this, safe in Magdalen College, Oxford, I felt a mixture of guilt and relief at my sheer good fortune.

The intensity of that time in Grahamstown stayed with me and

I followed the fate of the dramatis personae there. Poor Clem Goodfellow did not last long at Roma. One day, while on a hike in the Lesotho mountains, he walked off a precipice, leaving a suicide note for his stricken wife. His friends blamed Winnie for having refused Clem his promotion: had he stayed in Grahamstown surely this would never have happened? I was in no position to say how just or unjust this was, so I was taken aback to receive a furious letter from Winnie. Word of how she was being blamed had reached her and, weirdly, she accused me of being the source of these reports. She was clearly in no mood to listen to my protestations of innocence, so I made no reply.

Clem was a great loss. But then Daantjie Oosthuizen died suddenly in his early forties. Daantjie had pressed into my hands a bottle of sherry for Gilbert Ryle, which I delivered personally to the great man when I got to Magdalen. Eric Harber soon followed me to England to do a degree at Cambridge, but Terence remained at Rhodes for the rest of his long life, dying in 2017 at the age of 91. Winnie Maxwell remained queen of her castle in Grahamstown until her retirement. Cedric Evans went to Columbia University in New York where he participated in the great student rebellion of 1968. This cost him his job, and he was last heard of in a Southern state working as a motorbike mechanic. The thought of Cedric, the complete philosopher, doing such a job always put me in mind of Robert Pirsig's famous book, *Zen and the Art of Motorcycle Maintenance*. They were a strange cast of characters and it was a bewitching time.

CHAPTER SIX

Africa in England

South Africa followed me to Oxford.[8] Despite the fact that I was British, like other young South Africans I found that England presented a mental challenge. Behind us lay such drama and danger. The 1964 British election campaign was in full swing but the parties were arguing about lower interest rates, of all things. This was incomprehensible. We were habituated to a politics of black and white, of good versus evil. In South Africa we had neither known nor cared about interest rates. This was, of course, a measure of our naiveté. The key line in Britain's class politics was between homeowners and the rest, so in effect Harold Wilson was offering easier entry to the upper half to legions of young couples. Even South African communists were not attuned to class politics: when I met Ronnie Kasrils and Eleanor Anderson, who, after many adventures, had escaped from South Africa to Golders Green, they too were nonplussed by the strange ways of the locals.

I loved Oxford and the sense that some of the world's great intellectuals were there, that there was so much to learn – a boundless sea. I also loved its eccentricity and the funny stories. I did a graduate degree in politics with a thesis on ex-French Guinea and also fell in love with French politics. Over the next 30 years I made regular visits to

---

8   For an account of Oxford in my time, see *Look Back in Laughter.*

France and wrote a big book on the French left, and France became a large part of my life. Of course, I never forgot South Africa though I studied many other African countries as well. By the time I finished I had already been invited to put in for a Fellowship at Magdalen, my own college and the centre of my affections.

I kept in touch with news of Barry and Mike. Barry had emerged from detention strangely subdued and silent. When questioned about detention, he said he would rather not talk about it: he looked sad and stayed silent. This ignited suspicion: had he made a deal with the security police? Worse, had he agreed to become a state witness? Such turncoats, who sent down their own comrades for lengthy sentences, were much despised. Word that Barry had bought his freedom in that way reached me even in Oxford. I had no idea what Barry had promised the police but realised that one might agree to anything under torture.

On emerging from jail, Barry went round to see his girlfriend, Sybilla (Billa), whose mother, Margery, had always opposed their liaison. While Margery was chatting to her friends, Barry pulled Billa to one side and told her that he had an escape planned to Swaziland. Billa said she would come too. But when? Well, right now, said Barry. They simply stepped out of the room – and vanished. Margery quickly realised what must have happened and, in her desperation to stop this adventure, actually called in the security police. But it was too late: Barry and Billa arrived in Swaziland where they happily consorted with other South African exiles. This was highly insecure: the security police might kidnap them or exert pressure until the Swazi authorities handed them over. Barry and Billa then sent out invitations to a large party, but vanished before the party was ever held. Barry, realising that there were bound to be spies in their midst, had used the party as a blind.

Barry and Billa thus arrived in Mozambique. Billa's family had friends in Lourenço Marques (today's Maputo) and they lived a life of some luxury for a while – there were tales of Barry dancing on tables and other such diversions. However, the Portuguese secret police, the dreaded PIDE, began to take an interest, so once more they fled, having arranged a lift from a group of guerrillas from the Frente de Libertação de Moçambique (Frelimo) travelling northwards, using the cover of a furniture removals van. After several hundred miles they dismounted, which was lucky: further down the road Portuguese troops shot up the van, killing most of the occupants. Ultimately, with further help from Frelimo, Barry and Billa were dumped in open country and told that the Rhodesian border was ahead. They walked a long way, unsure whether they had crossed the border or not, but finally discovered they were indeed in Rhodesia. By this time Barry was suffering badly from an impacted wisdom tooth. From Rhodesia they reached Zambia where the British High Commission helped them to get to England.

All of which Barry retailed to me when he suddenly arrived at my rooms in Oxford. He stayed for over a week, sleeping on my couch, punting and playing croquet. He and Billa stayed in London for a while before removing to East Berlin, where Barry edited the ANC newspaper, *Sechaba*. I could not have imagined anything worse or less suitable: *Sechaba* was a Stalinist journal with an ironclad line and no sense of humour at all. After a while Barry and Billa returned with dreadful stories of South African exiles sunk in drink and depression. Barry had resented the repressive uniformity of *Sechaba* and never worked for the ANC propaganda machine again.

I had arrived in Britain still a member of the Congress of Democrats and thus completely aligned to the ANC, so I naturally socialised with Congress people when I went down to London at weekends. This led to rapid disillusion. Most of the exiles only knew other South African exiles and even after being in Britain for a few years had almost no English acquaintances. They were ignorant about the country and rather contemptuous of it. They were all deeply homesick – not only for the physical country of South Africa but also for all its ethnic, political and local loyalties. Then there was the singing. In Durban, cheerful evenings had often ended with the singing of Congress songs at midnight but here people would stand around at a party having little to talk about and some would start singing Congress songs, first at ten o'clock, then at nine and then even at eight. It was desperate.

But it was the politics that killed it. As a supporter of the Congress of Democrats, I was a Marxist and pro-ANC but I still believed in free speech and individual conscience – while most of the exiles did not. They were in England as a revolutionary minority entirely dependent on British traditions of tolerance and free speech – traditions they were quick to invoke when needed. Yet almost to the last man they belonged to a Stalinist party, the SACP. The Party had supported the repression of workers in the East German rising of 1953 and the crushing of the Hungarians in 1956. Even Stalin's crimes were never discussed. Elsewhere, right across Europe, Eurocommunism was transforming the communist parties into social democrats but there was no echo of that in the SACP.

The reason was simply their deep South African parochialism. They were totally gripped by the South African confrontation, and if the Soviet bloc was on their side this meant they were loyal to the Soviet side. So ANC cadres, self-styled revolutionaries, often lived in the Soviet bloc for years without ever realising that this was a revolutionary situation in which people would overthrow communist rule the minute they got the chance.

The other thing was racism. One of the ANC's main appeals was that it was non-racial – its Freedom Charter said that 'South Africa belongs to all who live in it', black and white. Its activists did nonetheless feel a deep suspicion of all whites. This was understandable and something one had had to deal with from the start. But I was quite unprepared for the open racial hostility I encountered. One of the chief offenders was Essop Pahad, who had a bullying manner and was gratuitously insulting. Yet I knew Essop was a senior man in the movement and a close friend of Thabo Mbeki (already seen as the crown prince) and, as a trusted communist, had been made editor of the *World Marxist Review* in Prague. If I continued to move in ANC circles, I would have to take orders from Essop and others like him – and there would be no room for argument or dissent. I realised I simply could not live with this.

So I drifted away. I remained sympathetic to the ANC, but whenever I encountered ANC activists I would be reminded afresh why I could not be one of them. I still saw Ronnie and Eleanor in London and I was actually instrumental in getting Ronnie into the London School of Economics (LSE). (Naturally, he saw this as an opportunity for student revolution and got no degree.) Ronnie was travelling a lot and spoke enthusiastically of the ANC's brother revolutionaries in Mozambique, Namibia and Angola, but word spread that this fellowship had been extended to include all manner of other revolutionaries such as the Palestinian Liberation Organisation (PLO) and, some suggested, the Irish Republican Army (IRA).

This was a delicate subject. Ronnie and other ANC activists were still engaged in armed struggle against Pretoria and went for military training in various Soviet bloc countries. Yet the British government still viewed South Africa as a friendly power (it had left the Commonwealth in 1961 and might rejoin one day), and it ran counter to all British practice to allow a guerrilla movement aimed at such an ally to base itself in London. Word spread that the ANC high command (usually meaning Oliver Tambo and Joe Slovo) had an implicit deal with MI5, the British intelligence service: the ANC would be allowed to base itself in London provided no military activity of any sort took place locally and the ANC also staged no mass anti-apartheid protests on British soil. Naturally, this agreement had to be secret; ANC activists regarded MI5 as demonic, and the movement could not admit openly that it was making deals with the devil.

Given that the ANC (and, in fact, the SACP) controlled the Anti-

Apartheid Movement (AAM), this was of great importance. The anti-apartheid cause was massively popular and could have put even more people on the street than the Campaign for Nuclear Disarmament (CND), Britain's biggest mass movement. The last thing the British police wanted was to have to deal with that, particularly since the righteous rage of anti-apartheid activists more or less guaranteed violence. So while the AAM called the occasional rally in Trafalgar Square it otherwise organised its other meetings indoors. The only occasions when mass anti-apartheid protest took place – for example, in Cambridge in 1970 – was when students beyond the control of the AAM took the initiative.

But in 1969 a 19-year-old South African exile, Peter Hain, organised the Stop the Seventy Tour campaign, disrupting that year's Springbok rugby tour of Britain and forcing the cancellation of the 1970 South African cricket tour. Hain had been a Liberal in South Africa and was beyond the control of the AAM. He greatly embarrassed the movement by showing what a potent force direct action against apartheid could be. Inevitably, one soon heard (ludicrous) murmurings in ANC circles that Hain was an MI5 agent.

Yet some MI5 agents were clearly irritated by the liberties allowed to the ANC in Britain, particularly after 1968 with the rise of the IRA and other terrorist movements in Europe, such as the Baader-Meinhof gang in West Germany and the Red Brigades in Italy. The Gaddafi regime in Libya gave assistance to such groups and Western intelligence services were keenly aware that a wide variety of terrorist groups were training in the Libyan desert – together with the ANC. Inevitably, these disparate groups met and tried to learn from one another. This hit a nerve in Britain. Conservative elements within MI5 have always fed titbits of information to the right-wing press, and there were repeated allegations from the Tory back benches that the ANC was collaborating with Britain's number-one enemy, the IRA. Ronnie was invariably cited as the chief culprit. Such reports were always denied by the ANC, but the truth was hard to know.

. . .

Gradually, the rest of my family joined me in England. The first to arrive were my older sister, Francesca, and my immediately younger brother, Philip. Francesca had attracted security police attention by her association with people like Ronnie and Eleanor and her flat had been bugged. This led to trouble.

When Mandela and the rest of the MK high command were on trial, a particularly noxious prosecution lawyer, Percy Yutar, had made himself the Vyshinsky[9] of the apartheid regime. Yutar was Jewish and particularly eager to prove that there were some 'good Jews' as well as the numerous 'bad Jews' on the left. Given the prevalence of anti-Semitism in National Party and security police circles, Yutar was swimming against the stream but he did so to a heroic extent, mocking the accused and shouting at them, and clearly aiming for death sentences. Francesca had confided in her friend Fern Levy that while she did not want to kill either Hendrik Verwoerd or John Vorster, it would give her great satisfaction to kill Percy Yutar. This was a mere expression of exasperation: Francesca wouldn't have hurt a fly. It later emerged that the listening security police took this rhetorical fancy very seriously: Yutar was warned that his life was under threat and given extra bodyguards. Francesca had to move to London.

Philip had committed the possibly greater crime of having a black girlfriend, Edna. Philip was fully aware that their relationship was highly illegal and tried to be discreet. To his surprise, the genial Asher Ntanga,

---

9   Andrey Vyshinsky, the state prosecutor in the show trials of the 1930s during Stalin's purges. He was known for his almost hysterical denunciations of the accused ('Shoot these rabid dogs! Down with these abject animals!' etc). He later did the same at the Nuremberg trials and also served as Soviet foreign minister.

though an ANC activist, angrily told him, 'White guys like you should keep away from our women.' Philip ignored this, so Asher tipped off the police, who caught Philip and Edna in bed together. They were both charged under the Immorality Act. Philip slipped secretly out of the country and soon arrived in London too.

Edna remained at risk, so Philip laid siege to the Home Office in London, demanding that they allow Edna to join him. When they refused, he sought help widely – Ben Whitaker, the Labour MP for Hampstead, was particularly helpful. Nothing seemed to work, so in the end he wrote to the Home Office saying that he could wait no longer: he would travel secretly back to South Africa, get hold of Edna, and escape back to England with her. If he was caught, he would surely go to jail, in which case a voluminous file of every piece of correspondence about the affair would be delivered to *The Guardian*, which would doubtless publish the fact that he, a British citizen, was in an apartheid jail due entirely to the resistance of the Home Office. This worked. Edna arrived shortly thereafter in London, where she and Philip got married.

Indeed, my old Durban life was reconstituting itself in England. By 1966 Rob Amato had also arrived on a Rhodes Scholarship – the previous year's scholarship had gone to Tommy Bedford. Rob elected to do a graduate degree. Being Rob, he only played at his thesis, as if he expected it to write itself, and he treated his regular meetings with his supervisor merely as enjoyable verbal jousts. His real energies were thrown into persuading the head of his college, Sir Alan Bullock, to allow him an extra subsidy to direct the annual college play.

To his delight he was successful. I was going out with a beautiful girl I'd met in Oxford, Anne Summers, and Rob told me that Anne and I had to attend: the play was *Twelfth Night*, and Rob said he had 'brought it up to date a bit' and generally 'improved' it. This filled me with foreboding. I feared the consequences of Rob 'improving' Shakespeare and I knew that Oxford audiences enjoyed Shakespeare comedies in traditional style, very much as Shakespeare had intended them. Rob's mother had also been pressed to come and we sat together in the front row. Mrs Amato knew her son well. 'Rob tells me he has been given a free hand with this production,' she said. 'So I think we should prepare ourselves for a considerable disaster.' Just how shrewd this was rapidly became clear when some of the actors appeared in space helmets. A cold shudder ran quite audibly through the audience. It turned out that this was only the first of many 'improvements'. By the end the audience had visibly thinned. Rob, looking a little perplexed, asked how we thought it had all gone. 'It was splendid, darling,' said the ever-gracious Mrs Amato, 'but I think perhaps the space suits were a bridge too far.' 'You mean it was too progressive?' said Rob intensely. 'Surely not. This is Oxford after all.' The reviews were calamitous and the play folded immediately. We were careful to avoid all mention of it thereafter.

. . .

I did a paper on African politics and also a thesis on Sékou Touré's Guinea. For both of these I worked under Thomas Hodgkin, which was a joy.[10] Thomas was a scion of a distinguished old Quaker family – for his grandfather had been Master of Balliol, his father Provost of The Queen's College and his aunt Principal of Somerville College. Both his wife and his cousin were Nobel laureates and his brother was foreign editor of *The Times*. Thomas himself was an old communist and still a Marxist but had the style and manners of a Balliol mandarin (which he was). He wrote like an angel and had a large sense of humour. Being around him was always enlightening and funny.

Thomas had become interested in Africa in the early 1950s and had travelled all round the continent on the back of long-distance trucks,

---

10   For more on Thomas, see *Look Back in Laughter*, especially pp 56–63.

making ends meet by writing articles for publication in London. He was one of the very earliest observers of the growth of African nationalism, and his *Nationalism in Colonial Africa* (1956) was the one and only book on the subject at the time. He followed this with *African Political Parties* (1961), a masterful summary of a whole new genre. This made him the principal go-to authority on African politics in the world. Moreover, Thomas had known most of the leaders of African nationalism, including Kwame Nkrumah, Tom Mboya and Julius Nyerere, and had even spent time in the FLN underground in Algeria with Frantz Fanon.

African studies in the 1960s was an exciting field. Even in Durban I had kept a map of Africa on my bedroom wall, marking off each new country to become independent. This wave of liberation and its rhetoric were intoxicating. Many of the new African leaders attempted to be philosopher kings, publishing their ideological manifestoes like so many Lenins. As is so well observed in VS Naipaul's *A Bend in the River*, many learned foreign academics pored over these works and wrote learned articles about them. Only gradually was it realised that all these 'philosophies' were threadbare. At the same time swarms of American academics descended upon the continent, writing earnestly about 'modernisation theory', 'charismatic leadership' and other such paradigms. Many intellectuals from the Soviet bloc and the Western left did the same, using the typologies and categories of Marxism.

This was about two things. First, there were over 50 African states, the biggest single bloc at the United Nations, and they were the object of fierce Cold War rivalry and competition. Most of the money and energy poured into African studies was about that. Second, African states and African leaders were, for a while, taken at their own inflated valuation. It rapidly became clear that the new elites were interested mainly in their own self-enrichment, and the new leaders – for all their theorising, charisma and ideology – disappeared under the accumulated weight of corruption and misgovernance.

This, however, took some time. For at least 20 years it seemed axiomatic that the cause of African liberation and that of the left were the same thing. Almost all African regimes claimed to be socialist, and most African leaders and their parties were either Marxists or *marxisant*, so it seemed natural that those who studied Africa shared similar attitudes. I was much influenced by Thomas. Later I suspected that he had smelt a rat early on, but he did not want to join the growing chorus of criticism of the new elite. He had run the Institute of African Studies in Ghana in the early 1960s, when the immediate excesses of the Nkrumah regime were becoming apparent. Notably, there was a Ghanaian cabinet minister, Krobo Edusei, who had mysteriously acquired such conspicuous wealth that he and his wife slept in a bed made of solid gold. Typically, Thomas had no critical words for Nkrumah (whom he always referred to as Kwame). He even had a rather ambivalent attitude to Conor Cruise O'Brien, the vice chancellor of the University of Ghana, who had a confrontation with Nkrumah over the issue of academic freedom, which ended in O'Brien's resignation. Thomas merely said, 'Well, Conor was always a good man for a fight.'

Thomas's emotional identification with African liberation was too strong to be qualified, so he simply avoided the growing signs that liberation was turning sour. He quietly left Ghana for Oxford, raising no issues of principle, lost interest in post-independence African politics, and instead devoted himself to pre-colonial African history. In the contemporary world he transferred his passions to the Vietnamese struggle, visiting Vietnam frequently (despite the heavy American bombing) and writing a history of the country.

Thomas's wife, Dorothy, for all that she had been Margaret Thatcher's tutor, held the Order of Merit and was chancellor of the University of Bristol, shared Thomas's views. She was a frequent visitor both to Vietnam and to Mao's China; I recall her telling me in 1966 that Mao's Great Proletarian Cultural Revolution was a much-needed purgative for a stagnant educational system. Even given what we knew then – let alone what we know now – this was an extraordinary judgement. The remarkable thing about Dorothy was the way she wafted through the corridors of the international establishment, receiving award after award, and maintained friendly relations with Margaret Thatcher, while quietly holding political views that would have scandalised many of her interlocutors.

Thomas once shocked me by pulling out a sheaf of photocopies of a typewritten text with handwritten amendments in the margins. He explained that Willie Abraham, the first African ever to be elected as a Fellow of All Souls College in Oxford, had had a study close to his in the University of Ghana. Willie, he knew, was ghost-writing for Nkrumah and had gone to see the president to get back the draft of Nkrumah's famous book *Consciencism*. Thomas heard Willie come back, but when he strolled over to see him, Willie had left his office. On his desk sat the draft with Nkrumah's emendations in the margins. Thomas, though feeling guilty, had been unable to restrain himself from making a photocopy of this interesting historical document, showing what part of the text was really Nkrumah's. Nkrumah was then at the height of his fame as a philosopher king and his writings were treated reverentially by African intellectuals. I was naively stunned to realise that this was somewhat bogus.

When Nkrumah was deposed by a military coup in 1966, the left-wing sympathisers who had gone to work for his socialist regime trickled back to England, many of them to see Thomas. I remember one Yorkshire couple, both Communist Party members, who were outraged by the military coup. They had come to Thomas for job references but they also wanted to stimulate student protests in favour of Nkrumah and asked Thomas which students they could talk to. He passed them on to me. They demanded that students must demonstrate against the new military government in Ghana and for the restoration of Nkrumah to power. I explained that this was a non-starter: British public opinion, students included, had heard too much about golden beds and about Nkrumah's shameful record on human rights, including his detention without trial of the opposition leader, JB Danquah, who died in jail. 'But Danquah was a reactionary!' they insisted. I pointed out that he had led the independence movement, had invited Nkrumah back to Ghana to be secretary-general of his party, and was a lawyer in good standing in British legal circles. In truth, it would be easier to get students to celebrate Nkrumah's downfall than to demand his restoration. The Yorkshire couple stared at me scornfully: 'And you call yourself a student!'

This was my first introduction to the travelling circus of left-wing sympathisers who greeted each new radical regime in Africa as the golden dawn of socialism. Many of those who had gone to cheer the heady triumphs of Nkrumahism turned up before long in Julius Nyerere's Tanzania. Once again, his admirers expressed adulation for this new leader and pored over his writing, this time on Ujamaa (brotherhood). Oddly, as socialists they disapproved in principle of the 'great man of history' theory, yet they hero-worshipped each of these leaders in turn, just as they hero-worshipped Fidel Castro and Che Guevara. Nobody wanted to notice the fact that Nyerere too employed detention without trial and that Ujamaa involved forced removals – roundly denounced when practised by apartheid South Africa. After Tanzania, the new great hope was Zambia. The circus moved on.

All this was surpassed, however, in 1969 when Basil Davidson published *The Liberation of Guiné* in which he recounted his time spent with the guerrillas of the Partido Africano da Independência da Guiné e Cabo Verde (PAIGC) in Portuguese Guinea (today Guinea-Bissau). Basil, a leading popular historian of Africa, was also very much on the left. He dramatically introduced the heroic figure of the PAIGC leader, Amilcar Cabral, whose writings on guerrilla warfare became as influential among Africanists as the writings of Che Guevara were for Latin

American progressives. Although Guinea-Bissau and Cape Verde were tiny territories, they were quickly assumed to have a world significance. Portugal's assertion that these were two separate territories that could never unite as a single state was regarded as a typical colonialist divide-and-rule tactic. The (equally heroic) guerrilla movement in Mozambique, Frelimo, was also revered. I met its leader, Eduardo Mondlane, when he visited Oxford to give a seminar. Although an attractive personality, he fell some way short of being a Guevara figure. (The American political scientist, David Apter, attending the seminar, told Mondlane that he sounded 'like a technocrat of revolution, not a revolutionary'.)

Basil Davidson had had a colourful career as an MI6 operative in wartime Hungary, had then been parachuted into occupied Yugoslavia to fight for Tito's partisans against the Nazis, and had then fought with the Italian partisans against the Germans. He was a tall, distinguished-looking man who smoked large cigars and enjoyed the mystique of having actually been on the ground, living with the guerrillas. His authority was reinforced not only by his war record but also by the fact that he was a generation older than the young progressives who flocked to hear him. For this was the high period of *tiers-mondisme*. Many on the left, influenced by the writings of Fanon and Mao, believed that only armed struggle could bring about a socialist revolution. Thus, the anti-Portuguese guerrillas were the real thing in a way that an Nkrumah or a Nyerere could never be. In 1974 Basil published *In the Eye of the Storm: Angola's People*, this time recounting his experiences with the Movimento Popular de Libertação de Angola (MPLA).

Basil was an intriguing, though difficult figure. Later, when a young Fellow, I had to prepare and edit (with Christopher Allen) a festschrift volume for Thomas Hodgkin's 60th birthday. We sought a contribution from Basil. Back came a rather hurried-looking chapter – for Basil wrote for profit and we were not offering a fee. We edited the piece into shape but there were still some glaring gaps, and we appealed to Basil to help us fill them. To our astonishment, back came a bitter tirade saying that young academics like us must doubtless look down on someone like him, for he had never been to university and we were clearly only concerned with advancing our careers. And so on and so on. We calmed him down but were amazed: we both admired Basil and it had never occurred to us that such an august figure might have such needless insecurities. In this we were perhaps naive, for in later life I not infrequently came across others with the same insecurities (for example, the South African newspaper editor Ken Owen). In vain one tried to say that one knew many silly academics and many clever non-academics. But this sounded patronising: one could not win.

In 1970, Portuguese mercenaries staged an invasion of Conakry in Guinea, next door to Guinea-Bissau. The invaders went straight to the presidential palace, clearly hoping to dispatch President Sékou Touré (who had strongly supported the PAIGC), and they also raided the PAIGC offices. In fact, both Touré and the PAIGC leaders were out of town, but the intent was clear. Since I was studying Guinea and had several contacts there, I gathered every scrap of information that I could about the event. I then sought Basil's advice. He averred that the invaders would surely have been helped and probably guided by renegade PAIGC fighters who had gone over to the Portuguese side. Were there such people, I asked. 'Oh yes, plenty,' said Basil. 'When I was with the Cabral brothers there were lots of very dodgy characters around – people who had mysteriously escaped from Portuguese captivity, and so on. I wouldn't have trusted half of them.' There had been no word in Basil's book about this – the guerrillas had been portrayed as heroic revolutionaries to a man. This was, of course, just a measure of my own naiveté, for Basil saw his own writing very much as serving his own political purposes, which is to say 'the progressive movement', so he would carefully omit information he judged to be inopportune. Some while later I reminded Basil of what he'd told me about the renegades in the PAIGC's ranks. He roundly denied that such people had ever existed.

The fact was that 'progressives' like Basil – and he was the most famous and distinguished of them – had invested much of their career in depicting Africa in romantic, liberatory terms. This had won Basil praise and awards from the African leaders he had supported, and he was certainly not about to revise his opinions now. But, like all the travelling circus of radical Africanists, he was doomed to one disappointment after another. Not only did Nkrumah, Nyerere and Kaunda all disappoint, but when Guinea-Bissau gained its independence in 1974, Cape Verde split away, just as the Portuguese had predicted. Worse, military coups soon followed and today Guinea-Bissau is mainly known for drug smuggling. In varying measures, the Frelimo and MPLA regimes also failed to live up to their advance billing: there were human rights abuses, massive corruption and great incompetence.

In the late 1980s I met up with Basil again. We both carefully skirted the question of what had happened to the heroic anti-Portuguese revolutionaries whose spokesman he had been. Instead he confided in me that he had at last found an African state that really was building socialism in just the way he had hoped: Siad Barre's Somalia. By 1991 this regime too had collapsed, revealing a completely failed state. The last time I saw Basil – by then he was old – he told me that what had gone wrong in Africa was that the colonial powers had imposed the idea of the nation-state on communities where this notion lacked any traditional basis: as usual, the colonial powers were to blame. I asked whether that meant it would have been better for colonial rule to have continued or perhaps better if Africa had just been left to its chiefs and warring tribes. Basil wanted neither of these alternatives. He would, I think, have liked to believe in a pre-colonial African golden age of peace and prosperity, but he knew this was a fiction. I longed to ask Basil whether his new insight that Africa and the nation-state did not belong together meant that all those movements for national independence had been mistaken and whether he now regretted supporting them. But that seemed too cruel.

I remember looking at him and feeling compassion well up. There was no doubt that Basil had fought the good fight. A war hero several times over, he had developed a passionate empathy with Africa's revolutionaries – a distinctly unusual choice for someone of his background. He had pinned his hopes on one chimera after another. They had all gone down in flames. He could have been pardoned had he felt – as many others ended by doing – that Africa had somehow let him down. But he was too respectful of history to feel that. He had always been aware that Africa was a tough, uncompromising place and difficult to know. He had spent much of his life trying to understand it. But Africa kept its secrets still.

CHAPTER SEVEN

Guinea

I had chosen to do my thesis on Guinea because it was then the most radical state in Africa. This was ultimately to lead me to make a research trip to Guinea, together with Anne Summers, straight after our wedding in 1968. (We had got married in Oxford and some of our guests arrived by punting up the river, alighting exactly at the rooms in Magdalen where we held our reception. Anne always kept her maiden name, which was then very unusual, though it has become commonplace since.) Our trip was eye-opening in ways that I had never anticipated. The experience remains forever fresh in my mind and was to change some of my views permanently.

When the Parti démocratique de Guinée (PDG), led by Sékou Touré, came to power, uniquely in Africa it abolished the chieftaincy. When the French president, Charles de Gaulle, put the new constitution of the French Union to the vote in 1958, Guinea alone chose independence by voting no. It adopted a radical foreign policy, removed itself from French tutelage, and boldly left the franc zone. Elsewhere in Francophone Africa the political elites were dominated by the graduates of the École normale William Ponty, the top *lycée* in French Africa. Touré alone came from humbler stock, and was a trade unionist and a radical populist. Francophone West Africa was dominated by Léopold Senghor (Senegal) and Félix Houphouët-Boigny (Côte d'Ivoire) – both Ponty men, both

Francophiles with large properties in France – but Touré was decisively different. He was, moreover, a remote descendant of the great Samory Touré, the greatest of all the leaders of pre-colonial resistance,[11] who in the late 19th century had fought the French to a standstill.

I studied all I could about Guinea in the libraries and archives in Paris. Visiting Guinea itself would be harder. The country was closed, suspicious and fearful of a French-inspired coup. It did not accept foreign researchers, seeing them as possible agents of imperialism. So I sought the help of the great French Africanist Jean Suret-Canale, with whom I was friendly. Suret, who sat on the central committee of the French Communist Party, was the sole exception to Touré's rule against foreign researchers – though even he had been expelled from Guinea because of his friendship with a group of intellectuals accused of a 'teachers' plot' against Touré. Nonetheless, Suret remained on relatively good terms with Touré, and his support was crucial to our getting visas to work in Guinea in 1968. We were, apart from Suret, the first Western researchers allowed in since 1958.

For the first few months we worked in the archives in Dakar, Senegal. Dakar then had many of the pleasant vestiges of French rule – attractive boulevards, good restaurants, and so on – and we enjoyed our time at IFAN (the Institut fondamental d'Afrique noire), which had a fine tradition of scholarship. A certain Cheikh Anta Diop was an occasional presence at IFAN but he was not highly regarded and had failed to secure a research position there. In his book *Nations nègres et culture* (1954) he had argued that ancient Egyptians were black people, part of a single African race, and that it was thus African civilisation that had produced the first writing (hieroglyphics) and invented mathematics. These achievements had been stolen from Africa, ending up in the hands of

---

11   See Yves Person, *Samori: une révolution dyula* (two vols, IFAN-Dakar, 1968), one of the greatest works of African history ever written.

the ancient Greeks, and thus becoming the property of Western Europe and the white race in general. Nobody took this seriously.

However, this gradually grew into a powerful current of African pseudo-history, known today as Afrocentrism. Suret threw up his hands in despair: apart from the fact that ancient Egyptians were a Nilotic people, there is no proof of their skin colour. Moreover, their portraits suggest features rather different from most Africans. But that was, Suret argued, beside the point. Intellectually speaking, it was unimportant whether the Egyptians had black skins or not: this was not an explanatory category and proper history could not be done that way.

But Diop's ideas gathered support in black America and elsewhere, such was the hunger of many blacks to 'discover' that they were really an ancient civilisation of a superior kind. Suret himself received some rough treatment for his dismissal of Diop's ideas (though he refused to change his views), as did American academics who objected to the wishful and racially based nature of Diop's work. Indeed, such was the black anger at those academics who criticised Diop – to do so was itself regarded as racist – that in most universities, respectable historians, while quietly rejecting Diop as nonsense, were usually careful not to say so out loud. Indeed, as Afrocentrism grew it went way beyond Diop's original formulation and today is a dominant force on black American campuses and in many parts of Africa as well.

The unhappy result is that in many departments of black studies in the USA and elsewhere, Diop is taken as gospel while mainstream history departments quietly ignore him. In Senegal itself the entire University of Dakar has been named after Diop. The result is a form of segregation in the academy that is both racial and intellectual. Those universities that espouse Afrocentrism are often regarded in much the same way as Southern fundamentalist colleges that refuse to accept evolution are – blockheaded and therefore inferior institutions. Presumably there was once such a division between flat-earthers and round-earthers.

...

We flew on to Guinea in an Air Guinée Antonov – the first of many Soviet touches. Conakry, the capital, was a humid, run-down place – a classic 'white man's graveyard'. After the comforts of Dakar, it was a shock. We were told that we were expected to present ourselves right away to the president to explain our purpose and present a letter of greetings to him from Suret. In practice this meant that for days we queued every morning at the presidency. The rainy season had begun and I was startled to see officials sauntering forth in tropical downpours, making no attempt to hurry or even to use umbrellas: the expectation was total that one was bound to get soaked to the skin, so why fight it?

Finally, we were ushered in to see Sékou Touré, a large, powerful man with an imposing presence – he was a macho figure who preferred driving himself at great speeds on the (bad) Guinean roads and was said to have an omnivorous sexual appetite.

Touré looked hard at us. We presented Suret's letter, which he read, and then he briefly asked after Suret. I explained to him that we were interested in Guinea's history and the growth of the PDG. He nodded as if that was the natural wish of all men and dashed off a few words on a piece of paper, which he then handed to us. This, it was explained, would be necessary if we wanted a visa to leave Conakry and travel into the interior of Guinea. We were specifically confined to Conakry until we could get the minister of the interior to grant us such a visa.

We devoted our first two months to work in the Conakry archives, which were situated right on the coast – the dampness got into every file and every dossier. The PDG regime had uprooted all the statues of colonial governors and the like and they had all been planted at the archives, staring blindly out to sea – a remarkable and symbolic sight. We were the only researchers at the archives throughout our time in Guinea, and as we worked mice and sometimes chickens would run beneath our feet while the archive assistants would approach us with dossiers hidden under their jackets, offering to sell them to us for money or American cigarettes. The air of neglect was total and we realised that the archives might not exist for very much longer.

Conakry was an unhealthy place and I soon contracted amoebic dysentery. I found I could not keep down any ordinary food and so resorted to a diet of nuts and bananas. This worked well, though I lost 18 kilos in weight. There was no public transport, so one had to take taxis everywhere. The taxis were already pretty broken down, and on one occasion the car's engine fell out onto the road. The driver stared at this sad sight. 'C'est cassé définitivement' (It is well and truly broken), he commented. And so it was.

There were few modern buildings in Conakry. The great exception was the huge Palace of People's Congresses and Culture, recently constructed by the Chinese. This was a subject of awe for most Guineans since the Chinese had arrived in force and worked day and night, under floodlights, finishing the whole structure in six months. No one had ever seen anyone work so hard. The Chinese builders and workers all lived in a large encampment and kept to themselves – this was the time of the Cultural Revolution. Anne and I thought it might be interesting to talk to them, so we went to their compound and asked if we might meet whoever was in charge. We were told that no one was in charge: everything was done by committee and our request was therefore impossible to accept.

Sékou Touré took himself seriously as a philosopher king and his Works rolled off the presses in many volumes. Essentially, they consisted of long and tedious party speeches, but now that Mao had made his Little Red Book famous, Touré produced his own Little Red Book of bits and bobs of revolutionary wisdom. One could occasionally see the book brandished by PDG activists. We bought most of our food at a Paterson Zochonis shop run by a rather gloomy Lebanese. ('It's very sad.

This whole country is just a disaster. But it's best to keep your thoughts to yourself.') The shop dealt only in hard currency because Guinea, in a defiant gesture of independence, had left the Communauté Financière Africaine (CFA), which was tied to the French franc, an arrangement that Touré denounced as neocolonialist. Once Touré could print his own money (with his own face on it) he inevitably printed however much he needed, with the result that the country experienced hyperinflation. No one wanted the Guinean franc and no neighbouring country would exchange its currency for it. This had led to the flight of hundreds of thousands of Guineans into neighbouring Côte d'Ivoire, Liberia, Sierra Leone and Senegal. Most of the old white and Lebanese communities had left too.

The calamitous state of the Guinean currency meant there was a considerable incentive to smuggle goods across the country's borders to earn hard currency. This was, indeed, what Touré's brother, Ismael – seen as the most left-wing minister in the cabinet – did with the entire production of the state-owned Sily cigarette factory. (Sily the elephant was the PDG symbol.) I was naive enough to be taken aback by this. The situation had also led the regime to set up its economic police, charged with tracking down illegal currency or trade. I remember going to Conakry's main market, where hundreds of market women sold their produce. The economic police stood around, Little Red Books in their hands. On all sides were posters denouncing capitalism, while down there in the market, capitalism flourished.

We were living in a rented house and discovered that our neighbours were obliged to go to PDG street committee meetings. As foreigners we were exempt, but when I asked about these meetings, I was told that it was understood that no one should ever criticise the president or the PDG and that it would, indeed, be dangerous to do so. Those who offended were dragged off to the sinister Camp Boiro and by no means everybody returned alive from there. Our neighbours were frightened by the thought of ever missing a meeting, for this could be taken as a sign of dissidence.

Conakry had become a refuge for failed radicals from elsewhere. The Black Panther leader Stokely Carmichael was there with his (then) girlfriend, Miriam Makeba. So was Kwame Nkrumah, having retreated there after being deposed. So was Djibo Bakary, the former leader of Niger's Rassemblement démocratique africain (RDA),[12] who had attempted, but failed, to get his country to follow Touré's example and vote no in 1958. And there too were Amilcar and Luís Cabral, the leaders of the PAIGC. Independence Day in Guinea was 28 September – the anniversary of the no vote – and on that day we attended the celebrations in a large soccer stadium. Touré was, of course, the star turn, but Nkrumah was there too, along with all these other revolutionary exiles. We met Luís Cabral, though not Amilcar. In fact, Luís turned out to be the only one of these exiles to return home in triumph. Nkrumah died in Guinea and Amilcar Cabral was assassinated there in 1973. Luís lasted only six years as president of Guinea-Bissau before being deposed in a coup. He died in exile in Portugal.

We were eager to go upcountry and visit all the main centres, gathering in the story of the PDG's ascent. We had to wait many days for an internal visa from the minister of the interior, though once we had shown him the scribbled note from the president, the visa followed. We set off on a bus to Kindia, about 95 kilometres up from the coast. Among our luggage was one suitcase full only of hyper-inflated Guinean francs. Halfway through the journey our bus was stopped by the economic police, who opened our case but said nothing – they were

---

12 The RDA was founded as a federal party across all eight states of French West Africa, so that parties such as the PDG were mere sections of the RDA. Until 1950–1951 the RDA was allied with the French Communist Party, which led to its repression by the French administration throughout West Africa. In 1951 Félix Houphouët-Boigny, the RDA leader in Côte d'Ivoire, quit the alliance with the communists, and some other RDA members followed his example. Djibo Bakary was among those who kept the true faith and refused to follow Houphouët.

looking for foreign currency or contraband. One passenger was escorted away in handcuffs, though it was not clear for what.

In Kindia we immediately sought out Ray Autra, who had played a leading role in the PDG's early days. Ray was something of a joker; his real name was Mamadou Traoré but he had pronounced Traoré backwards to produce Ray Autra. Something I have noticed throughout my life is that revolutionaries almost never have a sense of humour, and Sékou Touré was no exception. By 1961 Ray Autra had fallen foul of the regime, had spent a spell in jail, and was then living quietly as a schoolteacher. He made us welcome and began pouring out fascinating anecdotes. But suddenly he stopped. 'Have you been to see the party secretary yet?' No, we said. 'Good God, you'd better go see him right away. Whatever you do don't tell him you've already been talking to me. Or anyone.' The party secretary was, he explained, the inevitable boss of each region and etiquette required that everything was done through him and at his behest. So off we set and called on the secretary. He assembled his committee who, they said, would recount the history of the PDG in their region to us. Fairly quickly someone suggested that they ought to call Ray Autra to help, so he was sent for. He elaborately pretended not to have met us before and we did the same. Things went well and afterwards we went off for a meal with Ray. The next day we did more of the same.

From Kindia we travelled on to Mamou in the Fouta Djallon, a wonderful upland area sometimes referred to as the Switzerland of West Africa. The Fouta was home to the great Foula chiefs and it was here that the PDG's struggle against the chieftaincy had been at its fiercest. The Foula were devout Muslims, and near Mamou we met with the Almamy of Timbo, the greatest Islamic figure in the country. He was an utterly charming old man. We asked how he felt about being dispossessed of his chieftaincy. 'No regrets,' he said. 'If it happened, it must be the will of Allah.' He even talked of the fact that some of the young people were less devout than in the past – 'but I don't worry. Even if Islam should disappear, that would mean that Allah had willed that too.' In effect he had become a Stoic, which, we realised, was also a sensible position since the PDG would always be suspicious of someone who had been such a mighty chief. His apparent fatalism rendered him harmless. We could not help wondering if this was what he really thought or whether he was giving us a version that, even if reported to the party, would not get him into trouble. Somehow, I doubted that a great Muslim leader would ever really feel agnostic about the possible disappearance of Islam.

Mamou was a pleasant place and we quickly introduced ourselves to the party secretary. He, like the rest of his committee, was fairly young. As soon as we began asking how the PDG had developed there in the teeth of the opposition of the Foula chiefs, they said they needed to summon some of the retired old party militants. This was done and we soon began to learn the fascinating story of how the Mamou section had been particularly left-wing and had quarrelled bitterly with the PDG leadership when it first came to power and began rewarding itself with big cars and other perks. The Mamou section saw this as a betrayal and wanted to know why the party leaders could not use bicycles. A row developed and the Mamou section was excluded from the party until it finally came to heel.

This was all exciting news to me. It took two days to get the whole story out of the old militants, but gradually friction grew. The problem was that the new young men now in charge kept breaking in and interjecting, 'What they mean to say is …'. The old militants did not appreciate this and would angrily interrupt in turn, protesting, 'What do you know? You were not here then and we were.' Anne and I found ourselves trying to soothe the tensions.

From Mamou we went on to Pita to repeat the process. However, we had barely started talking to the PDG secretary there when we were informed that orders had been received from Conakry that 'le jeune couple Johnson' must return to the capital immediately. We were mystified and rather upset. An open lorry rolled up, we clambered into the back along with a dozen other folk on their way to Conakry, and off we set like the wind.

Once back in Conakry we gradually discovered that before we had arrived in Mamou there had been a lot of friction between the old party stalwarts and the new men of power. Things had become so heated that Touré himself had had to intervene to make peace. Then we had arrived and stirred things up. Indeed, the day after we had left Mamou serious trouble had erupted between the PDG leaders and the old stalwarts. News of this had reached Touré, who was furious, demanding to know how the strife had started this time. He was told that 'le jeune couple Johnson' had provoked it by asking all kinds of sensitive questions. So he had ordered us back to Conakry right away. It was clear that we were now in disgrace. Several people hinted that it might be wise to leave the country.

We were reluctant to go and decided we could profitably do more work at the Conakry archives. Meanwhile we began to get urgent summonses from the minister of the interior. We went several times to the ministry before we finally managed to see the minister. What he wanted were the interior visas he had earlier granted us. We realised that Touré was now probably angrily demanding to know who had authorised us to go and stir up trouble in Mamou, and the minister was keen to get the evidence and, presumably, destroy it. The fact that Touré's own signature had helped us get the visas would not count for very much now. Touré was not a man to cross, no matter what one's excuses. We handed back the visas and the minister looked deeply satisfied.

After a while we realised there was no more to do in the Conakry archives and that our time would be better spent finishing off in Dakar, so on 18 November 1968 we left Guinea. This turned out to be providential because the next day there was an army coup in Mali, which overthrew the regime of President Modibo Keita. Keita had been a militant in the PDG in the early days[13] and Mali and Guinea remained close. So Sékou Touré took fright and immediately arrested all the whites in Guinea. Had we stayed just one more day we would have seen the inside of a Guinean jail, which, from all we heard, was a fate to be avoided at almost any cost.

I was 26 when we returned from Guinea. It took me some time to assimilate the experience. I realised that my excited identification with radical African nationalism had essentially derived from my emotional reaction against apartheid. The truth had to be faced that Guinea had been a disappointment. Touré had installed a one-party state and thrown his enemies into jail at will. Diallo Telli, a Guinean, had been the first head of the OAU in 1964. When he retired back home in 1972, Touré was jealous and feared Telli might make a bid for the presidency. So he threw him into Camp Boiro, where Telli was deliberately starved to death. It was a ruthless system. There was no freedom of the press and, in effect, very little freedom of speech or association. I could not forget the fear ordinary people had of missing a street committee meeting or expressing open criticism.

Moreover, there was no development. Guinea has the largest bauxite reserves in the world and some of the richest iron ore deposits. Ten years after independence, neither was being exploited. People were poor, the currency was a disaster, there was a lot of corruption, and while Touré's many defiant gestures were magnificent in their way, they did not help anyone to eat or find work. Much of Touré's 'philosophy' was just warmed-over vulgar Marxism, without any serious intellectual interest. Many of the most enterprising citizens had fled. The truth was that PDG

---

13   This was not uncommon. Members of the RDA, like Keita, finding themselves in neighbouring countries, would simply join the RDA section there. It was as natural as a Labour Party member in Wales moving to London and joining his local Labour Party branch there.

rule was a sort of African Stalinism. Touré had the power of life and death over his subjects, just like Stalin had, and, like Stalin, he had a paranoid suspicion of intellectuals.

In the years that followed, many leading Guineans whom we had met ended up in Camp Boiro, usually dying there. One such was the fat and jolly Karim Bangoura, a prominent coastal-region politician who had become Guinean ambassador to the USA. He was arrested on trumped-up charges after the abortive coup in 1970. In the wake of the mercenary invasion Touré had all manner of suspects rounded up. Bangoura was one of them – I remember seeing his picture in the paper with some sort of placard around his neck, being paraded as a suspect, a look of awful misery and terror on his face. He was executed without trial. The minister of the interior who had been so unpleasant to us met a similar fate. Modibo Keita was thrown in jail after the 1968 coup in Mali and he died there in 1977. It was difficult to feel too much sympathy for him, given that he too had installed a one-party state and imprisoned opponents without trial.

When Touré died in 1984 the whole PDG regime came crashing down with him. All Touré's predictions of how Guinea would chart the way to a new radical Africa were simply dust. With Sékou gone, Ismael Touré attempted to take over – he had meanwhile become the ruthless chief prosecutor at Camp Boiro. He was quickly executed by the new military rulers. The PDG ceased to exist and the military ruled until 2010, when Alpha Condé was elected as president. Condé is widely accused of corruption and election-rigging.

So the democracy promised to Guineans when the French left has never actually arrived, and Guinea remains one of the poorest countries on earth. I started writing up all our research, but over time my enthusiasm flagged and I published relatively little about Guinea. It had been a cul-de-sac. In 2018 I gave my large collection of materials about Guinea to the University of Cape Town library. It is probably the best single collection of material on Guinea between 1900 and 1968 anywhere in the world. The PAIGC, whose guerrilla war in Guinea-Bissau I had cheered on, was an equal disappointment.

...

As I absorbed these disappointments, I realised, first of all, that I had been far too cavalier in ignoring – and thus implicitly accepting – the way that personal liberties and liberal institutions had been abandoned in Guinea. There had been clamant groups of Guinean exiles both in Paris and Dakar who had bitterly criticised the Touré regime. I had listened to them but had quietly – and unfairly – said to myself that this was what exiles sounded like the world over. In fact, they had been quite right. It had been too easy to accept the regime's story that personal liberties might suffer in the general cause of development and building socialism. But there had been no development. In any case, I realised anew that personal liberties really mattered and they were basic. You simply could not build a democratic society without them; they were non-negotiable.

Second, it was clear that if you wanted to improve living standards you had to be pragmatic. It was all very well for Touré to say that the CFA franc system was neocolonial. Maybe so. But it provided – and still does – a stable currency accepted by the world, one that investors are happy to use and trade in, with permanent low inflation. Only a certain number of the world's central banks are trustworthy. And people will vote with their feet and their money to have their currency tied to one of the trustworthy central banks. The CFA franc was tied to the French franc and today is pegged to the euro. It continues to work. You can see the alternative today in countries like Zimbabwe or Venezuela. No one trusts their local central bank: they trust the US Federal Reserve, the European Central Bank and the Bank of England. And such trust is immensely valuable. Once Zimbabweans and Venezuelans lost confidence in their own central banks and their currency, it became virtually impossible for those banks to regain their trust.

My mistake was obvious. Faced with the horrors of apartheid, radical African nationalism had seemed to me to be a key part of the answer. Clearly, it wasn't. And there might not be any simple 'answer' at all.

I was reminded of something my father had told me. 'If,' he said, 'you look at, say, Catholics or communists in England, they're the salt of the earth – good people devoted to the poor. But you can't judge any movement by looking at them where they are a small, protesting minority. You have to look at the way they behave when they have power. So have a look at what Catholicism is like in Spain or Ireland and what communism is like in Russia or East Germany.' And that was the point. In South Africa I had sympathised with African nationalism as a persecuted outgroup. It was a story of sacrifice and devotion to ideals. In Guinea I had seen African nationalism in power and it was a very different story.

CHAPTER EIGHT

Thoughts of Home

In Oxford I had become an expert on French politics, but I always had more than half an eye on events in South Africa. The Soweto rising of 1976 rekindled my interest and I sat down to write *How Long Will South Africa Survive?* (1977). By this time, I had become discontented with the ANC and Marxist interpretations of events and was, in my own mind, a determined realist – wherever that might lead. I was fascinated by the complex interplay of South Africa's political economy with the international political economy, which, I realised, usually had a determinant effect. I was gripped by the way in which commodity prices, particularly the (falling) gold price, had exercised enormous pressure on the Pretoria regime – and the way in which the price had clearly been manipulated by the USA.

I also realised that South Africa was a decolonisation problem like no other. Accordingly, I developed a model of metropole-periphery relations that enabled me to make more sensible predictions about the likely trajectory of events. One result was to make me realise that white supremacy still had further to run than many thought – many ANC friends were confidently predicting an immediate revolution in 1976. But my study of the Soweto events made me realise that for all their drama and violence they did not really challenge the survival or even the stability of the apartheid regime. The ANC faced a conundrum too, for while it wished to encourage such insurrections, it neither controlled them nor really knew what to do with them. Provided township unrest stayed confined to the townships, it could never really threaten white power.

These were not fashionable ideas: in left-wing and liberal circles in Europe the ANC version was rather romantically accepted, and even conservatives thought the white regime's life was limited. On the other hand, I had been struck by the success of the 1974 revolution in Portugal and the triumph of Frelimo in Mozambique and the MPLA in Angola. Guerrilla warfare seemed the inevitable way ahead; it was hard to see how Ian Smith's Rhodesia could withstand the guerrilla threat that would come from the Zimbabwe African National Liberation Army (Zanla), which was based in Mozambique. In the longer term, the same would surely apply to MK and South Africa. I concluded that white rule in South Africa would finally end in the early to middle 1990s, which meant it would survive longer than the ANC and SACP (and many others) were saying at the time. It was an erroneous explanation (MK never came close to challenging the regime militarily) that nonetheless produced an accurate prediction of the time left for white South Africa.

It was a young man's book. I had a heavy teaching load and could only write in the evenings. Many a time I wrote right through to breakfast and then went to teach another day. In the end I wrote the book's 130 000 words in just 100 days. It was in a way a product both of Oxford and of the thorough dousing in African reality that I had had in Guinea. The two things combined to influence my study of politics. They made me impatient of ideological wishfulness and determined to seek the real determinants of any situation. In a way Oxford has that effect upon you. All around there are very clever people impatient with conventional views, seeking the deeper keys to human events, and the notion sinks into you that this is the way you should proceed.

I have always been struck by the way Oxford influences even those who spurn study. Thus, to take two people whom I knew, Tariq Ali and Christopher Hitchens; both did very little academic work and spent their time on essentially frivolous pursuits. They both got Third Class degrees, virtually a disgrace. But both of them had been infected with the idea that the thing to be was a proper intellectual, a gentleman scholar. So although Tariq devoted his life to agitprop of a very 1960s kind and Christopher to a sort of knockabout humorous journalism, both of them also attempted to write serious books to show they were proper intellectuals. But neither of them had ever really been a scholar, and it showed. In Christopher's case it led to his public downfall when he wrote a 'serious' book on Tom Paine and *Rights of Man* only for it to be shown up in a deadly review by a real Paine specialist in the *London Review of Books*. (Mary-Kay Wilmers, the *LRB*'s editor, told me that Hitchens never spoke to her again after that.) Tariq's work at least avoided such ignominy but reviewers often mocked his efforts as wishful and insubstantial.

My first South Africa book had a curious history. It sold well initially and got good reviews. In South Africa, it was first banned and then unbanned. But then my publishers were sued for libel by the Zambian president, Kenneth Kaunda, of whom I had made fun in the book. I was furious because my manuscript had been expensively read by a major firm of libel lawyers who had given it the all clear. However, the publisher panicked and withdrew the book from publication. Whereupon the libel lawyers admitted that they had never actually read the manuscript but had just flipped through it. For almost a year the book stayed in the deep freeze. Finally, Kaunda realised that if he wished to sue for libel this would lead to a court case in London – and the Zambians recoiled with horror at the thought of stories about Kaunda being tested publicly in open court. With that the case collapsed.

. . .

I was invited back to the University of Natal in 1978 to give some lectures. Given the circumstances under which I had left in 1964, I was nervous. When I visited Pretoria the state authorities insisted on providing me with a driver whose job it clearly was to keep tabs on me. But nothing could spoil the fact that returning home was wonderful. The university atmosphere had improved considerably. Given the Soweto riots and the rise both of a black trade union movement and of the Black Consciousness Movement, the security police had their hands full and were clearly no longer monitoring the English-speaking university campuses so closely. I was astonished to see works by Marx, Che Guevara and Régis Debray on sale in the university bookshop, all of which would have been banned when I was a student.

I questioned members of the political science department about the new developments in the country – but drew a complete blank. Nobody had done any research about any of these developments. Indeed, they suggested that I give talks to them about such things, which was ridiculous. I learnt more when I met Alec Erwin, then a lecturer in economics and a trade union activist. But the real find was Lawrence (Lawrie) Schlemmer, by some margin the best social scientist in the country and a great fund of information about all manner of things. He was also the director of the Inkatha Institute, established by Mangosuthu Buthelezi, chief minister of the KwaZulu Bantustan and at that time easily the leading personality in black politics. Lawrie's open identification with him was seen as a very daring move, talked about by other whites with bated breath. It was about the most left-wing option available.

In fact, the situation was complicated. At that time, few people knew much about Nelson Mandela, for the ANC kept very quiet about him and the other Robben Island prisoners. This seemed to be based on a fear that Mandela might cut some private deal with the authorities in return for his release or at least partial freedom. In which case the ANC would have to disavow him – so better to say nothing about him to start with. (In fact, Mandela refused any possible compromise with his jailers, though they tried hard to tempt him.) Meanwhile, Buthelezi gave the authorities no end of trouble – denouncing apartheid, campaigning for universal suffrage, and demanding the unbanning of the liberation movements and Mandela's release. This earned him such a large black following that when Lawrie teamed up with the German scholar Theo Hanf[14] to carry out the first systematic survey of black opinion, Buthelezi ran comfortably ahead of the ANC leaders.

It was a fatal moment. John Vorster and then PW Botha were continually tempted to place Buthelezi under preventive detention – only to be warned that they would have to deal with millions of angry Zulus. So in the end they always backed off. The security police then decided to take Buthelezi down a peg or two. Elections were being held in KwaZulu where, normally, there was just one (Inkatha) candidate per seat. Suddenly independent candidates blossomed everywhere, talking the language of an extreme Zulu traditionalism. They were quickly bullied into standing down and even apologised publicly to Buthelezi for having dared to challenge him. Lawrie had been interested and told me that he had tracked down the fact that the security police had put these independents up to it and paid their expenses. Moreover, they had enlisted the support of Buthelezi's nephew, the Zulu king, Goodwill Zwelithini, who was jealous of his uncle's pre-eminence.

Lawrie asked the security police why they had done this – for Lawrie was willing to talk to anyone. Well, they said, we know Buthelezi sees the ANC exiles every time he goes to London and that he is under pressure from them to move further left (for the police had excellent intelligence sources). So we thought we'd put up these Zulu conservatives as a warning to Buthelezi and so that he feels pressure from the right as

---

14   Hanf was the director of the Arnold-Bergstraesser-Institut in Freiburg im Breisgau, West Germany.

well as the left. It was an interesting indication of the relative sophistication of the security police. When Buthelezi learnt of what had happened, he warned the king never to interfere again. The whole story was exposed at length in the Zulu newspaper *Ilanga*.

I also met up again with Frederik van Zyl Slabbert, now the leader of the Progressive Federal Party (PFP), whom I had first met when he was an Abe Bailey scholar at Oxford. And I travelled down to Cape Town for a marvellous week with Rob Amato, who was ensconced in a splendid house in Constantia.

Rob had originally gone to work for his father in East London, where the business was humming along. Rob, now married with three children, had fallen in with the newspaper editor Donald Woods and the Black Consciousness activist Steve Biko. Ultimately, Ben exchanged the business for a textile plant on the Cape Flats, a move that had suited Rob, who could indulge his love of theatre. Keen to discover and patronise the new black dramatic talent of the time, he had set up a theatre called the People's Space where he produced, directed and sometimes acted. The Amato household was full of black and white theatrical people, all helping themselves from the fridge and the wine cellar. It was a jolly scene.

Rob eagerly showed me the People's Space, obviously the centre of his Cape Town world, though I never got a clear picture of these new dramatic folk or their talents – they all seemed like bit-part players in Rob's larger drama. Both Rob's parents had died. His mother had committed suicide by walking out into the sea – 'She really didn't want to be an old lady,' said Rob. It sounded like a sad and eerie end, and I wondered if her motives had not been more complex. She had made it clear enough that she did not think Rob should ever be in charge of anything too important, and now he was in charge of the family business, the family everything.

I was anxious to see Rob's business, but he seemed bored by it. Finally, I persuaded him to take me there. Rob went off to talk to an accountant while I strolled around. After ten minutes Rob was ready to go. As we drove back to Constantia Rob talked happily about the theatre, the business already forgotten.

In Stellenbosch I made friends with a number of Afrikaners – Hermann Giliomee, André du Toit and Marinus Wiechers. I had never really had many Afrikaans friends before and I learnt a lot from them. Wiechers had attended the South West Africa constitutional talks at the Turnhalle, in Windhoek, as a legal adviser to the moderate Democratic Turnhalle Alliance. However, he discovered that the internal delegation from the South West Africa People's Organisation (Swapo) had no clue how to proceed, so he had ended up advising them too. This had greatly annoyed Prime Minister Vorster, who had openly attacked him for having joined hands with Swapo, a mortal enemy. Marinus felt that it was his perfect right to advise any accredited delegate and had indignantly gone to see Vorster to complain. Vorster himself had answered the door and said, 'Ag, Marinus man, come in and have a drink.' Which they did. It was an interesting window into the fact that Afrikaners were still a small community where such familiarities were common. No English-speaker could have access to that different world.

I was invited to a party in Stellenbosch by some younger faculty members who told me I would meet someone interesting there. This turned out to be the Reverend Allan Boesak, already a rising star in coloured politics. He sat perched on the arm of a sofa, confident and smiling. He was a perfect party animal – gregarious, fun-loving and a charmer with an eye for the ladies, who also had an eye for him. The only incongruity was any idea that he had the remotest thing to do with religion or a church. Indeed, watching and listening to him it was difficult to believe that this was a man of any sort of principle, religious or political. Holding to principles of any kind implies discipline, self-denial, even a kind of austerity, and of this there was no sign. Nothing that happened to and around Boesak in the years that followed – the womanising, the corruption, the endless refusal to own up and accept blame – ever really surprised me, for there was always this picture in my mind of the perfect party animal perched on the couch.

I was greatly invigorated by my South African return. The country was as lovely as ever but its politics had opened up and become a lot more real. There had been a major seismic shift with Biko's murder in September 1977. As a result, France joined the arms embargo against South Africa, and since it had provided Pretoria with its Mirage jets, Alouette helicopters and much else besides, this was a huge stride towards Pretoria's isolation. It also caused a major shift within the exiled ANC. The rise of Biko and Black Consciousness had alarmed them, especially since the Soweto students had acknowledged the leadership of Biko, not that of the ANC, The danger threatened that the ANC could lose control of the liberation movement. This was why the ANC had maintained warm relations with Buthelezi: he at least gave the exiles in London contact with a major grassroots figure and organisation within South Africa. Buthelezi, for his part, visited the ANC president, Oliver Tambo, whenever he was in London, though he told me he was deeply shocked to discover that the Tambo daughters could speak no African language.

Biko's death presented the ANC with an opportunity. While Biko had been alive the party had been a player in a three-person game and needed an alliance with Buthelezi to help them beat off Biko's challenge. Now, with Biko gone, it could dispense with Buthelezi. Moreover, the Schlemmer-Hanf poll showing Buthelezi's popularity had given the ANC a nasty shock. The party had carefully refrained from publicity about Mandela, saying it wanted to 'avoid the cult of personality'. But if the price of this was to see Buthelezi become the most popular black political leader in South Africa, then that was intolerable. So not only did the ANC find a pretext to break with Buthelezi in 1979–1980 but it also launched its 'Release Mandela' campaign.

As we now know, the ANC's Soviet backers took a firm hand at this point.[15] They were critical of the ANC's relative inactivity, pointing out that MK was having no military impact. The Russians too had been shocked at the ANC's loss of the initiative to Black Consciousness. They had poured large resources into the ANC for decades and did not want to write that off. So they suggested that the ANC take a new, far more active role – not only the 'Release Mandela' campaign but also the declaration of a 'people's war' within South Africa. The ANC had to impose itself everywhere by force, take control of townships, squatter camps and the English-speaking campuses – turning them into bases – and try to overthrow the various Bantustan rulers.[16] This led to a bloody war with Inkatha both in Natal and on the Reef, and violence mounted in strikes, kangaroo court executions and elsewhere. The death toll mounted.

Lawrie Schlemmer pointed out to me that South Africa had always consisted of multiple segregated political universes. When National Party politicians spoke to *die volk*, that is, to their own caucus and the party faithful, they were at their most sectarian and reactionary. They adopted a moderate tone when they addressed English-speaking whites and a yet

---

15 See Irina Filatova, *The Hidden Thread: Russia and South Africa in the Soviet Period* (Jonathan Ball Publishers, 2013), pp 244–245. Moreover, the Soviets suffered a serious loss of faith in the ANC at this point. The Soviet military stated flatly that MK could not win an armed struggle and a memorandum was circulated to the Soviet Communist Party's Central Committee by the Soviet Foreign Ministry saying that while the ANC's struggle would continue the Soviet Union should hedge its bets by establishing relations with South African academics, businessmen and even the Pretoria government.

16 The myth has grown up that the ANC derived the concept of 'people's war' from a visit to Vietnam in 1979. This is not true. In the Soviet Union from the mid-1960s on the Soviet military taught a secret course for Third World guerrilla movements called Military Combat Work (MCW). Over 90 per cent of all ANC cadres visiting Moscow attended this course and notes from the course circulated widely. MCW explicitly talks about 'people's war'. And Joe Slovo's document, 'Planning for People's War', was based on MCW. It was also the Soviets who told the ANC to send a delegation to Vietnam in order to study how they had successfully implemented a 'people's war'. That is, the visit was about implementation. The concept had been around for years before that and was already standard ANC doctrine. See Filatova, *The Hidden Thread*, pp 319–320.

more liberal tone when they defended South Africa's policies abroad. The ANC similarly took an ultra-revolutionary and ideological tone when they addressed their own activists, which they moderated when they were talking to sympathisers at home or abroad. The same was true for most South African political movements and the key was the existence of these multiple, separate audiences. But inevitably a speech intended for one audience would leak across to another audience for which it had not been intended, setting off endless ripples and reactions.

It was an immensely complex structure yet each audience was told that things were simple. There was the *swart gevaar* (the black peril), people's war, *baasskap*, revolutionary justice, and so on. Inevitably, though, as things moved towards a climax these barriers were coming down, so there would be more of a single national conversation. This, however, was a graduated and complex process and many moves remained hidden. For example, after the arrest in South Africa of a Soviet spy, Colonel Alexei Kozlov, in 1980, secret relations began between South Africa's National Intelligence Service (NIS) and the KGB. In 1988–1989 two KGB officers, generals Artiomov and Ivanov, travelled to Pretoria, met with President PW Botha, and were royally entertained by Niël Barnard, the head of NIS.[17] Similarly, secret contacts were taking place between the government and the ANC.

South African politics, I realised, were just as complex as anything I had studied in France. And for years the main actors were all offstage – the ANC leaders in exile, Mandela, Sisulu and company on Robben Island, and the National Party leadership in a little world of its own – so one seldom had inside information about the inner working of these separate universes. And since there was no formal communication between these various groups, there was no proper public debate. South African politics were thus in an unreal way, all symbolic images and pure

---

17   Ibid, pp 430–432.

principles. Only if one made the assumption that politics in South Africa worked in much the same way as politics did elsewhere could one begin to pierce through the mythology.

A classic case was the Rivonia Trial, which had sent Mandela and his co-accused to life sentences on Robben Island and thus became the epicentre of South Africa's 20th-century history. All South African political discussion still returns to this pivotal moment and the trial has become myth-laden. Yet it is worth examining it afresh just to see behind those myths.

Anthony Sampson, in his biography of Mandela, records that there was substantial support for Mandela and the Rivonia accused in Britain, even in the Conservative Party, and that Sir Alec Douglas-Home, the foreign secretary, offered to send a private message to Verwoerd about the trial. But Home thought that open British pressure could be counterproductive. However, it was quite clear that the trial was fixed and the verdict known in advance. Major-General Hendrik van den Bergh, later head of the Bureau for State Security (BOSS), told the British embassy in Pretoria that there would not be death sentences and that the prosecutor, Percy Yutar, would not ask for them. A week before the verdict was given, the defence lawyer George Bizos was told by the British consul-general, Leslie Minford, 'who was thought to have intelligence links': 'George, there won't be a death sentence.'[18]

The realpolitik behind this was that the UK and USA were still protecting Pretoria from the wrath of the UN General Assembly, pleading for more time for South Africa to reform and pressing it to do so. This protection was immensely valuable to Pretoria, so it was unsurprising that Verwoerd would listen when these powers made it plain that the Rivonia accused must not be hanged. Quite apart from the possibility that negotiations with the ANC would be necessary some day, the

---

18   Anthony Sampson, *Mandela: The Authorised Biography* (HarperCollins, 1999), pp 194–195.

execution of black leaders would create major problems for the Democrat administration in Washington, which depended on black votes. The British, for their part, had seen the Commonwealth nearly tear itself apart over the South African issue in 1961 and knew that Mandela's execution would enrage not only Ghana and Nigeria but also Canada, India, the West Indies and others.

Mandela, meanwhile, was desperately insisting at the trial that he was not a communist – for that alone would bring automatic and heavy penalties. The most embarrassing piece of evidence was Mandela's own essay on 'How to be a Good Communist', which included such statements as 'Under a CP government South Africa will become a land of milk and honey ... There will be no unemployment, starvation and disease.'[19] This was supported, moreover, by oral evidence from Bruno Mtolo, who told the court how Mandela had preached guerrilla warfare and had also told his audience in Durban that the communists – who dominated the ANC – should conceal their own beliefs, which were often unpopular in South Africa.

Even such sympathetic listeners as the defence attorney Joel Joffe thought that after such evidence Mandela and Sisulu were at best fifty-fifty for a death sentence.[20] Then, however, Mandela eloquently addressed the court, likening his relationship with the communists to that of Churchill with Stalin during the war, and praising the British and American political systems.[21] Justice Quartus de Wet seemed nervous as he gave his verdict: although he found the accused guilty, he had decided against the death penalty.[22] There was a gasp of relief in the courtroom. Almost everyone – including the accused – had expected

---

19   Ibid, p 190.

20   Ibid.

21   Ibid, p 193.

22   Ibid, p 197.

the death penalty. Several of the prisoners said happily: 'We got life!'[23] Mandela himself fully expected a death sentence.[24] According to the happy mythology of the trial, Mandela had proved that he was not a communist, and his dramatic speech and his lawyers' heroic efforts (particularly Bram Fischer) had won the day.

The truth was rather different. Mandela, as we now know, was not only then a communist, but was on the Party's Central Committee – the SACP itself boasted of this after Mandela's death. So Mandela was lying throughout about his beliefs, just as the Party required him to do. Moreover, even Mandela acknowledged that his speech was not his own. Bram Fischer and, through him, other SACP intellectuals had contributed extensively. For Fischer was a pre-eminent communist and had been involved in the Rivonia circle himself. His co-advocate, Arthur Chaskalson, had wanted to join the SACP but had been dissuaded by Fischer, who felt he would be more useful as a secret sympathiser.[25] Thus Mandela's defence was largely in SACP hands.

Mandela was not normally an eloquent speaker and it is unlikely that he would, on his own, have come up with analogies to Churchill and Stalin, or known much about the British and American political systems. Similarly, references in Mandela's speeches to the Magna Carta, the Petition of Right and the then recent sentencing of Bertrand Russell in England for his anti-nuclear activities all suggest the work of other speechwriters – points inserted to impress liberal opinion in Anglo-America. But the key point is that what turned the tide was British and American diplomatic pressure, not Mandela's speech.

For the British and Americans to know the trial's outcome in advance,

---

23 Ibid.

24 Nelson Mandela, *Long Walk to Freedom* (Little, Brown, 1994), p 360.

25 This emerged from an extensive correspondence in the pages of *Business Day* following Chaskalson's death in December 2012. Ken Owen, a former editor, claimed that Chaskalson had been an actual SACP member, while his defenders made the point above.

they must have received assurances, which could ultimately only have come from Verwoerd himself. Which in turn means that both Percy Yutar and Justice De Wet were under political control, doing what they were told. (De Wet, who had been appointed a judge under Smuts, would probably have preferred a less drastic sentence than death anyway.) On his own, Yutar would doubtless have demanded the death sentence. No wonder De Wet seemed nervous as he gave his verdict, which he may have feared would provoke an angry roar of political criticism.

This fact of political control enables one to understand a number of steps in the case favourable to the accused. Thus, De Wet interrupted Yutar, insisting that he had failed to prove that guerrilla warfare was ever decided on by the accused. Yutar, flummoxed, said that preparations for guerrilla warfare had been made. De Wet again, to the delight of the defence, replied that he knew that, but the defence had said they had, at the time of their arrest, taken no actual decision to engage in guerrilla warfare (in itself an extremely dubious assertion). Since Yutar could not disprove this, De Wet ruled that the defence argument must be accepted as the truth, an extraordinary concession.

Fischer then rose to tackle two cardinal points made by the prosecution, that guerrilla warfare had been undertaken and that effectively MK and the ANC were the same thing. To Mandela's delight and astonishment, De Wet interrupted Fischer before he had begun in order flatly to concede both points. Fischer was amazed.[26] Moreover, De Wet conceded that the crime of which the accused had been convicted 'is in essence one of high treason. The state has decided not to charge the crime in this form. Bearing this in mind … I have decided not to impose the supreme penalty which in a case like this would usually be the proper penalty.'[27] But why had the state deliberately pulled its punches in this way?

---

26   Mandela, *Long Walk to Freedom*, p 357.

27   Ibid, p 362.

The security police had penetrated both the ANC and SACP and must have known perfectly well about Mandela's Communist Party membership – and the evidence in court was pretty obvious. The accused were being perfectly realistic in expecting death sentences. Yet the court accepted that Mandela was not a communist. This was clearly nothing to do with the legal brilliance of Mandela's defence team; even someone as sympathetic as Joel Joffe thought that the evidence against Mandela was damning. However, if we allow that the judge and the prosecution were both under political control, it is easier to surmise what was going on.

Verwoerd knew full well how provoking to the National Party parliamentary caucus and its electorate was the sight of black revolutionaries plotting the violent overthrow of the white regime. If, in addition, their leaders were proven to be communists, thus vindicating the bogeyman constantly held out by Verwoerd, a death sentence would be unavoidable. For if they were found to be communists and only given life sentences, it would be very difficult to explain to angry National Party followers why they had not been hanged. Thus, once he had agreed with the Anglo-Americans that the prisoners would not be hanged, it was in Verwoerd's interest to soft-pedal the prosecution and to find them not to be communists.

If even the sacred myth of Rivonia could be so easily deconstructed, then what else was possible? So much of South African politics was obstructed by a fog of naiveté and parochialism that it was much more interesting to take a realist approach. Ever since the writing of my first South Africa book in 1977 I have attempted to do just this.

...

After my 1978 trip I organised a family holiday in South Africa for Anne and our children, Rebecca and Richard, in 1980. We had a wonderful time. However, when we came to stay with Rob Amato in Cape Town, we found he and his family were living in somewhat reduced circumstances in Rosebank. Of the theatrical hangers-on who had flocked to Rob's previous house, there was no sign. It emerged that the textile business had gone bust and the house was now all that was left. Rob's hands-off management style had clearly been disastrous. But this he fiercely denied, saying that the fault had been entirely his father's for leaving the business encumbered by debt. It was not my business to argue.

A lawyer representing Rob's sister in London then phoned. Rob was mystified: why did she not phone him herself? When she did, Rob couldn't understand why she was so angry. She explained that all their father's assets had been held in trust for his grandchildren – Rob's children and hers. Now Rob had wiped out almost all of that and she was thinking of suing him. Rob slapped his forehead: 'My God, she's right! I had entirely forgotten about the trust.' Only Rob could have forgotten such a cardinal fact. In the end his sister mercifully held off, for all that Rob had left was the roof over his family's heads.

Although Rob was now bankrupt, he made no effort to get a job. Instead he talked about plays and novels he wanted to write, and then decided to try to raise funds for a new theatre in Cape Town of which, of course, he would be the director and impresario. Unsurprisingly, this never came to fruition.

These two journeys launched me into a decade-long pattern of further trips to South Africa. My friend Mervyn Frost, the professor of political science at the University of Natal, invited me back time and again to teach a term in Durban during the Oxford long summer vacations. This allowed me not only to keep up to date with South African developments but also to write about them for the British press. It also gave me a ringside seat as the English-speaking universities were desegregated and a vast tide of black students flowed in. The tide of change was exhilarating and I realised that I had to come back altogether.

But my 1984 trip to Durban hit an obstacle. A deputation from the (then still white) SRC, which was by then strongly committed to the United Democratic Front (UDF), an ANC front organisation, told me they were embarrassed that their money had paid for my trip, which might be in breach of the academic boycott (which they supported). Previously, no one had checked up, but now they were alarmed by this possible political sin. They asked me to an interview where I would be grilled by the whole SRC, a difficult and hostile occasion. First, they asked me the standard UDF question: had I consulted 'the anti-apartheid forces on your own campus' before I came? I explained that in Oxford everyone was anti-apartheid – the Labour Club, the Tory Club, the rugby club, even the Gliding Club. Whom exactly should I have asked? Moreover, at Oxford, my own college, Rhodes House and occasionally student societies all consulted me on South African issues, on which I was seen as something of an expert. They would not have understood if I had asked them what I should do.

My interrogators were discomfited. So next they asked me what I thought about freedom of speech on campus. I said I was in favour. Ah, they said, we are all against. Freedom of speech would mean that Inkatha speakers would be allowed on campus and that would never do. I explained that in my time on the Durban SRC we had fought strongly for freedom of speech. I could not regret that. I found it difficult to imagine that times could change so much that freedom of speech was a bad thing, but it was up to them to make policy now.

Finally, they demanded to know what my attitude was to the academic boycott. I was tempted to say it was a lot of nonsense, but just such an answer had recently got Conor Cruise O'Brien into a great deal of trouble down in Cape Town. Instead, I said there would always be two views about it, but, in any case, I couldn't believe it applied to me. I had grown up here in Durban and even been on their SRC. I was coming home. Surely they approved of that? Didn't they all believe that the ANC and other exiles should be allowed home? The meeting broke up untidily and without further consequence.

It was a warning, though. As the anti-apartheid struggle moved to a climax, the ANC was pulling strings behind the UDF and most student politics too. And the ANC was still a highly disciplined and authoritarian movement. The combination of its pervasive influence and the rising excitement and commitment of the younger generation was producing a sectarian and intolerant atmosphere, particularly on the English-speaking campuses. I had already drawn criticism of my South Africa book for the way it did not follow the ANC script. Even such a distinguished visitor as Conor Cruise O'Brien had been physically threatened and his lectures disrupted. In the end the University of Cape Town had buckled and cancelled his lectures, a shameful retreat from academic freedom – and Wits University had quickly followed suit. This spoke volumes about the climate emerging on university campuses. Before he departed, Conor had made a prescient prediction that at this rate South African universities would have to face their own equivalent of the Red Guards of the Cultural Revolution. Until then I had worried exclusively about threats from the right. Now, clearly, the threats could come from both sides.

CHAPTER NINE

The Roaring Eighties

Back in England, Barry Higgs died suddenly in his mid-forties. I always put this down to the police torture he had endured, though, to be fair, Barry had lived a hard-drinking and unhealthy life. I was desperately upset by his death and to this day I have his picture on my wall. Melville Fletcher had also been forced into exile. He had a job at a power station down in Kent but he was a fish out of water and most unhappy. I heard he was dying too and rang him for a last and very emotional conversation.

Meanwhile I heard that Thami Mhlambiso had joined the exiles in London but fallen foul of Thabo Mbeki. Mbeki was notorious for his sharp elbows, and the moment the smooth, well-spoken Thami arrived, Mbeki seems to have seen him as a rival and worked to marginalise him. Ultimately Thami was sent away to be the ANC representative at the UN. In 1975 the so-called Gang of Eight were expelled from the ANC; these were African nationalists who objected to the dominance of the SACP within the exiled ANC. Although Thami did not join this group, Mbeki engineered a situation in which he was expelled as one of them. Thami thus automatically lost his ANC job in New York. However, by then he was well known in that environment and got a job working directly for the UN. This seemed to enrage Mbeki, who flew to New York expressly in order to get Thami sacked, presenting a letter announcing that Thami was unknown to the ANC. (Mbeki had presumably got Oliver Tambo to sign the letter.) The UN authorities, knowing this was ridiculous, concluded correctly that it was an intra-ANC squabble and so Thami kept his job. The situation was nonetheless tragic. The ANC had been Thami's life and now he was an outcast, marooned in a foreign country. Even later, when Mbeki was president, Thami felt it was unsafe to return to South Africa and made only flying visits. Exile life was full of such unhappy stories.

Back in South Africa, there was effectively a stalemate, with the mass movement of the UDF and the government glaring at one another. The UDF leaders Archbishop Desmond Tutu and Allan Boesak strongly denied that it was an ANC front. Their denial turned out to be untrue; when the ANC was unbanned from exile in 1990 it immediately wound up the UDF and took its place. Suddenly it was accepted universally that the UDF had indeed been an ANC front. Yet there was always a difference because Tutu and Boesak were both churchmen and not under ANC discipline. This caused considerable strain with Mbeki, who resented the UDF leaders' 'unmandated' position. For Boesak and Tutu would make spontaneous pronouncements about sanctions and boycotts without knowing much about the issue. At the same time, some ANC cadres demanded that the UDF leaders help smuggle arms into the country or at least help fund such supplies.

President PW Botha was utterly determined not to give ground except on his own terms. The result was a sterile period – the autumn of the patriarch. Economic growth and investment ground to a halt, the value of the rand fell, and apartheid began to collapse too. Critically, the government revoked the sections of the Immorality Act forbidding inter-racial sex in 1985. There were more and more mixed-race couples living together in defiance of the Group Areas Act. White rule remained but depended ever more openly on the police and the army.

The Progs' leader, Van Zyl Slabbert, told me that he often had to share platforms with Tutu and Boesak, an embarrassing business since they were both prima donnas who clearly hated one another. The minute that one of them slipped off to the bathroom, Van told me, the other would pour out bile and grievances against the absent party, declaring him to be mad. Boesak was, however, rather outshone, for when protests and demonstrations took place Tutu would appear resplendent in his scarlet robes and episcopal hat. He stuck out a mile and, affecting a prayerful pose, would make it virtually impossible for the police to touch him. Boesak, on the other hand, coming from a fundamentalist offshoot of the Dutch Reformed Church, had to wear a sober dark suit. This placed him at a considerable disadvantage, and he apparently resolved to have a new dark but shiny suit made. This progressively became a grey and then a silver suit, made at some expense. However, by the time the suit was ready, news of the Boesak corruption scandals had broken and, much to Van's amusement, Boesak never got to wear his silver suit.

I was in Oxford when the news broke that the Danish church charity, DanChurchAid, was taking steps to recover the $1 million it had given to Boesak's Foundation for Peace and Justice (FPJ) in 1985. A considerable portion of the money, intended for poor black children, had been spent by Boesak on himself and his new white wife, Elna. Tutu also happened to be in Oxford and had just stepped out of a college chapel where he had held a service when BBC TV arrived to ask him his views on the Boesak scandal. It was a bravura performance, particularly given that Tutu had been a trustee of the FPJ throughout the time of Boesak's peculation and might have expected some awkward questions.

Instead Tutu curtsied and danced and shimmied before the cameras, all smiles and prayerfulness. He could hardly believe, he said, the crimes alleged 'against my brother in Christ, Allan', but what could be more wicked than stealing from poor African children? He offered his prayers that Allan would make a clean breast of everything. So, while expressing a great deal of brotherly love, he left no doubt that Boesak was a thief and that everyone must now pray together for his soul. The BBC was overwhelmed. Tutu emerged snow white but his words had stuck a dagger deep into Boesak's heart. Tutu then lodged a complaint relating to the R423 000 he had handed the FPJ on behalf of singer Paul Simon (takings from the *Graceland* tour). This too had been stolen and misspent. In truth, anyone who was around Cape Town in the 1980s had heard innumerable stories about Boesak's extramarital affairs and spend-thrift habits.

In Johannesburg I met Mike Kirkwood again, now running Ravan Press, an anti-apartheid publishing house. Mike told me that originally Walter Felgate had owned the company and, as usual, he had attempted to engineer a deal whereby Mike would do the work and Walter would get the profits. Mike had been burned too many times for that. Not that there was much profit: indeed, Ravan depended heavily on the usual Viking gold from the Scandinavian churches. At one point, Mike was pressed to employ an out-of-work Anglican priest who then dismantled their computer system and reduced the company to chaos. After several warnings, Mike sacked him. Inevitably, the man then alleged that he was the victim of white racism. To his horror Mike found that the Scandinavian churches felt they had to take such a complaint seriously, so the Viking gold dried up. Had they not consulted Ravan's patron, Archbishop Tutu, Mike enquired. Yes, they had – and Tutu had refused to vouch for him. Alarmed, Mike went to see Tutu, only to find him holding court before a whole roomful of junior clerics singing his praises. When he asked Tutu why he had not vouched for him – and Mike's anti-apartheid credentials were solid – he simply said that Mike had not been to see him for a while. Mike felt this merely meant that he had not sufficiently paid court. For Tutu was by then undeniably a prince of the church.

Van Zyl Slabbert always had funny stories to illuminate the gloom. He was a rare spirit, serious and thoughtful but with a wild sense of humour. One Prog MP told me how he had been to see Slabbert over an issue brought up by one of his constituents – an important man and a major donor to the party. Van had tried his best but could make no headway with the issue and showed him the letter he had written to the constituent in question. In it, Van explained that he had handed the issue to the appropriate shadow minister, who had taken it up with the minister in question but had drawn a blank. Questions from the floor of the House had also not worked. Finally, Van brought up the matter during his monthly meeting with PW Botha but still made no headway. So in the end he wrote to the constituent that the party had tried its best but could get no further at all: Van advised that it was better just to let the matter drop. However, Van, a victim of his own anarchic sense of humour, had then signed his name and added in his own hand: 'In other words, please fuck off.'

Naturally, I renewed my friendship with Rowley and Jackie Arenstein. Rowley had done a spell in jail. Both of them were still banned but quite indomitable. When the Party had ordered that its activists should not leave the country but must stick it out in South Africa, whatever the cost, Jackie and Rowley, though they had ceased to be Party members, took it seriously. Jackie expressed contempt for the many leading SACP members who had decided, despite the Party's instruction, to leave the country rather than risk jail. She particularly scorned the Johannesburg SACP leaders who had made hurried pilgrimages down to Durban to seek out second- and third-rank Party members so that, when they got to London, they could claim that they had 'consulted with the Party' before quitting. Naturally, this had increased Rowley's alienation from the SACP and he had renewed his friendship with Buthelezi, whom he had known for many years and to whom he had once offered a place in his law practice. Ultimately, Rowley became a full-blown Inkatha supporter. Jackie did not follow his example and seemed disenchanted with politics altogether. Quietly she muttered to me that Rowley was something of a megalomaniac.

My main jobs in Durban were to write for the (London) *Times* and to teach. The university was changing rapidly as a torrent of poorly qualified black students poured in. Naively, I felt that this need not matter much. The same faculty was in place and would keep standards up. This turned out to be quite wrong. There was enormous pressure to pass at least some of the black students, who were always on the verge of failing. There was much 'affirmative marking' because 'you can't fail them all'. The failure rate was still high. Even the best academics were trying to massage students through at the bottom, so concern with standards at the top just vanished. So the pass level fell, ineluctably. The academics knew this and there was much worried talk about the necessity of maintaining standards.

Black students picked up on the word 'standards' and denounced it as intrinsically racist. This created an impossible situation. Academics were desperately concerned about standards but also forbidden to pronounce the word. Most simply caved in. Some years later, at the University of KwaZulu-Natal, or UKZN (as the university was renamed, the province having changed from Natal to KwaZulu-Natal in 1994), this led to a final piece of tragicomedy. Black students, noting that most of their number were grouped near the pass/fail borderline, demanded that, in order to avoid the threat of white racism, which they suggested was marking them down, in future all exam papers should bear not names but numbers allocated to students. The faculty happily agreed. In truth, far from marking black students down for racist reasons, they were generally marking them up for affirmative reasons. Everyone now marked the numbered papers but, since English was usually an African's second language, one could still guess the racial origins of examinees.

One day I found myself becoming increasingly irritated at the sheer illiteracy of many of the scripts. I then hit an even worse script and decided that I could not pass (and thus award a degree to) a third-year student who was so illiterate. I made a marginal comment about bad grammar and spelling. An hour later the professor came by my room. The student in question had retrieved his essay and had led a deputation to complain. He agreed he was not very literate but if that was so important, why had he been passed through first and second year? Not a bad question.

The professor looked anguished. 'Okay,' I said, 'this is your department. If you want me to pass illiterates, then I'll do it.' Please, he said. So I did. Within a year the professor himself had left for a job in the UK. The result of this sort of thing being repeated over and over again may be imagined. Most universities, with a naive faith in marketing, responded to this situation by boasting ever more loudly of their 'excellence' – or of their being 'world class'. Yet if you visit Oxford or Harvard nobody talks about being 'world class'. What produces such claims is not high standards but status anxiety.

...

In Natal these were the years of the UDF/ANC war with Inkatha, often a one-sided struggle, for the UDF/ANC always had a tail of sympathetic NGOs, churchmen and lawyers attempting to cast all blame on Inkatha. At the scene of a massacre one always found the Inkatha representatives standing dumbly, knowing full well they had no such folk on their side. At times the sheer 'noise' of UDF/ANC propaganda was overwhelming, for there was no doubt they were the 'progressive' and fashionable side. The situation on the ground was always a lot more fifty-fifty.

Occasionally I saw Walter Felgate, now Buthelezi's right-hand man. He lived in Ulundi, the capital of the KwaZulu Bantustan, and was at Buthelezi's beck and call. This sounded fairly tough, for Buthelezi was a workaholic. Walter told me it was nothing to be woken at 4 am and told that Buthelezi needed a new speech by 7 am. Walter would not have been Walter had he not commanded a good salary for this. Walter's wife,

Sue, worked as Buthelezi's secretary. She was a sweet-natured woman but Walter tended to change wives fairly frequently and Sue was no exception.

Walter had always had a strong streak of absolutism in his character but the struggle seemed to have made it worse. When I tasked him about the terrible violence of the war with the UDF he would dismiss it, saying, 'That's merely the idiom of African politics.' He also declared that as far as he was concerned, he was in a struggle for which he would gladly give his life. But when I spoke to other people in Inkatha, they all complained that Walter was unnecessarily confrontational. He was certainly blamed for giving Buthelezi some fire-and-brimstone speeches to read, often of enormous length. Oddly, Peter Mansfield was once asked to fill in for Walter when the latter had fallen sick. Peter wrote shorter and far more moderate speeches, all of which Buthelezi delivered without demur.

Rob Amato had also drifted up to Durban, having parted temporarily from his wife, Hildur. Rob had somehow squeezed money out of his family trust to finance him to do an MA in English at the University of Natal, where he also did some lecturing, which he did well – he had an enormous enthusiasm for literature. He had decided he would like to get an academic job in that subject.

The problem was that Rob had grown up with the consumption habits of a rich man's son, which meant he was always short of money. I heard rumblings from the city's arts festival, which Rob had prevailed upon to fund him to put on a play. Rob had allocated himself a comfortable salary as director and producer and there were complaints that this had left too little to pay for the actors, costumes and props. There had also been trouble at the university, where *Hamlet* was a set book in the English department. Rob had advised the other teaching staff that the play was being put on in Johannesburg. He offered to organise a trip, block-booking the tickets and hiring a Kombi, which he would drive. His colleagues had enthusiastically agreed, but once they arrived in Johannesburg Rob vanished, and when his colleagues rolled up at the Wits theatre they discovered that no tickets had been booked. The trip was a shambles and, they claimed, Rob had arranged it merely to provide himself with money and transport with which to visit a Johannesburg girlfriend. This created a good deal of bad feeling and if any mention was made of Rob getting a full-time lecturing post in the English department, there would be angry speeches about how this could happen only over various dead bodies.

Rob himself was cheerfully oblivious of the impression he had created and talked happily of his intended future as a full faculty member. I was very fond of Rob and sought his company, but I could hear the other side only too loudly. I tried to hint that his ambitions to be a lecturer might not come to pass, but such concerns would be swept away with a grand gesture. Inevitably, his academic ambitions came to nothing.

Disappointed, Rob drifted down to Observatory in Cape Town, a pleasant hippie area though with a high crime rate. Rob founded a neighbourhood watch scheme, which then produced a community newspaper. Of this he was immensely proud, though I was a little shaken to see that one issue carried separate articles by each of Rob's three children as well as an editorial by Rob. He wanted, of course, to turn the paper into a paying proposition: 'All it needs is an infusion of capital. I've been thinking about approaching Rupert Murdoch about that.' I was at the time writing for two London papers, *The Times* and *The Sunday Times*, both Murdoch-owned, and I could not imagine why Murdoch should be interested in a community paper. 'Well,' said Rob, 'my thought was that I would need to talk to him man to man. You know, as one press baron to another.' These dreams too came to nothing and Rob angrily abandoned Cape Town, saying it had not come up to his expectations. Soon he drifted back to Durban.

Cathy Brubeck, then back in Durban with her husband, Darius, ran the university's Centre for Jazz and Popular Music. She told me that Rob had come to her at one of Darius's concerts and told her that he wanted to reinvent the art of storytelling. 'Just think, Cathy, this is the origin of all literature – men sitting round a fire in the evening while a Homer or a Virgil tells them stories. Of course, one would have to bring things up to date – the stories would have to shock and move faster – but it could be done.' 'Well, I suppose so,' Cathy replied.

This was all Rob needed, and as Darius finished his number Rob charged onto the stage, seized the microphone, and announced to the somewhat mystified audience, 'Right, now I'm going to tell you a story. Let me see. Well … when I was a boy … (there was a long pause and Cathy realised, to her horror, that Rob was making this up as he went along) … when I was a boy, we had two, er, two dogs. Called Fuck and Shit.' (This was clearly the modern, shocking bit.) With great presence of mind Cathy switched off the lights, announced there was a power cut, shortly to be restored, and then switched the lights back on as Darius started a new number. Rob, though a little indignant that he had not been able to finish his story, demanded of Cathy: 'Surely you get the idea? Can you not see how well that could succeed?' 'Yes,' said Cathy carefully, 'I suppose I do. But I think it still needs some work.'

With apartheid now under continuous challenge and the economy stalled, there was an atmosphere of decline. We were nearing the end of white rule. Somehow, in my mind's eye, Rob became a metaphor for this. I learnt he was living in a *khaya* – the servants' quarters behind the main house. The house in question bordered a large and growing squatter camp in Durban, a situation that normally generated speedy white flight. Rob good-heartedly insisted that the squatters were fine people whom he was happy to have as neighbours. He then came home to find them carting off the last of his furniture. After that he moved into a dosshouse. Rob, though as charming as ever, now had few visible means of support. Most all his old friends peeled off, complaining that he took loans he never paid back, that he was a schnorrer (Yiddish for sponger).

Some of Rob's former friends warned me: did I not know how he had short-changed this one or that one? I was forced to consider my answer. Partly it was just for old times' sake, for the precious skein of common memories one has with only a few, but there was also always the memory of how generous Rob had been when he was young and better off than me. He had been only too happy to share whatever he had then and he had always been in the giving situation, something he clearly never allowed to count. I had never felt beholden. Now that the positions were reversed it seemed only fair that I should return a little of that generosity and in the same spirit.

But these criticisms could not be easily denied. Rob sometimes tried to strike bargains with me whereby I would have to make a lot of cash available up front in return for a cheque post-dated to some distant time. I learnt not to make such bargains: for Rob, a post-dated cheque was no more than wishful fancy. Once, when I pointed out that such a cheque had bounced, he told me I was 'an insufferable prig'. I was ambivalent, disliking his schnorrer habits but feeling that few others came up to his standards of warmth, intelligence and humour. This ambivalence matched my attitude to the decline of white South Africa. I liked the sophistication and warmth and the echoes of my youth but also knew its decline was inevitable and, in a sense, right. One of the things I loved about Rob was his sheer brio and his blithe belief that everything would be all right. He would alight on old friends in Durban and misbehave, but happily assume that there would always be old friends happy to put him up. His warmth and cheer were infectious, so there always were.

Poverty makes the maintenance of dignity difficult. The traditional way is to exhibit an ironclad honesty – handing money back when given too much change, and so on. Rob's ego did not allow of this. On more than one occasion I saw him steal the tips I had left for waiters. As we got up from the table he would hang around as if sunk in thought, ruminating. Suddenly the tip would be gone and Rob would be heading smartly to the exit before the waiter arrived to find his labours unrewarded. It was demeaning, or would have been had he been caught or confronted, but he wasn't. It is one of the odd features of such a situation that the person who pulls such scams tends to believe them invisible whereas everyone else sees them immediately. But Rob still had his dignity and would bristle with indignation if anyone let on that they could see what he was up to. So when we saw him steal a tip, we, his lunch companions waiting at the door, would stifle our laughter or indignation as he walked up to us, the change jangling happily in his pocket.

One could feel trouble coming. An old friend from UNNE, Rogers Ragavan, turned up from England and I drove him round Durban. Everywhere we saw the vast, burgeoning squatter camps and the signs of lawlessness. 'This is going to take a good while to sort out,' said Rogers nervously. 'A good long while.' He returned to England quite quickly.

At one point, Rob agreed to house-sit the residence owned by the professor of music, who was off on sabbatical. We had a fine dinner there together. Clearing away the dishes with Rob afterwards, I noticed that he was happily sweeping whatever remained on our plates into the rubbish bin, including our knives and forks. These I rescued, but Rob waved my concerns away: 'A knife or fork here or there, what does it matter?' One of Rob's duties was to maintain the house's swimming pool – chlorinating the water, sweeping for leaves, and clearing out the pump. Rob soon announced that he had decided to let the pool become 'more natural'. It was, he said, ecologically better if one allowed water lilies to grow, let the odd frog enjoy a swim there, and so on. Swimming was much healthier, he claimed, in this more natural environment. When the music professor returned there was a major explosion, not only over the state of the pool but also because there was no cutlery left in the house. Rob was indignant. 'She's a complete harridan,' he said. 'Shouting and carrying on. No sense of proportion, no sense of gratitude.' But nothing ever seemed to get him down. Like Jay Gatsby, he had an unlimited belief in the future.

Yet there was one remarkable situation that Rob failed to savour. When his father died, Rob organised a funeral in the Jewish cemetery in Cape Town, but suddenly found the cemetery invaded by hundreds of Orthodox Jews wearing black hats. They elbowed Rob aside, declared he was not a proper Jew, and said that they had come all the way from Kinshasa to give a proper burial to the man who had saved all their lives. For these were the former Jews of Rhodes, who by then controlled most of the Congo's import/export trade. Somehow or other word had leaked to them of Ben's death and they had flown down en masse to Cape Town. They could never forget Ben Amato's foresight in helping them to get well out of Hitler's way. Rob was furious at their incursion and stormed out of his own father's funeral. 'You should have stayed,' I said. 'What a tribute to your father!' But Rob was not someone who took a public rebuke well. 'I have zilch in common with those black-hat bastards,' he exclaimed bitterly. 'Zilch.'

Darius and Cathy Brubeck had a beautiful old red Datsun 260Z roadster. It was a car with a throaty roar and acceleration to match. As usual, the Brubecks were off to Europe on some jazz tour when Darius caught me eyeing the Datsun.

'Want to borrow it? There's no reason why not.'

'Man, don't tempt me. It would be crazy. I've got my own car. I don't need yours. Yes, I'd love to.'

'Always give in to temptation. Here's the keys.'

It was as easy as that. Suddenly I had this dream car. That evening I went out with Rob and somewhere in the conversation he mentioned Hildur, then teaching at a college far to the north in Giyani, the capital of the Gazankulu Bantustan (in what is now Limpopo province). I hadn't seen Hildur for years. Nor, it turned out, had Rob, though he had often spoken to her on the phone. Now he spoke of her wistfully.

'You know, we could drive up to Giyani and see her,' I said.

'Christ, couldn't we just!'

'But she'd have to be able to put us up for a day or two. It's at least a thousand miles each way.'

'I'm sure she could. I'll phone and ask.'

'We could take the Datsun roadster. It would be perfect for such a trip.'

'We'd share the driving?'

As he well knew, this was tricky. Rob had not been able to afford a car for many years, had no insurance, and had no recent driving experience. He also could not afford to pay for petrol. I breathed in deeply. I decided it was time to pay for that ride to Maritzburg in 1963.

'We share the driving fifty-fifty. I'll deal with insurance. The petrol's on my account.'

And so it was decided. We started at dawn. First I drove, up that magical road towards Maritzburg, with the subtropical plants turning to pines and oaks and then to aloes and cacti. It had become a motorway, and we swept past Maritzburg imperiously and then burst into the Natal Midlands – a green, fertile area full of English farms with English names and English private schools. We charged through Howick, Mooi River and Estcourt and then turned north to Ladysmith. I knew I had to bite the bullet. 'Do you want to drive?' I asked.

'Do I want to drive? Holy cow, just let me get at this machine!' Rob almost tumbled over me into the driving seat and off we went. It was all about power. Sometimes, when Rob had nagged me into loaning him money, he would simply stand with the cash in his hand and say what a great feeling it was, having some power in his hands again. He had been brought up to be a boss, had loved using power. But when the money was all gone, so was the power. This may have been why Rob never got an ordinary job, even when he was broke, and why he was always trying to convince possible donors that they should fund 'a theatre of light', with him in charge. He instinctively invented a boss role for himself. He never achieved it. Instead he would write plays and novels that were never published or enacted, smoke marijuana, and talk about his next book.

Part of the power Rob was missing so badly was the power that comes with driving nice cars. Now he had his dream machine in his hands and off we went, far too fast. It was exactly like Toad in *The Wind in the Willows*. He was half-mad with the euphoria of speed, the sound of the engine and the incredible glamour of the open road.

And the open road was glamorous. South Africa is a great big country with (then, at least) fine roads and low traffic density, a motorist's paradise. The country is endlessly diverse and beautiful beyond the singing of it, as Alan Paton used to say. As we roared past Glencoe and Dundee – old battlefields of the Anglo-Boer War – I pointed out to Rob that our petrol was very low. 'We'll just about make Newcastle,' I said, 'but we definitely have to stop there.' But as we swept through Newcastle Rob slowed not a bit. 'Rob, you've passed a garage,' I shouted. 'We must stop and go back.' 'Stop?' he asked. 'Certainly not. I'm having far too much fun as it is.' So we roared on with the petrol gauge flat on zero. Somehow I communicated my extreme anxiety to Rob: if you run out of petrol in South Africa anything can happen – mugging, murder, carjacking. When we swept into the next tiny hamlet with a petrol pump, Rob stopped, thrilled at having won his bet against the petrol gauge. I was in a state of complete nervous exhaustion and sat for a while with my head in my hands before I could get back in the car. 'C'mon,' said Rob, 'you ain't seen nuthin' yet.' Nor had I.

We tore on, skirting Swaziland. We were now approaching the Kruger National Park. It wasn't until we were plunging on into the Northern Transvaal (today's Limpopo) that I managed to get the steering wheel back off Rob at Potgietersrus (today's Mokopane).

We talked all the way. Rob was fascinated by Dante, and by the

Portuguese poet Luís de Camões and his creation Adamastor, the giant spirit that personifies the Cape of Storms and lies in wait for sailors. Rob had the notion of writing a book that would somehow weave all these themes together. Sadly, he never did. But we also talked about politics, as we always had. The difference between us, however. was that Rob, despite his own diminished fortunes, was always vastly optimistic about the country's future. Everything would come right: it always did.

At length we turned off to Giyani, where Hildur worked. She occupied a detached cottage that gazed out at the endless landscape of the bushveld, a feeling of eternity stretching away, completely flat. From what Hildur said, things were far from right at her college but she was hanging on to her job. Already one could sense that apartheid would soon be over and with it the whole bizarre nonsense of Bantustans. Anything might happen then. The college authorities clearly wanted to turn the place into something more profitable, like a casino.

We stayed for about four days and then set off southwards again, this time more gently, breaking our journey overnight at Pilgrim's Rest. We laughed and talked all the way to Maritzburg, where I deliberately arranged that Rob would drive us the last 80 kilometres to Durban. Rob rattled on happily, occasionally bursting into song, as I relived that magical drive down to Durban of 25 years before. Rob didn't even remember it, but he was in the same boisterous good mood as he had been on that first occasion.

Sadly, our friendship did not end well. Gradually Rob had squeezed more and more money out of the family trust, which was supposed to exist purely for his children's benefit. I had learnt to hold my tongue about many things but I upbraided Rob about taking this money from his children. He was, of course, furious. 'Have you gone mad? I demand that you apologise right away.' I said I couldn't. He slammed down the phone.

A few months later I heard that Rob had been killed by an out-of-control Mercedes driver. As he lay dying in the wreck of his own jalopy street children picked his pockets and took all his scant belongings. Hildur (with whom he had reunited) arrived just too late. But the image I keep of him is not the shattered man lying in that wreck but the free spirit at the wheel, Toad of Toad Hall, alarming me, charming me and with a warmth that washed over me, banishing my anxieties as unworthy. I cried at the news of his death and realised I did not know why I was crying. Does one cry simply at the loss of a dear friend? Or is one really crying for oneself in one's loss? Or is it really a weeping for those lost and magic times of adolescence that we shared? All of them, perhaps.

CHAPTER TEN

The End of Apartheid

By 1989 Andries Treurnicht's Conservative Party (CP) was making considerable gains, and other formations of the extreme white right, particularly the Afrikaner Weerstandsbeweging (AWB, or Afrikaner Resistance Movement), had also made headway. Driving around the Bluff area of Durban, I found a virtual forest of AWB posters.

This made sense. The Bluff is a long, narrow promontory guarding one side of Durban Bay. When Vasco da Gama first came this way in 1497 he described it as being 'where a hill comes down into the sea'. In the 19th century, after the murder of Piet Retief by the Zulu king, Dingane, and the bloody fate that met many of the early Boer raiders who set off to 'teach Dingane a lesson', there were frequent scares among Durban's whites in which rumour had it that the Zulu impis (regiments) were marching on the city. In the ensuing panic there would be a general flight to the Bluff. Its narrow width made it easily defensible, and if the worst occurred, one could retreat to the end and escape by boat. So it seemed logical enough that the local tough guys of the AWB were preparing to make their last stand on the Bluff.

The feeling that apartheid could not last much longer was scary for many lower-class whites, who were most unsure how they would fare in a post-apartheid world. In effect, the AWB leader, Eugene Terre'Blanche, promised them that if they rallied behind him they would defeat or at least head off the threatened 'black communist revolution'. It was, of course, an illusory promise – in effect, they were fighting demography. Treurnicht played on the same theme – his posters in 1989 read 'It's later than you think.'

I was intrigued by the rise of the white right. When there was a municipal by-election in the Addington ward – a white working-class area near Addington Beach – I went to mingle with their activists. They were in high spirits: 'We've really got the surfer vote locked up,' they told me, this being a significant social group in Addington. I kept quiet about the fact that I had recently taken part in a march to integrate nearby North Beach. The racial integration of the beaches was, it emerged, a local surfer nightmare.

But the real test would be the 1989 general election. The nearest constituency where the CP had a clear chance of winning was Newcastle in northern Natal so I went up there for the last week of the campaign. The local National Party MP took a firm line: it was obvious that South Africa had to change, so there could be no kow-towing to the CP. This seemed a risky strategy, and the CP seemed confident of victory. I got to know some of the CP activists. They were often the salt of the earth, though from time to time they would let drop a gross but almost unconscious piece of white racism. On election day I sat at their table for an hour or so. At one point a tall, tanned young soldier strode up. He was asked what he had brought back from the border. He grinned and turned down his collar to show, hidden beneath it, an AWB badge.

To the general surprise the NP held Newcastle quite easily. When people had been brought right to the edge, they had backed away. There was a more general lesson here about the sociology of the right. The right's appeal peaked when people were frightened and thought there was still a chance to defeat the changes that threatened. But once the moment of change arrived, the right fell apart as its followers looked around and quickly decided to take whatever individual actions they could to protect themselves in the new dispensation. The last thing they were interested in was Terre'Blanche's crazy military adventures.

Returning to Oxford, I rang *The Times* and told them that it was quite certain that the new president, FW de Klerk, would abandon apartheid altogether as soon as Parliament met again. It suddenly seemed quite obvious. *The Times* agreed to send me back to South Africa to write a series of articles based on that premise. I also spoke to Van Zyl Slabbert, then on a visiting Fellowship at All Souls College. Van confided that he had just been visited by agents of the NIS who wanted to discuss with him the unbanning of the ANC and PAC, thus confirming that this was in De Klerk's mind. Logically that implied complete democratisation. Van had told them not to make the mistake of retaining the ban on the Communist Party. Clandestinity had suited the Party, he pointed out, since it made its actions and influence invisible and deniable, but if it was unbanned and brought blinking into the light, some ANC leaders would probably leave it rather than associate with it openly, and the Party would have to be publicly answerable for its actions.

On my flight back to South Africa I found myself sitting next to the wife of the Tanzanian ambassador to a neighbouring state. She seemed a nice woman and plied me with questions about Nelson and Winnie Mandela and what De Klerk was up to. I said De Klerk was about to negotiate his way out of power and hand over to the ANC. She felt there had to be a catch. I told her that South Africa was lucky to have a man like Mandela waiting to walk out of jail. She nodded enthusiastically. What about Winnie? She was, I said, brave but disturbed and dangerous, a serial killer of children. The Tanzanian lady couldn't believe this and had clearly got Winnie marked up as a political saint. 'So what happens then?' she asked. What happens, I said, is black majority rule. She was visibly shocked. 'No, you can't do that, I've lived through that and seen what happens,' and she reeled off a list of power cuts, failure to maintain infrastructure, corrupt police, the country falling to bits. 'Whatever you do, you mustn't do that,' she said. At first she had been a politically correct black woman, cheering on her side. Now she was the middle-class lady horrified at the loss of amenity.

The world's press would inevitably concentrate on Mandela's release from jail, so I decided to skip that. Instead I thought I would roam around some of South Africa's backwaters and try to catch the mood in a time of change. Sure enough, on 2 February 1990 De Klerk announced the end of apartheid, Mandela's release and plans for a negotiated democracy. The floodgates were opened.

I tried to see Treurnicht at his constituency in Waterberg but could only get his agent, a tough middle-aged Afrikaner. This resulted in a peculiar and very hot evening in which I was, in effect, repeatedly challenged to refight the Anglo-Boer War. My host led off with a series of bitter remarks about the British royal family, clearly intended to rile me. I happily said I was a republican. Stunned for a moment, he was quickly back on the attack. I refused to fight and kept steering him back to the events of the day. His main reproach against the ANC was that they were 'a lot of black Englishmen'. The impact of the revolutionary changes decreed by De Klerk seemed to be that my host no longer cared one whit about his party's policies. De Klerk's speech had rendered them obsolete.

The CP's Koos van der Merwe, who had helped me get this interview, had told me that the main thing in the Northern Transvaal was whether 'you can stand your man with a *witblits*' (drink the local, explosive moonshine round for round). And, indeed, as the evening wore on the *witblits* (white lightning) played its part. Finally the agent confessed that his real problem was that his party's followers included a number of young men, some recently out of the army, who often talked about the solution to the racial problem being a raid into the local township where, using automatic weapons, they would kill a few hundred blacks, the idea being to reduce the black population somewhat. This was not entirely surprising; I remembered such genocidal fantasies being quite common around the time of Sharpeville. A certain sort of young white, made uneasy by the rising tide of black nationalism, would often expatiate about such schemes over a drink. Nothing ever came of them. The lone exception was in 1988 when Barend Strydom, a former policeman, went on a killing spree in Pretoria, murdering seven black people. This was punished and treated as an individual pathology.

But the CP agent was scared that his young men might really do what they talked of doing. He had spent a great deal of time trying to dissuade them and talk them down. But, I said, that means that in effect you are working to make young Afrikaners accept the direction of change ordained by De Klerk. 'Yes, I know,' he said with some desperation, 'but what else can I do?' Later I mentioned this to Lawrie Schlemmer. 'Ha!' said Lawrie, 'it's the problem of the tannies (aunties).' He explained that in the sort of small towns where the CP ruled, the white population tended to be respectable and church-going and this was particularly true of the tannies, the women of middle age and above. They were a numerous and pivotal group, strongly conservative and upright, and they had great influence in determining the local political mood. They would be absolutely horrified by the crimes of violence the wild young tearaways were dreaming of. So if anything like that happened, the CP would be forced to denounce their own young men rather than risk alienating the tannies. Just the sort of choice they would never want to make.

I then flew down to Umtata, the capital of the Transkei Bantustan, to interview its ruler, General Bantu Holomisa, an engagingly open man – when I had rung from Oxford the general himself had picked up the phone to make the appointment. Holomisa's office looked out over a sort of parade ground where several hundred MK soldiers in battle fatigues were marching. Holomisa, who seemed unimpressed by MK as a military unit, explained that there was a firm rule that equal facilities would be offered to the PAC. Just as with the young Afrikaners who had frightened the CP agent, there was a strong element of play-acting: it was a period in which even Winnie Mandela appeared dressed in battle fatigues. There never was any engagement in which such 'soldiers' ever came close to fighting anyone. This sort of make-believe was about advertising one's allegiance and one's militancy.

Far more serious was the constant smuggling of AK-47s into Natal. These had been supplied to the ANC by the Soviet Union on the understanding that they would be used against the government's forces. This never happened: attacking the SADF would be suicidal. So instead they were used against Inkatha in a war that was killing 200 people each week. There were buses plying the route between Umtata and Durban bringing up a great deal of dagga, which is a major crop in the Transkei. The weed was often used to conceal the weaponry underneath.

Holomisa was charming and easy to talk to. He was sure that the Transkei would be reincorporated into South Africa and he would cease to be president. He seemed happy with that. At that time there was a great deal of agitation over a 'rebel' England cricket team, captained by Mike Gatting, that was touring South Africa in defiance of the sports boycott, a huge issue for the ANC. Knowing that General Holomisa was a keen sportsman, I asked what he felt about the Gatting tour. 'Well,' he said, 'they're not bad. But their bowling's a bit weak.'

I then interviewed the Inkatha leader, Mangosuthu Buthelezi. On the one hand he emphasised that no one had campaigned longer and harder then he for the end of apartheid, the unbanning of the liberation movements and the release of Mandela. On the other hand he found himself at war first with the UDF and then quite openly with the ANC. Buthelezi insisted he was a man of peace and a strong Christian and that he wanted to meet with Mandela to try to stop the violence. I knew that Rowley Arenstein had phoned his old friend Mandela to request such a meeting. Mandela had agreed but the hotheads inside the ANC would not hear of it.

The problem was that Buthelezi was the man in possession. He still controlled the KwaZulu Bantustan and many of the rural areas of Natal. The ANC was determined to displace him. Any truce would leave Buthelezi in charge and the ANC militants would never accept that. Indeed, they passionately resisted a Mandela-Buthelezi meeting, let alone a truce. I had heard Inkatha militants complain that in the old days a Zulu leader would simply unleash the impis and tell them to keep fighting until the problem disappeared – a sort of all-out extermination purge. Why did this not happen now? Buthelezi said he had heard only too much of such talk but would not countenance such a drastic 'solution'.

I ended up in Mafikeng, the capital of the Bophuthatswana Bantustan ruled by Lucas Mangope. 'Bop' (as it was called) was the most prosperous of the homelands, drawing considerable income from the local platinum mines. The result was evident on the streets of Mafikeng, where one could see a comfortable black middle class. The University of Bophuthatswana (known as 'Unibop') was, similarly, a cut above other homeland universities and had attracted a number of radical white academics who had been banned in South Africa proper. Recently, however, there had been trouble between the academics and students and the Mangope administration.

When I had set up an interview with Mangope, the administration had insisted on providing me with a driver who, I feared, might make sure I only saw the 'right' things. I had asked to meet a representative group at Unibop and when I arrived there were 30 to 40 people waiting, anxious to explain how oppressive the Mangope government was and how it had interfered with academic freedom. To my relief my driver just sat there, grinning, as his employer was denounced. The most prominent speaker was a black academic whom I took to be the ANC leader on campus.

I was then asked to address the audience. I had made careful note of the discussion and said that I had an interview with President Mangope the next day and that I would bring up all the issues mentioned. As an academic myself I knew that academic freedom was non-negotiable. I would also raise the particular cases they had mentioned to me. This caused a sort of collective mutter: they didn't like the idea of anyone meeting with Mangope.

I suggested they ought to consider carefully. We had just spent all day hearing people trash the Mangope government. This had taken place in the capital, on a campus built by the government with a government employee (my driver) present throughout. Clearly, they all felt free to speak their minds. Moreover, I knew how these things worked – some of the audience were clearly ANC activists and I had no doubt they used university stationery, telephones and fax machines to promote their cause. (I noticed the presumed ANC organiser nod at this.) They might reflect that this degree of tolerance was unusual in Africa. Nyerere, Nkrumah, Touré or Banda would never have stood for such behaviour: they had closed down universities and thrown students and academics in jail. Things might not be fully right in Bop but they should take stock of their situation with care.

I then threw out a general question. The fruits of Bop's comparative affluence were all around – all those well-paid civil servants, plus Bop Radio, Bop TV and the airline, Bop Air, all providing jobs. And everyone knew that when the UDF had called school boycotts on the Reef, parents there had sent their children to safer and better schools in Bop. Now, the ANC insisted that Bop had to be reintegrated into South Africa with the rest of the homelands. When that happened the money that had made all this possible would go straight into the national treasury and it would doubtless get spent on projects outside Bophuthatswana. In other words, the territory that was now Bop would become poorer. How did everyone feel about that?

This produced a furious speech from the presumed ANC organiser. I had it all wrong, he shouted. Bop's reincorporation would end much exploitation and everyone would be much better off in Bop, in Soweto and everywhere else. This seemed to be the general line, for no one dissented.

Next morning I spoke with Mangope, a pleasant man of late middle age. I told him of the complaints I had heard at Unibop about violations of academic freedom there. Universities were like flowers, I argued: they could do much good for the lives of young people – but they were fatally easy to damage. It was as easy as breaking off the bloom of a flower; once you did it, the flower did not recover. A look of great tiredness came over Mangope's face. You don't understand, he said. Whatever open spaces we leave, the ANC immediately invades them and uses them to try to undermine and overthrow us. Over and over again we face the choice of whether to allow them to get away with that or close down those spaces. It's absolutely relentless, there's no possibility of compromise. I knew enough of the ANC to understand his dilemma. They had the revolutionary bit between their teeth and were certainly not interested in compromise.

Over the years those two scenes – first at the university and then that tired look on Mangope's face – often drifted through my mind. Bophuthatswana became part of the new North West province, with Mangope evicted from power. All the jobs in the Bop civil service, radio, TV and airline vanished. ANC governance proved no blessing. It was here that the police carried out the Marikana massacre in 2012, shooting down 34 black miners, wounding 78 others, with hundreds more tortured in police custody. Under the premiership of the local ANC boss, Supra Mahumapelo, the province's administration became corrupt and authoritarian to the point where, in 2018, it produced a large-scale popular revolt. The province had been looted to a standstill and almost nothing worked: Mahumapelo was furiously pushed out. Unibop, meanwhile, was merged with Potchefstroom University (today North-West University) and lost its radical young academics to greener pastures.

...

De Klerk's 2 February speech had propelled South Africa into an era of turbulent change, culminating in the first democratic election in 1994. I managed to acquire funding for a study of that election, which was bound to be a watershed in South Africa's history. I recruited Lawrie Schlemmer to help me and based myself in Durban at Oscar Dhlomo's Institute for Multi-Party Democracy. Oscar, previously a headmaster and then secretary-general of Inkatha, was a shrewd and impressive man with a very practical grasp of politics. At that stage, for example, there was much anticipation of the expected boom in housing for blacks. Oscar commented, 'Well, the question is, will land near the cities be released for housing? If you look at the current situation in Durban what that comes down to is whether Tongaat-Hulett, the big sugar combine, will release sugar-cane areas for urban housing. That won't happen in a hurry.' This turned out to be exactly right.

Oscar talked sadly of Inkatha, saying it was no longer the same movement that he had originally joined. On the other hand he had seen a great deal of the ANC's 'people's war' up close and recoiled from that. Mandela's imprisonment had, he felt, been a cross for all black people to bear, and his release something to be greatly celebrated – and he had a good relationship with Mandela. The day before the 1994 election I asked Oscar how he would vote. He sighed. He could not vote for Inkatha, he said, nor could he vote for the ANC. In principle his heart was with the small (and then all-white) liberal Democratic Party (DP) – 'but that's not my party either'. In the end he said sadly that he had spent all his life campaigning for universal suffrage but now that the great day had arrived, he would abstain.

Working with Lawrie was great fun. As always, he produced an endless flow of shrewd insights, but he also had a great supply of funny stories. Together we carried out a large series of opinion surveys, calling press conferences to publicise the results. Lawrie always arrived late for these occasions, cursing and swearing at whatever had delayed him. I thus had no idea what he was going to say, which did not make it easy for us to present a united front. Once he took away with him all the survey data, so that I rolled up at the press conference without any idea what was in it. Lawrie's colleagues from his earlier job in Durban had given him a cartoon of himself depicted as what the French call a 'turbo-prof' – endlessly running for planes, giving papers and seminars on the run.

We attempted to maintain good relations with all the parties, offering them free presentations of our data. This worked well with everyone save the ANC, which was suspicious of anyone who was not an ANC member. In their eyes Lawrie was associated with Inkatha and I was known for writing that did not take the party line, a sin in itself. For at that time most journalists, domestic and foreign, tended to take the 'progressive' (ie ANC) line – and the ANC expected no less. It was thus a surprise when the ANC called one day, asking for Lawrie. Their call related to a traumatic incident in Lawrie's life.

At his Centre for Social and Development Studies (CSDS) at the University of Natal, Lawrie had been among the first academics anywhere in South Africa to employ black researchers. One Saturday morning the security police had arrived at the CSDS, demanding to search the office of one black researcher. After some negotiation Lawrie agreed to open the office, provided he was allowed to stay to see fair play. The police were confident that the researcher in question was actually working for MK because, they said, he had multiple car registrations in his name. This was always a sure sign, for MK guerrillas infiltrating South Africa needed cars and did not want to get caught for car theft so they used one of these false registration plates. And, indeed, the police quickly turned up all manner of MK material in the man's office. They then demanded to know where the researcher was. Somewhere in Umlazi township, Lawrie replied: there was no phone number and he would not see the man again until Monday morning. Once the police left, Lawrie phoned the researcher, telling him to get out of the country fast.

Not long afterwards this man contacted Lawrie from Lusaka. He felt that he owed Lawrie a good turn and so he was writing to tell him that a number of 'the comrades' in Lusaka, riled by Lawrie's association with Inkatha, were talking of assassinating him. Lawrie told me: 'What the hell was I to do with that? Death threats are a dime a dozen in South Africa. You can't allow yourself to be put off by that.' So he ignored it and carried on as before. But after the founding of the UDF things changed. Not only was a full-scale Zulu civil war (Inkatha vs UDF) being waged within a stone's throw of the university campus but the advent of the UDF had also swept all manner of student radicals along in its wake. This made Lawrie extremely unpopular with the 'progressive' camp, which frequently denounced him.

One day Lawrie had gone to work to find his university office on fire. He could only watch as he lost the books and papers of a lifetime. Realising that whoever had firebombed his office might have similar intentions towards his flat, he rushed home to find it on fire too. Luckily, his wife, Monica, had gone out shopping but, again, she and Lawrie lost everything. He could not but note that the student radical who had been his chief critic vanished from the campus from that day on – without doubt the culprit.

So, years later, this was why the ANC was ringing Lawrie. The radical student in question, who had ended up in an MK prison camp in Tanzania, had returned to South Africa and was asking for a pension or lump sum on the grounds that he had played a part in the struggle by burning down Lawrie's office and flat. But the ANC, lacking all records, needed to check his story with Lawrie. He sat patiently as this miserable story was recited back to him. 'Ha!' said Lawrie at length, 'he's the bastard all right. He set fire to my home and my office. Oh hell, why don't you give him the money?' He put the phone down and, turning to me, said,

'You know, I often wished that guy an unpleasant fate. But never anything as bad as an MK prison camp.'

The election study was fun but exhausting. Conducting opinion surveys was a hazardous business, for there were many no-go areas and our interviewers often feared for their lives. At one point I made a trip down to the Eastern Cape, driving back up to Durban through the Transkei Bantustan. Nearing the border with Natal, I suddenly saw a road block and Transkei police checking the cars. I had quite forgotten that theoretically the Transkei was still an independent country – it seemed such a nonsense. The police were checking passports and I had no passport with me. I turned the car, retreated a bit, put my shirt on back to front to create the impression of a clerical dog-collar, drove back, and apologised heartily for my lack of a passport. I was, I said, a bishop on the way to a church synod: it was desperately important that they let me through. Which they did. 'Bless you, my child,' I said.

Our election book remains a monument in the political sociology of South Africa.[28] As the election approached, many NGOs were keen to play a role, particularly with voter education. The ANC effortlessly colonised many of these NGOs so that their 'voter education' material was really ANC propaganda. The National Democratic Institute (NDI), the Democrat part of the US National Endowment for Democracy, played a considerable role. It adopted a strongly pro-ANC stance, which presumably went down well with black voters in the US (and these were the Clinton years, during which the Reverend Jesse Jackson exercised great leverage over the NDI.) The NDI decided to hold a series of large voter education conferences. Arriving at the first one in Cape Town, I looked around to see a number of the SACP's leading lights holding key positions as chairmen and moderators. As usual, the key was the

---

28   RW Johnson and L Schlemmer (eds), *Launching Democracy in South Africa: The First Open Election, April 1994* (Cambridge University Press, 1995).

front organisations. Apart from having several members on the ANC delegation to the conference, the SACP had several more on the Youth League and Women's League delegations, most of the Congress of South African Trade Unions (Cosatu) delegation and several on the South African National Civic Organisation (Sanco) delegation – as well, of course, as the SACP delegation itself. I knew the lady then in charge of the NDI in South Africa, sought her out, and asked her if she was aware that the SACP was effectively in charge of the conference. She dismissed this out of hand but I got the impression she was aware of what was going on. Sure enough, as the conference got under way, Essop Pahad, a leading SACP man, played the leading role.

I attended a session on the new electoral system. The speaker, a Scandinavian professor on his first visit to South Africa, professed astonishment at the extreme form of proportional representation that had been chosen. He would, he said, have expected the ANC as the dominant party to insist on a majoritarian system, thus guaranteeing them a huge majority. The chairman, Pahad, interrupted to insist that the ANC were true democrats, happy to have all shades of opinion represented. I could not let that pass. The system was, I pointed out, designed to give the party bosses absolute control over the electoral lists, so the whole political system was patronage-based. The party bosses could choose the order of candidates on the list, thus determining who got elected, and could also sack any MP who showed indiscipline, and swap MPs with members of the provincial legislatures. Under such conditions there could be no real parliamentary government. The system was essentially a deal between the National Party (which would at least keep 20 per cent of the seats) and the SACP. The SACP's problem was that it had many white and Indian cadres who could not possibly get elected if a constituency-based system was chosen. But under this system the party bosses could simply push SACP cadres into electable positions all over the ANC list. I saw heads jerk up in astonishment as the penny dropped.

Pahad was furious. He insisted he could get elected anywhere and challenged me to stand against him. When the conference ended I was told that unfortunately there would be no room for me to attend the two planned follow-up conferences. A black friend on the organising committee tipped me off that Pahad had demanded that I be excluded 'for harassing the comrades' – and of course, because the SACP really *was* in control, he got his way. I wrote up this affair for a Washington journal, *The National Interest*, pointing out that these SACP manoeuvres had been funded by US taxpayers. Back in South Africa, I knew my card had been marked.

...

The last days of the election campaign were crazy. I happened to be up in Kosi Bay on the Mozambique border when Buthelezi, who had previously boycotted the election, decided that Inkatha would participate after all. As I drove back south through Zululand to Durban I saw vast crowds of Inkatha supporters – veritable impis – being mobilised everywhere, an extraordinary sight. Passing by the Mfolozi Game Reserve I saw a rhino with an ANC poster pasted to its back – heaven knows how that had been achieved.

I proceeded to the black township of Wembezi, outside Estcourt in the Natal Midlands, a scene of bitter warfare between Inkatha and the ANC. Improbably, the ANC leader there was one Teaspoon Mkhize and the Inkatha leader was Spitfire Dlamini. So Teaspoon versus Spitfire. The township was completely divided: there were Inkatha footpaths and ANC footpaths, Inkatha bus stops and ANC bus stops. I decided to talk to both sides about the election. Spitfire, a long-standing boss, was fairly relaxed. He said voting could take place as long as Inkatha people were able to vote in 'their' voting stations and ANC people in 'theirs' – though he expected the ANC to cheat. Teaspoon was tougher. Outside his house sat a boy of 13 with an AK-47 on his lap – always the ANC weapon of choice. He frisked me and spoke with a voice of command. I asked him how old he was and about his job. He turned an icy stare on me. 'You don't need to know those things and you should know not to ask.' I then had a tense conversation with Teaspoon, who said exactly the same things that Spitfire had. He expected Inkatha to cheat.

On election day I voted in Red Hill, Durban, near where I'd grown up. It was a farcical scene. The returning officer was a coloured woman who was a girlfriend of a friend. I knew her well: she was quite prominent in the ANC. Indeed, I'd attended parties in her house that had been full of MK and ANC militants. She allowed ANC activists to wander into the polling station to 'assist' voters. Outside there were young men filling in photocopies of a blank ID document with their own or bogus names, allowing them to cast multiple votes. It was not fair but it was not violent.

As was to be expected, there was huge confusion over the vote count in Natal. The counters staged a strike and a rebellion and had to be got rid of and replaced. Both sides made accusations of cheating, no doubt correctly. As the votes from the country areas came in, Inkatha pulled ahead, producing a frantic reaction from the ANC and its assorted NGOs and lawyers. The idea of an Inkatha victory was simply unacceptable to them. Deadlock ensued, whereupon one of the election monitors pointed out that if the deadlock continued there might be panic in the markets when they opened. The ANC spokesman, Mike Sutcliffe, retorted: 'Well, fuck the markets then.' Only Mandela's intervention settled the matter: he announced that the results must stand and Inkatha had won the province. This was wise: after all, the ANC had won the whole country and seven of the nine provinces. It could well afford to concede Natal to Buthelezi.

I spoke to the USAid representative about the chaotic scenes I had witnessed. 'I know, I know,' he said. 'It was the same in Vietnam. I lived where I could see Viet Cong activity. Often they were using guns we had given to the other side only a day before. I saw things you can't imagine. The end of a regime is never tidy and it's usually violent and at least a little surreal.'

After the election my old history professor, Jeffrey Horton, invited me to his cottage in the foothills of the Drakensberg at Upper Loteni, a wild and gloriously beautiful spot. Jeffrey was the only white person living for miles around. He employed a local Zulu man as a nightwatchman. Then, for two or three nights in a row, the nightwatchman did not appear. Jeffrey was worried, and when the man appeared again, demanded to know he where he'd been. The man looked unperturbed: 'Some men came from the next valley. They killed my brother.' Jeffrey apologised and was concerned: 'Why, that's terrible! I'm so sorry. Are you all right?' The man nodded: 'Is all right now. We have killed the men who have done this thing.'

It was as simple as that – an inter-valley feud that had been going for ever, with regular raids and stock theft. There was no thought of going to the police. These things were settled privately. One glimpsed an older Zulu world that had probably never been encompassed by colonialism. Even apartheid had never really penetrated here. Things had continued in the old ways, and now that white power was shrinking they would be unchallenged. Soon afterwards Jeffrey, recognising the inevitable, sold his property to his black neighbour.

· · ·

The end of apartheid was a release for everybody. (The ANC liked to take credit for this but actually De Klerk revoked all the major apartheid legislation in 1990.) No more bannings, house arrests, exile, no more detention without trial and no more Group Areas Act. We all experienced it differently.

I was particularly struck by this when I visited my old friend Bruce, in Johannesburg. Bruce lived not far from Parkview police station, a fact that had dominated his life. When his first marriage broke up, Bruce had depended on a motherly black domestic, Beauty, to look after his two children. This had worked well but after some years Bruce had fallen for Precious, a black schoolteacher who taught at a school in Soweto. Precious had moved in with him, but Bruce was acutely aware that he was breaking the Immorality Act and the Prohibition of Mixed Marriages Act. He was concerned lest his new domestic arrangements catch the attention of the Parkview police, but luckily by then the increasing crime wave had led everyone, Bruce included, to build high garden walls, thus providing some measure of privacy.

Bruce's household now worked in reverse. Every morning, when a vast human tide flowed from Soweto to work in Johannesburg, Precious would set out against the tide for Soweto. But Precious, like any other woman, had cast a quick eye over Bruce's house and pronounced it not clean – 'You men never notice these things.' She asked Beauty to clean the house properly but Beauty was hardly keen for extra work and refused, saying that Precious was 'not a proper madam'. Bruce remonstrated with Beauty and said she must accept Precious's authority as the new lady of the house. If she could not manage that, she would have to go. This immediately brought an explosion from Bruce's children: 'Beauty looked after us and virtually brought us up after Mum left. There is no way that we could ever accept Beauty being sacked.' A classic South African domestic tangle.

This left Bruce stumped, but Beauty could see that the situation was untenable so she soon introduced a new girl, her cousin, Anna, who was about 15. She informed Bruce that Anna would help with the housework and live in the spare room. As Bruce soon discovered, Anna was no cousin of Beauty, but just a country girl come to Joburg to look for a job. Beauty had found her at the railway station and told her that if she wanted food to eat and somewhere to sleep, she had better do exactly what Beauty said. Thenceforth Anna laboured mightily and if she ever protested that her load was too heavy, Beauty would just say, 'Do you want to eat? Do you want to sleep on the pavement?' There was thus little finesse as far as labour relations went. In theory, the three African women were hardly on good terms but often when Bruce came home he would find them all together, talking and joking in Pedi in the ironing room. In the last analysis, they were all African women with much in common. When Bruce appeared they would roar with laughter and he would realise they had been talking about him. 'I'm beginning to feel as if I'm the guest here,' he commented wryly.

By then a new worry had overtaken Bruce. He lay in bed at night, he told me, thinking about how MK was training its fighters in East European countries like Bulgaria or Romania. It seemed obvious to Bruce that any sensible MK unit would set up a mortar on the far side of Zoo Lake and lob a few mortar shells across the lake at Parkview police station. But, since the quality of military training in Bulgaria and Romania would be pretty ropey, they would probably miss and hit Bruce's house instead. So now the police station brought a different kind of threat. Bruce, it should be said, was my only friend likely to have his sleep disturbed by worries over the quality of military training in Bulgaria.

Finally, Bruce pensioned Beauty off, hired Anna as her replacement (so she now got properly paid), and he and Precious had two children together, hiring a young au pair to help with them. Apartheid had gone and Bruce and Precious could live together quite openly. The au pair, however, had a boyfriend at Parkview police station and would often wheel the pram with her two charges in it down to the station. There, the policemen would greet her warmly and ask after Bruce and Precious, about whom they had clearly known for a long time. Indeed, as black people themselves, they had taken their side. 'So now I have a nice warm feeling about that police station,' Bruce explained to me. 'I feel my whole life can be divided into chapters according to my changing attitude to that station.' I didn't manage to see a whole lot more of Bruce before he died, but several times I drove past his house and heard happy childish shouts from the garden. To me that symbolised what the end of apartheid was really meant to be.

CHAPTER ELEVEN

Campus Interlude

The events of February 1990 plunged South Africa into an atmosphere of tension and high excitement. The impending regime change made the ANC the new men of power and there were frantic, indeed quite blatant acts of 'repositioning' by many individuals keen to curry favour with them. This was especially marked among journalists and businessmen. I attended several meetings in which leading businessmen and civil servants were trying to ingratiate themselves with the ANC, often with grimly fixed smiles. Others threw money and directorships at the new men, who happily snapped them up. The bribery of the new black elite was quite breathtaking, but the ANC were more than up for it.

I recall Cyril Ramaphosa, the ANC secretary-general, visiting the Durban Club, a pillar of the old Durban, which was now looking around for black members. Women, whether black or white, were still not officially allowed inside and had to be sneaked in through the garage entrance. Ramaphosa began with, 'On my way here I was wondering whether we should nationalise the Durban Club,' which was clearly meant to frighten the audience. Throughout his speech he threw out other speculations about nationalising many more enterprises and industries. It was so stagey and calculated that it was difficult to believe anyone could be taken in, but, sure enough, at the end of his talk there was a long queue of frightened businessmen keen to contribute to the ANC.

Old stalwarts of the Natal Indian Congress and many Indians who had been prominent in the UDF proudly put themselves forward, hoping for ministerial positions. They often retained this hope for several years, only to be smashingly disappointed by 1994. There were far too many ambitious Africans pushing themselves forward for Indians to have a chance. During the struggle, the NIC always had several speakers on every ANC or UDF platform party. But, despite its passionate protestations of democratic intent, never in its entire history had the NIC conducted elections, so there was always a lot of muttering about 'the cabal'. Moreover, the NIC was a closed shop not just ethnically but for a limited number of Indian families. And the NIC's passionate anti-apartheid line had often seemed like a cry of rage that Indians were being classed with Africans. Africans were liable to sniff this out fairly quickly.

The realisation that they were now relegated to the back of the queue created considerable bitterness among many Indians. An old student friend, Mewa Ramgobin, was alone in denouncing the NIC, saying there was now no place for ethnically defined bodies and that he was joining the ANC. This was smart, since Mewa was not an NIC favourite. It earned him a seat in Parliament – but that was all. Knowing of Mewa's gigantic ego, I doubted that this would be sufficient. Sure enough, Mewa was permanently torn between trying to ingratiate himself with the new men of power and then, when that failed, denouncing them (though not to their faces) as simpletons not worthy to darn his socks·

These contradictions were intensely felt on the University of Natal campus, where I was an occasional visitor. Fatima Meer had at last come into her own, her status heightened by her friendship with Winnie Mandela, who had somewhat dubiously been accorded the title of 'mother of the nation'. Fatima now presided as a professor, an angry, brooding presence, over an Institute of Black Research, which never did any research or teaching – it had been created just to show the university had its heart in the right place. (Similar deals were struck for a few other

black academics, including Blade Nzimande, later leader of the SACP.)
When I tried to renew my old acquaintance with Fatima, she seemed so
consumed with racial bitterness that it was difficult to talk with her. She
was also in charge of Phambili (Freedom) school in central Durban, an
institution set up by the UDF with Scandinavian donor money (Viking
gold again). The idea was that the numerous black children expelled
from government schools for acts of defiance would all attend Phambili.
Naturally this grouped in one place a lot of children who were quick to
feel – and express – a sense of grievance. This would send Fatima into
towering rages – she had a pronounced authoritarian streak – and she
would come storming down to the school, threatening vengeance.

When Winnie Mandela came to town she invariably teamed up with
Fatima. Even by the late 1980s both judges and policemen were afraid to
hold Winnie responsible for her many criminal acts so, naturally, everyone
else was afraid too. Shopkeepers were terrified that she might appear in
their shops for it was well known that she would order luxury goods,
never pay her debts, and threaten anyone who tried to make her pay.

My own introduction to the Winnie phenomenon came in 1988
when I attended a meeting addressed by Winnie and Fatima. There had
recently been demonstrations and protests against Fatima's authority by
the Phambili students. Fatima responded with autocratic fury, expelling
pupils, sacking teachers and peremptorily closing the school down. At
the time of the meeting this had just happened again.

The meeting got under way before a packed hall. A large bouquet
was brought up to the podium. Fatima rose to accept it but then had to
sit down rather quickly since it was, of course, for Winnie. Fatima spoke
first but had hardly got into her stride when a procession of protesting
Phambili children entered the hall with placards denouncing Fatima for
closing down the school and for her alleged denial of democracy. Fatima,
clearly discomfited, looked across at Winnie, who immediately ordered
the Mandela United Football Club to deal with the intruders. The young

men of the club – they were really just a band of thugs – leapt into the aisles and bundled the children out into the foyer, where they beat the living hell out of them. Hearing the thumps and screams, I went out to the foyer to see the children running for their lives, leaving their banners and placards behind them.

Winnie's football club already spent a great deal of its time beating up children in Soweto at Winnie's behest. All told, at least eight children died thus under Winnie's orders, though the journalist John Carlin put the number of murders at 16 and other estimates were even higher. I marvelled at the strange path Fatima had trod from the passionate Gandhian I had known in my youth. Walter Felgate, her former mentor, was now Buthelezi's right-hand man and Fatima almost squealed with hatred at the mention of his name.

. . .

My teaching stints in the political science department at the university were pleasant affairs, but there was always a slight tension between me and the department's most junior member, Ian Phillips. Ian was a dogmatic communist and the effective leader of the left on the campus. There was always a group of ANC and SACP activists around his office, particularly Simphiwe Mgoduso, the head of the Black Students Society, and Ian clearly exercised authority over them. Ian also tended to exercise a degree of leadership within the department, for he would often announce what the future was to be – clearly the result of discussions within the SACP. If someone mentioned a possible curriculum change, Ian would say, 'There is no point discussing that. A decision to do something quite different has already been taken.'

The universities would soon be 'massified', Ian told us, and students would appoint all the academic staff and decide the curriculum. Fascinated, I asked him if he knew whether any other universities in the world had ever worked on such a model. No, he said proudly: this model was partly based on Cuban experience but a lot of it was unique to South Africa. Did it not worry him, I asked, that no one else had ever made a university work like that? Well, the Party has decided, he would say, which, for him, meant that the policy was now inscribed on tablets of stone. It turned out he was right about much of this: huge numbers of black students soon poured in, with no increase in the number of their teachers. And students sat on academic selection committees, often exercising pressure for affirmative appointments. Whether this 'worked' was debatable, for standards fell, institutional memory was lost, and many campuses were racked by unrest.

Although I avoided arguments with Ian, he was well aware that I did not share his views or, indeed, accept his intellectual leadership. I had enough experience of the sectarian spirit of South African communists to know that that made me a sort of enemy. Ian was also an MK activist and often carried concealed guns, so he sometimes clanked as he walked. Often, I worked late in my office and was aware that Ian's office was a blaze of light, with much coming and going by black activists. Naturally, they used the departmental phones, fax machine and photocopier for MK and Party purposes. A great deal of their effort was devoted to the war against Inkatha. Ian refused to discuss this, but he made it clear that it was sensible, in the old football phrase, 'to get your retaliation in first'.

Ian was short and thin. His face was badly pockmarked and often somewhat bloodshot, for he drank heavily. He never shouted, but his manner bespoke a great sense of purpose and discipline. Yet if one discussed either Marxist theory or communist politics with Ian one could not but be struck by his doctrinaire naiveté and, often, ignorance. (Once we discussed the Rivonia trialists and I discovered that he thought Ahmed 'Kathi' Kathrada was a woman.) In effect, he was an old-style Stalinist. I happened to be teaching a comparative government course with him in 1991 – I did the French, British and American sections while he did the Soviet Union. Ian immediately announced that the Soviet Union was so important that he would need a lot more than a quarter of the students' time. I knew that Ian was extremely hostile to Mikhail Gorbachev's perestroika and glasnost policies, so I was fascinated when, just as his lectures began, the Kremlin hardliners staged a coup against Gorbachev on 19 August 1991. What would he say?

Ian excitedly announced special lectures because this was an event of enormous importance. As it happened, I had to give a public lecture the day after the coup and was asked what the prospects were for the new hardline regime. I took a public bet that it couldn't last a week. So, rather incredulously, I asked Ian what made him think the coup would last. 'Oh, it will definitely,' he replied. 'You see, the minister of agriculture has gone over to the new regime and that means that the new government has the support of the peasants.' I could hardly believe that even Ian could reason in such a fashion. By 22 August the coup had indeed collapsed, with the hardliners arrested or, in some cases, committing suicide. I decided not to mention the subject to Ian, who had very publicly lost face. He in turn never mentioned it again, resuming the same steely air of discipline.

Ian was, nonetheless, a powerful figure. The university had a formal rule against allowing political meetings on campus but in practice the university's leadership bent the rules in favour of the ANC. Shortly before the election the university invited Nelson Mandela to give a public lecture. Naturally, he treated this as an election rally and gave his normal election speech. Three people sat on the podium – the vice chancellor, Mandela and Ian Phillips – a remarkable acknowledgement that although Ian was only a junior lecturer, in effect he was already a big political boss.

Ian went on to become an ANC MP and then a close adviser to Jeff Radebe, a leader of the local ANC who had been trained in East Germany and was also an SACP member. After 1994 Radebe became a leading cabinet minister, which made Ian even more powerful. He would probably have become a cabinet minister himself had he continued. But Ian was gay and had contracted HIV, though he affected an Aids denialist stance similar to that of Thabo Mbeki. He died of Aids in 2007.

I always had my suspicions about Ian. He had done his first degree at Rhodes, where he was known as a right-wing activist. In that era the apartheid government frequently inserted police spies onto the English-speaking campuses, which were already pulsating with political dissidence. Typically, these informers had a double role, attempting to organise resistance to the left on the campus as well as informing the security police about the left's key personnel. Sometimes, in order to do this, the informer would himself join the left and play a leading role in it in order the better to gather information and ultimately to sabotage it.

My own guess – there is no proof – is that Ian may well have started out as a police informer at Rhodes, but when he moved to Natal he was able to re-emerge there inside the Communist Party, a move he could not have made credibly at Rhodes. It was also striking that although Ian travelled to Moscow before 1990 and subscribed to various Soviet sources and newspapers (though I don't think he spoke Russian), he was never detained, banned or restricted in any way. Normally that would have been the fate of someone who was so openly and actively a communist activist. Indeed, Ian always seemed quite unbothered, almost nonchalant, about the risks he was supposedly running. If he was a police informer, this would account for his surprising immunity.

However, these were wild and turbulent times, and, if this supposition is correct, at some stage Ian must have realised that by joining the SACP and ANC he had joined the winning side, so that what may have started as a bogus loyalty became a real one. At that time there were many political entrepreneurs playing a variety of such roles. For example, also active in the UDF/ANC cause on the Natal campus at that time was Mike Sutcliffe, a lecturer in town planning. Mike was able to attract large-scale donor support (Viking gold yet again) for his Built Environment Study Group (BESG), which was theoretically devoted to building community centres, clinics and so forth for black communities in Natal. In fact, little actually got built but the BESG was effectively used as an ANC front, sending paid organisers all over Natal. Mike was so good at his anti-apartheid fund-raising that this made him an important man in ANC circles. He became the city manager of eThekwini (Durban) municipality on a large salary, a post he then used to launch a successful business career.

...

With the ANC and SACP back in the country and openly fighting for position, the full cast of forces was now engaged. The ANC-Inkatha battle continued but there were many other struggles in process too. The old white military and police forces were still very much present and there were recurrent rumours that some rogue elements within their ranks had constituted a 'third force'. Eugene Terre'Blanche and the AWB were still in full cry, while the ANC decided to try to topple several of the Bantustan leaders. There was no real need for this: with the advent of democracy and the reincorporation of the Bantustans into South Africa, they would soon disappear anyway. But the ANC wanted some 'revolutionary' victories and also wanted to establish control over as much territory as possible before the election. For power had become very territorial – where one party ruled, that area immediately became a no-go area for others.

In September 1992 the ANC decided to organise a mass march in Bisho, the capital of the Ciskei Bantustan, ruled by Brigadier Oupa Gqozo, an unpleasant thug. Clearly, the ANC hoped to force Gqozo out. A local magistrate, alarmed at the potential for violence, ruled that the ANC's 80 000 protesters could not enter the capital itself. Inevitably, the ANC decided to ignore this, but the Gqozo forces had erected razor wire to prevent the marchers entering the town. Ronnie Kasrils led a breakaway group of marchers in an attempt to storm through this barricade and break the lines of the Ciskei Defence Force (CDF) drawn up behind the barricade. Gqozo's men were determined not to let this happen and opened fire with automatic weapons, killing 28 of the marchers and one of their own; 200 more were injured. It was a major disaster and the ANC forces hurriedly retreated. The Goldstone Commission condemned Gqozo and the CDF for the massacre but also denounced Kasrils for his 'irresponsible' behaviour in leading the charge that had forced the confrontation.

Knowing Ronnie as I did, I could not feel terribly surprised. When I bumped into him in Durban a few days later we discussed the Bisho events but he showed no hint of remorse. He was at pains to insist that the men who had charged had been full of revolutionary enthusiasm as they did so. I asked how anybody could possibly know what had been in their minds in their last minute on earth? To this he made no reply. But even if Ronnie's assessment had been correct, how could that justify such a pointless waste of human life?

...

When African students began to flood into the University of Natal in the mid-1980s the university made the mistake of failing to insist that its student residences should be equally multiracial. Instead they filled up with large numbers of African youths who had little notion of the rules and civilities that had previously been the norm. The wardens presiding over the residences soon found their jobs impossible and moved out: the students were unruly and played music at full volume at all times of the day, making it impossible for anyone to study. Inevitably, the students were also unwilling to accept the authority of the (invariably white) wardens. White and Indian students in residence soon found conditions intolerable – particularly women, for rape was not uncommon – and moved out. Each residence became a monolithic ANC fortress, quite beyond the control of the university authorities.

There was an interesting footnote to this. In the 1980s one of the most militant UDF speakers had been Jerry Coovadia, a distinguished medical professor. At one meeting Coovadia was urging the necessity of school boycotts when one of his audience objected that this was hardly fair given that Coovadia's own sons were at Michaelhouse, an exclusive private school, where they would not suffer any such boycott. At the time this seemed to cause no ripple on the UDF side but by the late 1980s I heard some of my African students discussing how they must 'drive the coolies (Indians) out of the residences'. I asked why they wanted to do that. They replied that Indians were hypocrites who called for school boycotts at African state schools while sending their own children to expensive private schools. Somehow the Coovadia example had been generalised to all Indians.

The feminists on campus were horrified by the rapes in the residences and by the fact that members of the (now all-black) SRC defended the right of African males 'to spear any women we want' (a phrase quoted in the student newspaper, *Dome*). The black women students I spoke to were too frightened to join any protest – 'You just don't know what goes on in the residences at night,' they would say. There was a nasty affair in one of the men's residences where a gang rape of a black woman took place publicly on a table tennis table. However, the woman vanished and made no complaint, leading to speculation that she might have been a prostitute, for it was clear that there was some prostitute activity around the male residences.

Meanwhile ANC supporters, black and white, were in a state of high political excitement: clearly there would be big changes and big opportunities ahead. Just before De Klerk's speech wrought the great change, the SRC had invited UDF leader Allan Boesak to speak on campus – thus breaking the university rule forbidding political meetings. The meeting drew a huge crowd, which Boesak worked up with passionate rhetoric in his rather reedy, high-pitched voice. With the meeting over, the large black crowd spilled out onto the road and gardens outside, where, however, they faced a large contingent of riot police, attracted by the illegal meeting. The black activists began to hurl insults at the police and spit at them, daring them to charge. The scene unfolded against an incongruous backdrop. At one side stood the statue of the King-Emperor George V, while a series of ladders had been erected against the university buildings on which a number of black workers were steadily washing the windows. For a while police discipline held, but the overwhelming impression was that here were two large groups of young men, hating one another and longing for a fight.

Soon the police charged and the black students fled in all directions. Overhead a police helicopter hovered and shot tear gas into the ranks of the black students. I picked up one of the smoking tear gas canisters and carried it away as a memento. The police chased the students into the university buildings, including the library, beating up a good number of them. Gradually the mayhem cleared to reveal King George V still staring vacantly out at Durban Bay below while the black window-washers continued their toil, apparently quite unbothered by the wild scenes milling around the base of their ladders. The windows still had to be washed, after all. Somehow this completed the impression of a monstrous charade. Some people had been thumped but there seemed to be no arrests. Boesak had been quickly spirited away, avoiding the trouble.

Then, in 1992, the Knowledge Mdlalose affair convulsed the campus. Knowledge, who was an SRC member, had been a student in one of my classes. He was academically very weak, seemed to do little or no work, and sometimes, when I attempted to talk to him, I wondered if he was psychologically disturbed.

At that time the vice chancellor of the university was Dr James Leatt, a churchman with a business school background. Leatt was one of the then numerous breed of 'facilitators' – individuals who put themselves forward as men of goodwill who could play an intermediating role between opposed sides. The beauty of being a facilitator was that you didn't have to believe in anything other than the virtues of compromise. The problem was that the ANC was a disciplined party full of authoritarian instincts and buoyed up by a huge sense of triumphalism. Its activists were little interested in compromise, and in order for a facilitator to strike a deal involving the ANC side – represented on the campus by the South African Students' Congress (Sasco) – one had to bend over backwards in their direction.

The first rumble of trouble came early in 1992 when the head of the political science department returned from a session with the vice chancellor. Leatt had told him, *en passant*, that he had just had to deal with a special request from Knowledge Mdlalose. Mdlalose had failed all his end-of-year exams – not for the first time – which meant that he was supposed to vacate his room in his residence. He had appealed to Leatt, saying that as an SRC member it was necessary for him to stay on – and Leatt, eager to show goodwill, had agreed. My professor friend was disturbed by this: the rules about vacating residence rooms were clear and well known. Mdlalose's failure would mean that he would lose his bursary and thus his ability to pay for fees or a room rental. No special case could be made for the faculty to accept Mdlalose back as a student again. He had failed too badly and too often, so on what basis could a non-fee-paying non-student be allowed to live in residence? There would be no end of other students whose failure had led to their exclusion who would wish to copy this example.

Sure enough, the faculty board announced that Mdlalose would not be accepted back as a student – and that he must therefore vacate his room in residence. Sasco protested, demanding that Mdlalose must be allowed to stay in residence and should, indeed, be readmitted as a student. The university authorities reiterated the rules and their decision. Leatt tried to broker a compromise between the Senate on the one hand and Sasco and the SRC on the other. The Senate sharply insisted that Leatt's job was to represent and implement university decisions, not to use them as mere bargaining positions. Mdlalose, for his part, refused to vacate his room, and a trial of strength began. The first thing that happened was that a Kombi belonging to the student sports association disappeared, clearly stolen.

At this point, several of us looked around for Simphiwe Mgoduso, leader of the Black Students Society. He was an amiable character and we thought he might help to reach a solution. He was a lot older than most students, having attended almost every university in the country. It was, indeed, pretty clear that he was really a full-time ANC organiser who had made a career out of organising students behind the UDF and then the ANC cause. In the 1980s there were many highly charged political funerals, with ANC activists turning them into virtual political rallies. Many of our Sasco students attended these occasions and frequently asked members of faculty to come along too, not just to show moral support but because these funerals often resulted in major confrontations between the police and ANC activists. For these were explosive occasions: the police were heavily armed and the students, after a great deal of singing and speechifying, were in a highly emotional state. Several of my colleagues who had attended such funerals spoke very warmly of how Simphiwe had more than once headed off trouble by negotiating a deal with the police whereby both sides stood down. But now that we wanted him, Simphiwe had vanished from the campus.

Mdlalose's supporters declared that all lectures were cancelled until he was readmitted. They sought to enforce this edict by physical force. This produced at least one very tense stand-off when, armed with sticks and clubs, they tried to shut down an engineering lecture, whereupon one of the engineering students drew a gun. Several times the Mdlalose forces recruited large numbers of schoolchildren from the giant Umlazi township, and, armed with sticks, they then swept through the campus, forcing other students and faculty members to run for cover. Then one day an unseen hand lobbed a grenade into one of the chemistry laboratories, virtually destroying it. The authorities stood their ground but the whole university was in crisis. A large faculty meeting was held at which several lecturers demanded to know how the situation had arisen whereby Mdlalose had been allowed to stay on in residence at all. His exclusion should have been automatic once the exam results were made public, but now his room was barricaded and he was hanging on grimly. Leatt, to my amazement, agreed heartily and said that one lesson that had been deeply learnt was that these rules must be applied absolutely and without exception. His statement drew applause, for it was not widely known that Leatt himself had been the one to make the exception.

The crisis continued for many weeks but, inevitably, the Mdlalose forces lost momentum as the end of term neared. Ultimately, the authorities were able to force entry to Mdlalose's room, remove its furniture, and padlock it shut. Word spread that inside the room there had been documentary evidence of a connection to the security police. With that the crisis at last ended.

During the crisis a young African reporter on the local morning paper, *The Natal Mercury*, asked to interview me. He was very pleasant and we spent an enjoyable morning together. He was a recent graduate of the University of Natal and had ANC sympathies. I asked whether he knew Simphiwe. He certainly did: at one point they had been detained together by the police. But, he said, there were many strange things about Simphiwe. He had been brought up in an Inkatha household – his parents were strong Inkatha supporters – and, the reporter thought, Simphiwe might have been a member of the Inkatha youth movement at one time. Then, when they had been detained together, Simphiwe told him, 'Let's go and talk to the security police. Some of them are good guys, you know.' Sure enough, Simphiwe had walked up to one of the policemen, slapped him on the back, and enjoyed a few jokes with him. Several other security policemen had come through the office and they all acknowledged Simphiwe with a smile. Soon, they were both released, whereupon Simphiwe told him, to his astonishment, that he had arranged a trip down the South Coast with one of his security police friends.

'Are you saying Simphiwe works for the security police?' I asked. The reporter was not sure but was certain that Simphiwe's story was not a simple one. I began to dig around. It emerged that Simphiwe had been the leader on the Wits campus of the Azanian Students' Organisation (Azaso) – a Black Consciousness organisation separate from and partly opposed to the ANC. He had also been a leader of the South African National Students' Congress (Sansco), the predecessor of Sasco. He had, I gradually realised, been a political entrepreneur, floating opportunistically on the tide of change. No doubt the ANC had paid him a pittance, so he had decided to increase his income by striking a deal with the security police as well. No wonder he had been so brave and successful at mediating with the police at those political funerals – he clearly had good friends on both sides.

Meanwhile detective work on campus amplified the picture. Simphiwe was strongly rumoured to be the man who had hand-grenaded the chemistry lab. The grenade itself must have come from MK sources. But Simphiwe had clearly also decided to go into business on his own account. He it was who had stolen the Kombi, using it to establish his own taxi service in Umlazi – where he had then been able to use his influence to recruit the schoolchildren there as soldiers for his cause.

While on the campus Simphiwe, I was told by several black students, had begun to build a business empire by setting up gambling, alcohol and prostitution rackets in the residence where Mdlalose had stayed. Simphiwe had lived on many different university campuses and must have realised that they were soft targets. When he had abandoned the campus to run his taxi business, he had needed an enforcer on the spot to keep the rackets going. This had been Mdlalose's role. No wonder Knowledge had been so desperate to cling to his residence room; it was providing him with an income from the rackets. So when the university resolved to exclude Mdlalose from residence they had been threatening a key part of Simphiwe's business operation. Naturally, he had resisted with might and main, using his influence with Sasco and the ANC students to get them to support Mdlalose's cause. My guess was that when the university authorities found evidence of a security police link in Knowledge's room, these would have been materials belonging to Simphiwe, not Knowledge, for Simphiwe had used Knowledge's room as his business base in the residence.

The beauty of the whole thing was that even at the end of the crisis the university authorities believed they had been involved in a dispute over academic rules: there had been Senate meetings, attempts at mediation and all the usual well-meaning procedures. In fact, though they never knew it, they were really involved in a ruthless game with a would-be township taxi boss.

There were a number of sequels to these events.

James Leatt was forced to resign as vice chancellor not long after the Mdlalose affair. His deputy vice chancellor, Brenda Gourley, who had sworn never to run for the post, was quickly elected as his successor.

I saw Boesak again at the ANC's 1991 conference in Durban, where he was bargaining for a leadership role while warning that the many devoutly Christian coloureds in the Cape (that is, his constituency) would not accept too strong a communist presence in the movement. Boesak's half-in, half-out position meant that he spent quite some time outside the conference hall where the discussions were going on. He relaxed in the sun, wisecracking with journalists – he had enormous self-confidence and felt sure that the ANC would want him to campaign for the coloured vote.

But it turned out that this was where his luck ran out – after a long, good run. Although he was selected to lead the ANC list in the Western Cape, Boesak lost badly in 1994. Mandela then named him as ambassador to the UN in Geneva, a plum post, but before that could happen the scandal broke about his stealing money intended for poor black children. This ended with a jail sentence for Boesak and the loss of his priestly status, which was, however, restored in time and he moved to the USA, where his style of hot gospelling is apparently appreciated.

Fatima Meer died in 2010 and Winnie Mandela died in 2018.

The end of Simphiwe's story is sad. The High Court at Bisho (today Bhisho) found Bonisile Grey guilty of Simphiwe's premeditated murder at a funeral near Mdantsane on 16 July 2005. According to several witnesses, after the burial Simphiwe was queueing for food when he was attacked by Grey, who had a knife and shouted, 'This dog is sleeping with my wife!' He inflicted multiple stab wounds, some of them fatal. Although numerous witnesses insisted that Simphiwe himself had no knife, Grey was later treated for a stab wound in hospital.

The lady in question, Boniswa Qaga, said she had had a relationship with Grey for some 14 years and they had two children together, aged 18 and 14. Grey insisted they had been married according to Xhosa custom. Boniswa denied this although she also said she and Grey had first met in 1987. She said she had only met Simphiwe in May 2005 but that they had soon become lovers and she had moved in with him.

I have no information as to what Simphiwe got up to between 1992 and 2005 – no doubt it is a tale of many chapters. The Knowledge Mdlalose affair had been a complicated one and Simphiwe had clearly lived a very complicated life. But his ending was a simple story of the eternal triangle. There is a terrible irony to the fact that Simphiwe, a successful veteran of so many political funerals where violence always threatened, died in the end at an ordinary country funeral, normally the safest of occasions.

CHAPTER TWELVE

Coming Back

The New South Africa dawned amid considerable euphoria, with Mandela lionised as a sort of living saint. I felt curiously mixed. I was delighted to see the end of apartheid, and I had spent so much time involved in the political excitements of change that I knew I wanted to return to South Africa and be part of this new era. But I had seen enough of the ANC in exile – an inept and shambolic organisation full of parochial attitudes and authoritarian instincts – to be dubious as to what sort of government it would make. South Africa was not only a difficult country to govern but it was also far more developed than any other African state. Nowhere else in Africa had African nationalists had to manage such a sophisticated economy. Anyone who had seen how quickly independent African states had developed into kleptocracies had to be worried: there was so much more to steal in South Africa that an enormous feeding frenzy was on the cards. And while I shared the general admiration for Mandela, his enforced isolation in jail for a whole generation meant that he was quite naive about many issues. He was, for example, publicly surprised and saddened to discover that there was corruption in the ANC, for there had been none among its members in jail.

As for me, by 1995 I had been teaching in Oxford for 26 years. I had loved my time at Magdalen, but teaching is ultimately a repetitive business and I needed a change. In addition, my marriage had broken up and both my children had grown up and left home, which left me free to move. So when I was offered the directorship of the Helen Suzman Foundation (HSF) in Johannesburg, I decided to take the gamble and accept. I was an odd man out amid the general euphoria of the time. Everything I knew as a political scientist suggested that the ANC would fail to rise to the challenge of governing South Africa well. I decided, however, that apart from doing whatever I could to assist the liberal cause, I would set myself the task of trying to understand, analyse and write about the dramatic new experiment that South Africa was engaged upon. It was a matter of where I could make the most useful contribution. I had spent 29 years of my life studying and working as a political scientist in one of the world's top universities. People with such skills were relatively rare in South Africa, whereas I knew that the minute I resigned my Oxford job there would be no shortage of top-class applicants to fill it.

I was conscious of swimming against the current. In the early 1990s a British-South African conference had been held in Durban, organised by my old friend Bernard Crick. I found myself in a study group discussing the post-apartheid economy. As always in those days, there was no shortage of politicised clerics full of a political correctness completely untethered to reality. (Later, the Truth and Reconciliation Commission suffered from the same over-supply of such clerics.) In this case there was much discussion of 'an ethical investment code', the general idea being that before any foreign investor was allowed to invest money in South Africa, he would have to subscribe to a set of ethical principles. Thabo Mbeki was sitting only two places away and I hoped (in vain) that he might step in and stop this nonsense.

In the end, I could bear it no more. I pointed out that all round the world countries were touting for investment. Nowhere else was anyone demanding that investors sign up to codes of ethics. South Africa had to join the real world and stop acting as if it was doing investors a favour by taking their money. One had to realise that shortly after independence two things had happened almost everywhere in Africa: their countries had ceased to be self-sufficient in food and had plunged into food deficit, and in many countries the electricity supply had broken down. What we should discuss was how South Africa could avoid these twin disasters. Almost immediately, Mbeki got up and left the room. I was then roundly criticised for having precipitated his exit by being 'conservative', 'reactionary' and 'negative'. Later events often caused me to remember that scene.

I discovered I really needed to found the Helen Suzman Foundation from scratch. It had no staff or money and had lapsed into complete inactivity. Helen Suzman herself was merely a patron, but since the organisation bore her name, she took a keen interest. She had now retired from Parliament but even President De Klerk acknowledged that in the end it was her ideas that had won the day, for in 1990 he had effectively carried out everything she stood for. I had always admired her but soon I got to know her properly. She was warm and smart and had a good sense of humour. One MP told me how, when she had retired from Parliament, DP MPs had thrown a party for her at a Johannesburg restaurant, where an imposing black major-domo showed them to their seats. One of the MPs, keen to share the occasion, turned to him and said, 'This is Mrs Suzman. She has spent her life fighting for human rights for black people and making sure that they too get the vote.' The major-domo, unimpressed and expressionless, replied in a deep baritone, 'Then she was wasting her time.' Typically, Helen joined in the laughter.

Many of the wealthier Johannesburg whites, enjoying their new friendships with the ANC, competed to invite ANC ministers to dinner or even to holiday with them. Some also hastened to join the ANC. Partly this stemmed from a desire to erase a less than glorious past, but it was also highly fashionable: everyone enjoyed being very 'progressive' and enlightened. The ANC took full advantage of this situation and enjoyed a rapturous honeymoon with the media. But there were already early storm warnings. Some of the ministers appointed by Mandela were completely inactive and incompetent, and some were corrupt. Almost immediately the state began to practise not just affirmative action but so-called cadre deployment, with semi-literate but politically favoured folk given senior positions. This was particularly evident in the civil service. Even when whites (me included) offered our services free, we were most unwelcome. The sight of hopelessly ill-equipped people being appointed to important positions throughout the state and parastatals clearly foreshadowed major trouble. Everywhere institutional memory and organisational capacity were being lost at reckless speed.

I decided that the only thing to do was to tell the truth as straight-forwardly as possible, which we did in the publications of the HSF and which I tried to do in my journalism. In this I was greatly helped by Philippa Ingram, who had worked on the London *Times* and now edited the HSF publications. There was a certain irony in her position in that she had been Thabo Mbeki's girlfriend when they were both in the Communist Party at Sussex University some 30 years before. Indeed, when Albert Luthuli had died in 1967 Mbeki had asked her to go out to South Africa to attend the funeral in his place. Philippa had long since moved away from the Marxist left but her recollections of that earlier period were sharp and amusing.

There was at that time a toxic mix in the media. On the one hand, there were many 'movement journalists' who had been politically committed ever since UDF times and were careful to make what they wrote acceptable to the ANC. On the other hand, the ANC exiles (the predominant group) had long been spoilt by a strong following wind in the international media. They were, after all, the heroes of the anti-apartheid struggle and they possessed 'the moral high ground'. In the eyes of newspapers like *The Guardian* and *The Observer* the ANC could do no wrong, and many international correspondents, keen to display or confirm their anti-apartheid credentials, lionised the new men of power. The results were sometimes fantastic. I remember opening the centre pages of the (previously centrist) Johannesburg *Star* and seeing four large articles occupying the op-ed space, all by prominent members of the SACP. Similarly, I remember Shaun Johnson, then writing for the *Weekly Mail*, telling me how Mac Maharaj, who was to become a powerful ANC minister, had threatened him for being 'too bloody independent'. A few months later Shaun brought out a book of articles, his book launch hosted by … Mac Maharaj. For people were not only keen to appear 'progressive', they were also scared of getting on the wrong side of the ANC. So the ANC was used to being able to control the narrative.

For anyone who had studied politics, such euphoria, and the accompanying Vicar of Bray behaviour, seemed very naive. In all walks of life, people were being appointed to complex and important jobs who were manifestly untrained or suitable for them, yet there was a general keenness to welcome such appointments in order to show that one was in favour of 'transformation'. No one wanted to mention that some cabinet ministers, such as Joe Modise, were gangsters, or that some of the new army generals had been torturers in the MK camps. Better to smile and find nice things to say about everything. This involved a lot of very deliberate pretending. To speak out about such matters was trouble-making and reactionary. Another ideological crime was 'Afro-pessimism', for, rather as in the people's democracies of Eastern Europe, optimism was now compulsory.

I did not want to go looking for trouble but I was also no good at pretending. The ANC still monitored the British press and were angry to see that I was failing to observe the right line. Friends would warn that there was such anger against me in ANC circles that they would not be surprised if something bad befell me. I could only shrug. Life is too short not to tell the truth. And in any case, if you are a writer, what is it all for if you don't try to tell the truth? Journalists often despise those of their colleagues who defect to become PR men at better salaries, yet there are many journalists who are little better than PR men for their adopted cause or party. And it is not a simple thing to tell the truth. Sometimes it means upsetting people you like or owning up to things that you really wish were not so.

Helen had retired from politics but she still had a politician's instincts and liked to be in the swim. She wanted to enjoy the New South Africa that she had fought so hard for, and she saw Nelson Mandela as a special friend – he was then living close to her in Houghton. They had first met when she had been investigating prison conditions. Mandela and the other Robben Islanders had been profoundly grateful for the improvements in their conditions that she had secured. In addition, Helen just found Mandela a very attractive man – she confided to me that had she been younger she might well have fancied him. At first, Helen was very much part of the euphoria of the New South Africa and she tended to gloss over her political differences with Mandela.

The problem was that the ANC had decided that my journalism in the British press had to be stopped. Anthony Sampson was quickly enrolled in this effort. Anthony had once chosen one of my books as his book of the year in *The Observer* and we had become friends, comparing notes about South Africa. But the ANC's advent to power presented him with a great opportunity to utilise his links from his old days at *Drum* to become Mandela's authorised biographer. In writing that book Anthony accepted uncritically as fact a great deal of ANC historical mythology that was far from true – for example, he solemnly suggested that the 1949 anti-Indian riots had somehow been the work of whites. A great deal of academic research had been done on the matter (some of which I had supervised myself) and there was not the slightest evidence for that. But the historical animosity between Africans and Indians was embarrassing to the ANC, which was, in any case, prone to blame the whites for everything.

I was surprised by Anthony's gullibility but, when I reviewed his Mandela book for the *London Review of Books*, I was staggered to see that he had also swallowed the obvious untruth that Mandela had not been an SACP member. When I pointed out this error, Anthony hotly disputed it, for his gullibility on that central question undermined his whole book. He could not acknowledge this fact without, in effect, admitting that Mandela had lied in court and to Anthony himself, his biographer. The controversy between us was written up by the rest of the British press. Sadly, Anthony died long before the SACP openly boasted that Mandela had been a member of its Central Committee. Nobody disputes this fact now and nor does it seem shocking. Mandela simply did what any other communist would have done. Indeed, he was under Party instructions to do so.

With the ANC in power Anthony became far more partisan, a virtual hired gun. When I saw him at a publisher's party in London, he attacked me bitterly for taking a neutral view of the struggle between the ANC and Inkatha. When I protested that this was the right attitude for any objective observer, he retorted angrily, 'Well, let's face it, the Zulus are all bloody stupid, anyway.' I objected that this was mere tribalism, whereupon he just walked away. Next, I heard from the editors of the various publications I wrote for that Anthony had visited them all in turn to tell them that they should not publish me. It is hard to believe that Anthony would have attempted such a move except at the express instruction of the ANC, for he was an old Fleet Street hand and should surely have known that this attempted censorship would not work and would also be resented. Every one of the editors rejected his demand.

I found it odd that Anthony had been a strong supporter of the Social Democratic Party (SDP), a rightward splinter from the British Labour Party, whereas I had stuck with the Labour Party through thick and thin. In my own mind I was a liberal social democrat in both Britain and South Africa, whereas Anthony was to the right of me in Britain but to the left of me in South Africa – where being an ANC supporter involved acceptance of many ANC leaders who were simultaneously communists. I put this down to fashion: the SDP had once been the height of fashion in Britain, just as the ANC was fashionable in the 1990s.

Anthony also acted as a sort of godfather to several young South African journalists. At the time Fleet Street editors were keen to get some good hard news from South Africa. They knew all about Mandela being a living saint but they wanted to know where his money came from, who his girlfriends were and how he came to have a big house in Houghton. Most of all, they wanted a 'warts and all' profile of Mandela-the-man. A number of young journalists were commissioned to write such an article but Anthony always counselled that this was 'not the right time', so no one ever wrote it. One editor I knew reacted with fury when his commissions only produced hagiographies with long quotes from Mandela speeches. 'Doesn't anyone there write real stuff?' he roared.

It was obvious that the ANC pressure to silence me was most likely to come from former London exiles who were in the habit of reading the British papers. This would point to people such as Mbeki, Essop Pahad and Joe Slovo. ANC people who had spent their time in South Africa were far more focused on the local press and were unlikely to read what appeared in London. However, Mandela's friendship with Helen Suzman was generally known, so the attempt was made to enrol Mandela in this censorship effort too. Quite regularly, Mandela would approach Helen with some clipping from the British press that he had been given and complain that these 'unfair' or 'inaccurate' articles were coming from the man who ran her own foundation.

Helen was disturbed by this and would call me in to discuss Mandela's latest complaint. The fact that I admired Mandela made it no easier.

I would simply hand Helen what I had written and ask for her opinion. Invariably she would say, 'Well, that's perfectly fair and accurate' – but of course she did not enjoy having this disturbance in her relationship with Mandela. The situation was made worse by the frequent visits of South Africans long domiciled in London but suddenly anxious to revisit their old country. They commonly had a naive faith in the ANC and still lived in a world in which criticism of the ANC almost necessarily stemmed from white racism. It was very provoking to be sternly lectured by people whose entire knowledge of South African politics had been acquired in Hampstead or Holland Park.

As the ANC government got into its stride it did many things that appalled Helen. She was extremely disappointed, for she had hoped for better – whereas I had expected pretty much what we got. She always remained friendly with Mandela but she stopped quizzing me about my articles and she and I now saw eye to eye. She was too astute to become one of the unconditional worshippers who tended to surround him. One afternoon she told me with some asperity that she had just walked out of Mandela's house: 'Irene Menell and Nadine Gordimer were there, praising him whatever he said, and Nelson just sat there boasting endlessly about how much money he had raised for the ANC. I just couldn't stand it and left.'

I could imagine the scene. Nadine Gordimer, the child of an affluent Jewish family in northern Johannesburg, had little experience of the real world even if she had a lively life of the mind. Almost her only venture from home had been to go to Wits as a teenager, but she quickly concluded that she had little to learn there and dropped out. She then lived in the same part of Johannesburg for the rest of her life. She was an eager ANC camp follower and her best book, *Burger's Daughter*, was a thinly disguised portrait of Bram Fischer's family.

In 2006 I interviewed Gordimer for *The Sunday Times* and was startled by the bitterness with which she denounced the Afrikaners and said they all ought to be punished for having brought apartheid on the country. I asked, 'But surely you cannot be in favour of collective punishment?' 'Yes,' she said, 'absolutely, they're all guilty.' I pointed out that the doctrine of collective punishment had been used to justify the medieval persecution of the Jews. More recently, it had been deployed by Hitler and in all the great genocides from Armenia to Rwanda. Guilt, and thus punishment, could only be individual, not collective. Briefly, she agreed with this but then returned to demanding that all Afrikaners be punished. I reflected that when she had headed the (ANC-aligned) Congress of South African Writers she had supported the ban on Salman Rushdie's *The Satanic Verses*, simply because ANC activists such as Fatima Meer had campaigned for it.

The Helen Suzman Foundation's problem was that it was nearly impossible to raise funds for a liberal organisation in the Johannesburg of the 1990s. The last thing those with money wanted was to be associated with an organisation that mounted a liberal critique of the government. Their donations to ANC causes were partly protection money but also acted as cover while they took steps to transfer their wealth out of the country. Several friends warned me that the ANC would simply find a way of cutting us off from all funds but we somehow soldiered on. Most of the time the HSF had just three employees but we worked hard, putting out two regular publications, *Focus* and *KwaZulu-Natal Briefing*. *Focus* was for some while probably the leading political publication in the country. We also completed a number of large research projects. I was director for six years, by the end of which we were running right out of money.

To my disappointment, several of my successors at the HSF managed to raise more funds but only by dint of giving up the publications and research projects and retreating noticeably from the foundation's avowed liberal purpose: the annual Helen Suzman Lecture was now given by ANC speakers. This sort of thing often happened in the New South

Africa. The *Sunday Times* Alan Paton Award, for example, was wholly taken over. The prize was regularly given to communists and often to rather poor writers to boot. Paton would have turned in his grave.

I had always thought of South Africa as a country full of brave people, willing to risk ostracism and worse in order to stand up for principle. Now all that seemed to have disappeared. To some extent, this was a question of sheer exhaustion: liberals who had fought the good fight for a generation had no stomach for a further struggle against an authoritarian ANC. A key difference was that the anti-apartheid cause always had massive international backing, so that many white South Africans were able to make their careers by playing to this foreign anti-apartheid gallery. Now the ANC enjoyed international favour, and if you wanted to play to that gallery, you had to be on that side.

. . .

Shortly before the 1999 election, Walter Felgate suddenly resigned from Buthelezi's employ, taking with him a lorry-load of confidential documents. Walter denounced Buthelezi and said that he would now use these purloined sources to expose his many and nefarious activities. Simultaneously Walter joined the ANC, who hoped to use him and the documents to undermine Buthelezi in the forthcoming election campaign. It was a startling turnaround: Walter had been Buthelezi's close confidant for many years and had been instrumental in the foundation of Inkatha.

A few weeks later, Walter rolled up to my office at the HSF, together with a new wife. He announced that he was going to deposit all the purloined papers with the HSF, that I should store and catalogue them and then write them up in order to expose Inkatha and Buthelezi to the world. As was usual with Walter, these instructions were delivered as a sort of binding order. I said the whole idea was impossible. We had no space to store such a load. I was already working flat out for the HSF and on a new book of my own. I simply had no time for these enormous new tasks that Walter wished to impose upon me. Moreover, Buthelezi was angrily insisting that the papers had been stolen from him. The HSF could not possibly take receipt of what were, on the face of it, stolen goods. Walter said that I did not understand how dreadful it had been working for Buthelezi. The man was impossible, a virtual slave-driver, and so on. I had heard such descriptions often before from embittered ex-employees. Walter must have heard them too and had disregarded them for 30 years, yet he now made the same remarks with the air of having just discovered this awful truth.

One of the few public figures with the requisite guts to face this difficult new environment was the new young DP leader, Tony Leon. We had our differences: he was an admirer of Mrs Thatcher, whom I had greatly disliked. But this did not really matter: his key virtue was the courage to stand up and speak truth to a very authoritarian government. Tony was rather annoyed that the HSF did not come out in open support of the DP but our constitution forbade that. Thus, when we carried out opinion surveys, for example, we made the data equally available to all the parties. At one point the PAC, by then a radical splinter group, asked for a presentation. I made a date to talk to them and then found that, as a result of the Queen making a state visit to South Africa on the royal yacht *Britannia*, I was invited along to meet the royals on exactly the same day. So I kept my word to the PAC. When they heard that I had passed up a chance of mingling with royalty they gave me a standing ovation, one of the funnier moments of my time at the HSF.

As the 1999 election neared, Tony became increasingly worried. The DP had begun to do well in municipal by-elections but there was little sign of recovery at national level from its miserable 1.7 per cent in 1994. Both Lawrie Schlemmer and I assured Tony that the results would come. Only the best-informed and most active citizens voted in municipal by-elections, but given this support from key opinion-formers, the DP would surely break through soon in the national polls. Tony was unimpressed by our confidence: he wanted to see hard data. Finally, with the election less than a year away, I went down to Cape Town to present to the DP caucus a new survey we had done. For the first time our data showed the DP up to 10 per cent. The caucus was thrilled, though as I looked down, I could see Colin Eglin, a former PFP leader and now an HSF trustee, fast asleep in the front row. It seemed like a comment on the passing of the torch to a new generation.

Tony had meanwhile hired Bill Clinton's former pollster, Doug Schoen (a former student of mine), to do the DP's polling. He also asked me to be part of the DP's general discussion of election strategy. I said I could only do that in a private capacity. Tony could not care less about such distinctions. Thus, I found myself happily working alongside Doug again. We compared notes on our respective surveys and found we agreed completely. Doug had brought with him another Jewish New Yorker, Stuart (Stu) Sheinkopf, an expert in political marketing. But the DP had also employed one of the big South African advertising agencies to come up with a marketing strategy for the DP's campaign, which meant that they and Stu were in direct competition. All of us met with the DP executive round a large table.

Doug ran through his poll, pointing out that Tony was more popular than the DP, and that the party was best known for the tough-minded way in which it had stood up to the government. Then the local advertising agency spoke. In a way typical of politically correct business people, they were worried that the image of Tony and the DP was too strong, even strident. So they suggested that the DP's posters should mainly feature little furry animals of a Disney variety. Voters would come to associate the DP with these cuddly little creatures, thus toning down the party's image. Tony should not feature too much on the posters, which would mainly feature rabbits, koalas and Bambi.

Stu declared this strategy to be 'absolute crap'. The voters, he argued, had no prior connection to such furry animals and would still be puzzled by their appearance by election time. Proper strategy meant leading with your strongest points, and in the DP's case this was precisely their fearless, fighting image, personified by Tony. The party should make the most of it, not try to hide it. Doug agreed, saying this was what had pushed the party up in the polls. And since Tony personified such tough-minded liberalism, the party and its posters should make the most of him.

The advertising agency people were clearly very nettled by this criticism. They angrily demanded what exactly the theme of Stu and Doug's proposed campaign would be. Doug and Stu were ready for this: a picture of Tony, they said, with the caption 'The Guts to Fight Back'. By this time tempers were rising and the following exchange took place:

Local agency: To be successful you can't have a slogan as long as 'The Guts to Fight Back'. It has to be shorter.

Stu: OK, then. Fight back.

Local agency: That's two words. You ought to be able to say it in just one word.

Stu: Fuck you.

The DP decided to take Doug and Stu's advice. As Doug confided to me – he was familiar with such scenes – 'The local guys always hate being shown up, but their tempers cool very quickly when they realise they're still going to get their fee.' He then got down to brass tacks. He realised that the DP had very little money, not many members and only the shell of an organisation. 'Look, he said, you guys cannot compete with the ANC or the Nats over the course of a whole campaign, they'll just outspend you. Your best hope is to put serious money into printing really good posters and then concentrate on getting them up quickly all over the country. The effect will be like a 100 metres runner sprinting away from the start in a mile race. You grab attention and become a big talking point and just hope to God the effect of that will last through the campaign. Because after that you'll be running on empty.' This was agreed and what was known as the 'Fight Back' campaign was set in motion. I was later much surprised to hear that this campaign had been devised by the DP's pollster, Ryan Coetzee, who was not even in the room when the above discussions were held.

Shortly before the election, Van Zyl Slabbert approached me. I had seen a lot of Van in Johannesburg – we often breakfasted together. But Van was in a strange state of mind. While he'd been leader of the Progressive Federal Party (by then the DP) he had had many meetings with Thabo Mbeki and the ANC exiles in London, suggesting they work together against apartheid. Mbeki said they could not work with a party represented in a whites-only Parliament. Van and Mbeki had a long and impassioned correspondence on this issue. In the end Van had astounded his Prog colleagues by suddenly announcing (in 1986) that change could never come from a whites-only Parliament and resigning not only the PFP leadership but his seat in parliament as well. Many Progs never trusted Van again after that. Helen Suzman refused to speak to him for several years.

Van then set up the Institute for Democratic Alternatives in South Africa (Idasa). This meant he had carried out his side of the bargain, and Mbeki then carried out his as the two of them together organised a famous meeting in Dakar of ANC leaders and a delegation of Afrikaners led by Van. This created a sensation and set the scene for increasingly frequent meetings between various South African elite figures and the ANC. Van, meanwhile, began a career in business and became a director of several companies.

Van felt he had established a close and warm relationship with Mbeki, whom he regarded as a real friend. Indeed, Van seemed to think that he had an understanding with Mbeki that they would run South Africa together. When the ANC came to power, he told me that 'They're going to need all the help they can get,' and that he was therefore going to work with them. I was surprised. The ANC was an authoritarian organisation that hated liberals. I could not see how the former leader of the main liberal party could fit in with that. This seemed to worry Van not at all. Indeed, he several times asked me what I thought of his becoming foreign minister. I said, well you would have to join the ANC first. Fine, he would do that. I was sceptical. I knew the ANC would never trust anyone they saw as an outsider, and Mbeki's reputation was that of a cold-blooded and ruthless schemer. He could be charming, but many fell foul of him, though their downfall was effected with sufficient subtlety that their fate could seldom be pinned on Mbeki. And Mbeki had not actually offered Van a position of any kind. I thought that Mbeki might be leading Van up the garden path or, possibly, that Van was leading himself up it.

Van continued in this vein for some time. Finally, I told him I didn't believe a word of it. He seemed a little hurt but mainly curious. 'Look,' I said, 'Joe Slovo (the SACP leader) is very influential in the government and over the years he has used his elbows very sharply to make sure that he is the only white man to have such influence at the heart of the ANC. And he is very used to the position where he is the cleverest man in the room – hardly difficult in a cabinet full of incompetents. But Mbeki is also of the view that he is the cleverest man in the room – and without doubt he is the most cunning. Mbeki is already speaking in quite racist terms against whites. Do you really think he wants someone like you, who will always argue his corner and who is a lot smarter than him, in a cabinet where you can contradict him? And, even more, do you think Slovo wants a white liberal there who is also smarter than him? Mbeki and Slovo don't like one another but the one thing they'll agree on is keeping you out.' Truth to tell, I was surprised that I needed to spell out such realpolitik factors to Van. He merely looked nonplussed.

However, Van then told me that he wanted to run for premier of the Western Cape, perhaps at the head of his own new party. I told him that if he wanted to run it had to be on the DP ticket: a new party would fizzle. He quickly accepted this. But first he prevailed on me to add a question to the survey I was about to do to test his popularity in the Western Cape. We phrased this carefully by listing a series of people who had left politics – FW de Klerk, Allan Boesak, Dick van der Ross, Van Zyl Slabbert, Cyril Ramaphosa, Franklin Sonn, Jakes Gerwel and a few others – and asking voters whom they would most like to see return to political life. The interesting result was that coloured voters did not give more than two per cent support to any coloured candidate: instead they plumped massively for De Klerk and Ramaphosa. Whites were much the same. Blacks were mainly ANC. Van still had a following but it was mainly confined to middle-aged whites and coloureds. However, I cautioned him that the DP had only got around 12 per cent in the Western Cape in 1994. It was simply impossible for the party to jump to 50 per cent in one election. That might happen in time but it would take growth through many elections. Van seemed rather crestfallen on hearing this. The implication was that if he ran, he would have to choose a coalition with either the Nats or the ANC.

Van still wanted to run, so I arranged a meeting at his house for Tony Leon, Lawrie Schlemmer and myself. At the last moment I was called away to Zimbabwe and could not attend. But I heard a full account of the meeting. Tony and Van had got on well but deadlock had ensued. Tony was already committed to the Fight Back campaign against the ANC government, while Van said that if he ran, it would be in order to go into coalition with the ANC so they could run the province together. Both Tony and Lawrie said this was impossible: it would effectively hand the province to the ANC, would hugely upset DP voters, and would contradict the Fight Back campaign. The only possible coalition was with the remnants of the National Party. Van, who had spent his whole career fighting the Nats, could not agree to that. Tony and Lawrie pointed out that things had changed a lot and that the Nats now pretty much agreed with DP policy, but it was no good: the meeting broke up without agreement. It meant the end of Van's political comeback.

The election was dramatic. The DP blanketed the country with posters of Tony Leon and the slogan 'Fight Back' or 'The Guts to Fight Back'. Since the DP lacked branches in many small towns and rural areas, a lot of midnight postering was done out of drive-through party vehicles. As these towns woke up to this poster onslaught they were often enthused and wanted to form DP branches. Both the ANC and the Nats, with hideous unwisdom, reacted sharply to the posters – with the ANC claiming that the campaign really meant 'Fight Black'. All this did was to focus attention on a party that had entered the lists with only 1.7 per cent of the vote: the publicity was priceless. Tony toured the country, addressing packed meetings everywhere, for Fight Back had stimulated great excitement. It also upset the more politically correct members of the DP – who would probably have been happier with the furry-animals campaign. Tony came under heavy criticism from within DP ranks, which naturally unsettled him. Doug Schoen told me that he fielded several phone calls from Tony asking whether he was really sure about the wisdom of the Fight Back strategy. Doug said, 'Yes, absolutely. Just keep on keeping on.'

The DP leapt up to 9.6 per cent, overtaking a whole slew of other parties. The party went from seven seats to 38. For the first time in South African history, the liberals had ceased to be a hopeless minority and were now the main opposition. Everywhere new DP branches were formed and membership increased. It was an utterly critical election, for thereafter opposition opinion naturally crystallised around the DP, or, as it now became, the Democratic Alliance (DA). Ironically, the new DA MPs included some who had criticised the Fight Back campaign – to which they owed their seats. Over the next decade the party's vote continued to climb and it captured both Cape Town and the Western Cape. It was by far the most multiracial party in the country, with substantial fractions of its vote coming from all four of the major racial groups. All this success derived essentially from what had been achieved in 1999.

Van seemed almost miffed by the result, announcing that Tony Leon had now 'painted himself into a corner'. Actually, the road was now wide open to the DA's expansion and it was Van who had really painted himself into a corner by allying himself to the ANC, which was, in the crunch, never going to give him what he wanted. The thought went through some minds that Van had wanted to run in the Western Cape in order to enhance his leverage with the ANC by having the ability to hand over to them a province that they greatly coveted, though I have no idea whether there was any truth to that.

Not long after the election, Van told me that Mbeki had asked him to chair a commission of enquiry on the subject of the electoral system. I said, 'Well, the system we have is a disgrace. It gives all the power to the party bosses. We desperately need a more constituency-based system.' Van pounced: 'Ha! I thought you'd say that! But if you have a first-past-the-post system then the ANC will win 90 per cent of the seats.' I pointed out that there were many alternatives to the Westminster system, and I thought the German system, which features both proportionality and constituencies, would work well. Van, who had not heard of this before, became very excited and said he wanted me on his commission. I knew immediately that Mbeki would never stand for that, which meant that Van would soon drop that idea. Nor did it happen, though Van's commission duly recommended the German system. But the government threw the report in the dustbin as soon as it was delivered, for the ANC party bosses liked the system just as it was. There had been public criticism of the way Van had been left out in the cold, so Mbeki had apparently invited Van to head this commission merely to give him something to do, without ever meaning to implement its report.

Van began to say that Mbeki had played him as a useful idiot. This was so obviously true that I found it too painful to agree. Sadly, Van's later years were clouded by a growing dementia and he died in 2010. It had been a sad waste – he was a man of enormous talent. In fact, he had been wrong to quit Parliament in 1986: political change, when it finally came in 1990, came exactly from there – which he had denied to be possible. Had he remained in Parliament he would inevitably have played a major role in the transition and could have had a major political career after it. For me it meant the loss of a fine friend of great warmth, intelligence and good humour.

Walter Felgate died in 2008. His last years were not happy. The ANC used him as an anti-Buthelezi weapon during the 1999 campaign but otherwise had little interest in him. (The stolen Buthelezi documents yielded nothing by way of scandals or exposés in the end.) Rather pathetically, Walter now claimed that he had always regarded the ANC as his real spiritual home – but the ANC would never trust a man who had been their bitter enemy for so long. Walter continued for a while as a member of the KwaZulu-Natal provincial legislature. But Arthur Konigkramer, the editor of the Zulu newspaper *Ilanga*, and himself a member of the legislature, told me that at lunch time in the legislature canteen Walter found that he was not welcome to sit down at either the Inkatha or the ANC tables, so Arthur would take pity on him and lunch with Walter himself.

It was a sad and curious ending. Walter had always been tremendously emphatic and convinced of his beliefs, yet here he was wandering around in no-man's land. Walter had also been a man of great intelligence and ability, his talents never properly used. I still cannot go onto the campus of what is now the University of KwaZulu-Natal without seeing, in my mind's eye, Walter roaring up to the Memorial Tower Building on his huge motorbike, with Fatima Meer on the pillion.

. . .

These were difficult years for anyone with eyes to see, for South Africa was clearly running down. Institutions and infrastructure were not being maintained, many skilled people were emigrating, and trouble was being laid down for the future. But none of that could be said out loud. Lawrie Schlemmer was one of the few people who were quite aware and quite frank about what was going on, but he was so much *persona non grata* with the new regime that no radio or TV station or newspaper wanted to hear his views. It was dreadful that this most informed and aware person should be shut out of the debate. Lawrie was philosophical about this, but he deplored what he called 'the loss of complexity'. It was a good term: with many people of education and wealth emigrating, all sorts of things such folk would once have sustained now went to the wall.

I always suspected that Lawrie's passion for old cars was a case in point. He never had fewer than seven of them on the lawn outside his house. But when he moved down to the Cape from Johannesburg, he had to sell quite a few of them. Worst of all, he could not find a buyer for his 1934 Chrysler fire engine (which really belonged on a Hollywood set). So when Lawrie bemoaned 'the loss of complexity', I always had it in the back of my mind that what he was really thinking about was the disappearance of the sort of collector who might have gone for a 1934 fire engine.

CHAPTER THIRTEEN

Zimbabwe

In 1997 we (the HSF) carried out a large international opinion survey in Zambia, Malawi, Zimbabwe, Namibia, Botswana and Lesotho. We used many of the same questions we had just used in a survey in South Africa so that we could compare the evolution of opinion across the whole subcontinent. The data suggested three ages of African nationalism. First, a rigid, authoritarian and Jacobin phase, with a strong stress on party discipline, Marxism, a hostility to traditional chiefs and so on: the prize exhibit was Namibia, followed by South Africa. Second, there was a phase in which just such a variety of African nationalism was clearly disintegrating – the key example being Zimbabwe. And third, there was the rest, where the original ruling parties had already disintegrated, giving way to multiparty politics. (Botswana, of course, had never had a Jacobin phase.)

The revelation was Zimbabwe. Outwardly there was no sign of discontent with the Mugabe regime but the survey suggested that an explosive situation was building up. In Bulawayo and Harare the ruling regime was rejected and even despised. This was not surprising in Bulawayo, given Mugabe's horrific repression in Matabeleland in the early 1980s. In the far larger Harare, the capital, despite its being overwhelmingly Shona (like Mugabe himself and his ruling party, Zanu-PF), the regime was particularly unpopular with the young and the better educated – ironically, given that the Mugabe government had spent enormous resources on educating this generation.

But there was the rub. After independence in 1980 Mugabe had spent heavily and run up debts, while his radical rhetoric scared investors away. The result was economically unsustainable: by 1997 the economy had ceased to grow, unemployment was mounting, and the country was deep in debt to the International Monetary Fund (IMF). The country rested four-square on the efforts of some 4 000 white commercial farmers, whom the World Bank regarded as Africa's best. These farms fed the country and produced a large agricultural surplus for export. There were some small-scale black commercial farmers but the bulk of black land was devoted to subsistence agriculture in the old tribal trust areas.

A land reform programme financed by Britain had been abandoned when the British discovered that the land they had bought from white farmers was being given not to poor African farmers but to Zanu-PF fat cats around Mugabe. Thereafter a farmer could buy or sell land only if the government wasn't interested in acquiring it. Normally, it wasn't. The regime seemed to have lost interest in land reform and decided simply to benefit from the farmers – who fed the country, produced most of its exports, and paid most of the taxes.

I presented the survey results in Harare. Although the meeting was strictly non-partisan and the data provided simply as a public service, the meeting soon acquired the atmosphere of an opposition rally. Our survey was the first ever done in Zimbabwe and it engendered considerable excitement. The meeting was packed out by young, educated blacks who cheered and clapped as they heard of the regime's unpopularity. A number of them gave such strong rhetorical expression to their feelings that I had continually to stress that I had had no political purpose in conducting the survey.

Thereafter I visited Harare regularly. On one visit I saw the demonstration by the Zanla war veterans, led by Chenjerai (Hitler) Hunzvi, which caused Mugabe to cave in to their demands for extra pensions and gratuities, although it was clear that many of Hunzvi's followers were far too young to have been veterans of the liberation war. The IMF said there was no fiscal space for these extra pay-outs. Mugabe told the IMF to 'go to hell' and in 1999 Zimbabwe defaulted on its IMF loan. All lenders now pulled back. The signs were clear: an explosion could not be long delayed. Increasing labour unrest was led by Morgan Tsvangirai, the head of the Zimbabwe Congress of Trade Unions (ZCTU). This Mugabe fiercely repressed.

I went to see Tsvangirai in his sixth-floor office. He told me that only two days earlier two Zanu-PF thugs had charged in and attempted to throw him out of the window. He was, though, a strong and burly man and had successfully fought them off. He was blunt: 'The minute we began to call strikes, all Mugabe's talk about the workers, socialism and Marxism – it all just vanished. The truth is that he wants to reduce us to the state of dependent peasants. That's the key to Zimbabwe. In the rural areas when there's famine you only get food or seeds if you can show your Zanu-PF card. The peasants live in terror of the government.' I liked Morgan and we became friends.

Another impressive man I met was Mike Auret, a mild-mannered and devout Catholic. His Catholic Commission for Justice and Peace (CCJP) had long ago carried out a full investigation into the Matabeleland atrocities but it had never been published. Mike told me that his bishop was extremely nervous about upsetting Mugabe, so he would never agree to publication. But somehow Mike fooled the bishop and got the report published, creating a major stir. Early in 1999 Mike told me he had decided that what Zimbabwe needed was a new constitution and had accordingly set up a movement for constitutional reform, the National Constitutional Assembly (NCA). I was sceptical: it was difficult to see how this could alter the harsh facts of Mugabe's brutal dominance. But I was wrong. Mike not only gathered most of the NGOs into the

NCA but also the ZCTU and Tsvangirai, giving it real muscle.

The NCA then toured the country, holding mass meetings to discuss constitutional change. Huge crowds participated and everywhere there was great enthusiasm for change. The government became nervous and started to organise its own constitutional discussions, which ultimately resulted in a draft new constitution that was put to referendum by Mugabe on 12 and 13 February 2000. Meanwhile the NCA morphed into the Movement for Democratic Change (MDC), headed by Tsvangirai, the first mass opposition movement that Zimbabwe had seen. Mike Auret's initiative had been crucial. He had brought together the intellectuals and the middle class with the muscle of the unions, an unparalleled feat. But, of course, the MDC quickly developed a life of its own.

Conscious of the rapidly changing political environment, I had put a new opinion survey into the field in January 2000. The MDC had only just been formed and did not campaign against the new constitutional proposals, but nonetheless Mugabe lost badly, by 54.7 per cent to 45.3 per cent. I checked the results against our poll, conducted only days before the vote. It was immediately obvious that there had been large-scale rigging. In Matabeleland South, for example, our survey found a large majority opposed to the government. Yet the official results showed a large 'yes' vote there – an impossibility. Other rural areas were somewhat dubious too. It gradually became clear that Mugabe had performed that rarity: he had lost a rigged referendum. The pro-government vote had been 'adjusted' upwards in rural areas where cheating was harder to spot, but the Mugabe forces had underestimated the tidal wave of 'no' votes in Bulawayo and Harare. For cheating was much harder in the cities, where the press, election monitors and NGOs were all on the alert.

Almost immediately land invasions began as Zanu-PF and the Central Intelligence Organisation (CIO), the secret police, led gangs of war vets and party activists to take possession of the white-owned farms. Despite the rhetoric, this had nothing to do with land reform. The point was that nearly 250 000 black farm workers, together with their families, lived on the white farms. Thus nearly half a million people lived under the umbrella of the paternalistic white farmers. The farmers provided schools for the farm children and, often, special facilities to look after Aids orphans. If there was a bad harvest or famine in the rural areas, the farmers, with their sophisticated irrigation systems, still produced enough food and nobody on their farms starved. Thus, unlike their peasant relatives, this large group of people did not live in fear of starvation nor of Zanu-PF. If they wanted to vote against Mugabe – and they did – they had felt free to do so. And they had tipped the scales against Mugabe.

So while the media concentrated on the awful drama of white families watching their farms being ransacked and their livestock butchered, this was not the whole story. The real target was the farm workers and their families. They were beaten and tortured while being made to sing Zanu-PF songs and, usually, to beat other farm workers and their families in hideous sessions often lasting many days. Then they were thrown out on the road, traumatised, jobless and starving. Over time, many thousands died. Just as Tsvangirai had said, they were being reduced to cowering peasants. The farms usually ended up in the hands of the Zanu-PF fat cats who knew nothing of farming. Production collapsed and today many of these farms are nothing but fields of weeds.

However, it took some time for this process to work its way right through the country, and in the meantime a parliamentary election was held in which the MDC, despite massive intimidation, torture and rigging, won almost exactly half the seats. I roamed around Zimbabwe writing for *The Sunday Times*. From that point on until at least 2008 I carried out many more surveys and almost invariably the result was Zanu-PF 20–25 per cent, MDC 60–63 percent. That is to say, although Zanu-PF 'won' several elections in that period, the reality was always an

MDC majority of at least two to one. Mike Auret had become one of four white MPs (with Trudy Stevenson, Roy Bennett and David Coltart) in the MDC parliamentary group of 56 MPs, and he told me how paranoid the mood now was inside Zanu-PF. When the MDC group sat in Parliament the random seating meant that its four whites were scattered among the group. One day several Zanu-PF MPs came up to Mike in the parliamentary canteen and told him, 'We have worked out why you MDC white guys don't sit together. Each of you has to control your own bloc of black MPs.' Mike tried, but failed, to convince them that the MDC was controlled by Tsvangirai and his front bench.

The publication of our opinion surveys greatly embarrassed Zanu-PF. Nor did my articles in *The Sunday Times* go unnoticed. The Zimbabwe High Commission in London faxed back copies of all articles about Zimbabwe in the British press, which were read by the CIO and the Zanu-PF bosses. Since my articles told the story of murder and mayhem, this made me a marked man.

Meanwhile the general economic catastrophe the country was undergoing produced a complete shortage of petrol and diesel. Knowing that foreign correspondents invariably flew into Harare – where one of my colleagues on *The Sunday Times* was stopped and put on the next flight back to London – I would drive up all the way from Johannesburg or Durban – vast, long drives of 2 400 kilometres and more, each way. I drove a large 4x4 and would stock up with cans of diesel, which took up almost the whole available space but which avoided the need for refuelling until I drove back into South Africa.

I tried to maintain a non-partisan stance, offering to give presentations of the surveys to Zanu-PF. They never wanted them and the government-controlled *Zimbabwe Herald* would routinely denounce them as lies. Finally, I went once again to Zanu-PF headquarters in Harare to offer a presentation and was told that if I did not disappear within two minutes I would be handed over to Hitler Hunzvi and his war vets. Hunzvi was well known for his 'torture clinics' and I had no wish to sample one, so I left quickly.

It became clear that I couldn't stay safely in any hotel, because it was too easy for the CIO to monitor people they did not like and snatch them. (I had heard something of their snatching proclivities from my former student Peter Godwin.) Often I would stay with Rhoda and Mervyn Immerman – Rhoda ran the Amani Trust (which helped torture victims) while Mervyn was a prominent lawyer. Sometimes, however, I stayed with Dave and Norma Kitson.

The Kitsons were a major story on their own. Both Dave and Norma had been SACP militants, and after Mandela and the rest of the original high command of MK had gone to jail, Dave had become deputy commander in a replacement high command. This had earned him a 20-year jail sentence.

Norma had gone into exile in London where, against SACP orders, she staged a permanent protest outside South Africa House, demanding the release of her husband and his comrades. The exiled SACP leadership tried to forbid this because of the tacit understanding they had with the British authorities that they would not stage street demonstrations. Naturally, since the ANC – and particularly the SACP – controlled the British Anti-Apartheid Movement (AAM) this restriction applied to that body too. Norma was, however, made of sterner stuff (she earned the occasional soubriquet of 'Stalin's Granny'). When ordered by the AAM to make no street protest, she simply founded her own organisation, the City of London Anti-Apartheid Movement, and under its banner she then sat, together with a few sympathisers, in all weathers outside South Africa House. This open defiance naturally infuriated the Party, making Norma a political outcast.

Dave was finally released in 1984, having served his 20 years – 'By the end the warders looking after me were guys who hadn't been born when I started my sentence,' he told me. A Johannesburg friend took him shopping for new clothes, a Rip van Winkle experience in which Dave was suddenly introduced to men with long hair, girls in miniskirts, new car models and such novelties as video and computer shops. When he got back, Norma was on the phone from London asking where he'd been. He started to tell her but was quickly interrupted: 'Bloody hell, Dave, I've been standing in the pouring rain in Trafalgar bloody Square and you've been ogling girls in miniskirts and bloody shopping.'

Dave proceeded to London. He was by far the most senior political prisoner yet released and had also been chosen by the AAM as its Prisoner of the Year. However, he then met with Joe Slovo, about whom he already had serious reservations. Dave had obeyed the SACP injunction not to flee into exile and had gone to jail, but Slovo had fled, living in comparative comfort as an exile in London. The fact that Dave had outranked Slovo within MK was a further potential friction point.

Slovo spoke only about the issue of Norma's indiscipline. He pointed out that the AAM would shortly hold its AGM, where Dave would be greeted as a hero and where he would have to give a speech. When he spoke, Slovo said, Dave would have to denounce Norma for her indiscipline. Dave protested that he could not do that to his wife, who had worked so tirelessly for his release. Slovo then declared that if Dave refused he too would have to face the consequences of his indiscipline. In the end Dave was expelled from the Party, from MK and from the ANC. The Party took steps to deprive Dave of the scholarship he had won at Ruskin College, Oxford. So the Kitsons, after all their sacrifices, became non-persons. They suspected that Slovo, seeing Dave as a rival, had engineered a situation in which Dave had no option but to refuse to denounce Norma.

Dave and Norma wanted to return to the new South Africa and experience, as it were, the fruits of their struggles, but being non-persons, shunned by all their old comrades, would not be a tolerable existence. They put their case before Mandela, who was horrified but who proved quite ineffectual in the face of Slovo and the Party's iron discipline. Dave and Norma retreated to Harare – a way of being back in the southern Africa they loved without suffering continual Party persecution. Norma, who now hated the Party, referred to it as 'the *chevra*', that is, the Chevra Kadisha, the Jewish burial society, for the Kitsons, like most whites in the SACP, were Jewish. 'That's what those bastards want,' Norma would say. 'They're there to see us safely buried. And they always have their *shomrim* (watchers).'

There was always something a bit sad about the Kitson household, festooned as it was by pictures and banners from anti-apartheid days in the UK. And, after all, they were still in exile. I spent hundreds of hours listening to Dave's riveting stories – he had a prodigious memory, unlike Norma, who would explain, 'I suffer from CRAFT, which means Can't Remember A Fucking Thing.'

Things got steadily more difficult in Zimbabwe. Once I had a car breakdown in a remote rural area and managed only to get to a small town – nearly bumping into a leopard on the way – that turned out to be Hunzvi's HQ and a torture centre. I had already filed a story about Hunzvi and the so-called war vets and realised he would probably get to read that story by Monday and come looking for me. Luckily, just in time I managed to hire someone to tow me in my broken-down car to Harare.

There were many difficult moments. I once went to investigate yet another land seizure by the war vets and as I hove into view of the farm gate I saw a number of well-armed war vets waiting for me. My phone rang. It was a colleague on *The Sunday Times* calling from the wilds of Sri Lanka, where he was hanging out with the Tamil Tigers, then fighting a losing war with the Sri Lankan army. One of the Tigers, he said, claimed to have played a key role in Mandela's election campaign in 1994. Was this true? I didn't know, I said, but riffling through my address book I told him that someone who would know was Stanley Greenberg, the ANC pollster in 1994. If he rang the New York number I then gave him he could get Greenberg's number. It was all done in a minute. I marvelled at the way modern technology had made such a hook-up possible. After some tense moments, I managed to talk my way through the war vets.

By this time it had become impossible to drive up to Zimbabwe – the immigration officials at Beit Bridge now had a list of names of people like me. Nor could I fly in through Harare airport for similar reasons. But I managed to ferret out the fact that at Victoria Falls airport, customs and immigration were not computerised. Almost nobody but tourists landed there, so arrivals were literally recorded in pencil in an exercise book. So I would fly up to Victoria Falls, hire a car, tell everyone I was on my way to see the Falls, and then drive in the opposite direction, to Harare. This turned out to be foolproof.

However, one day I flew to Victoria Falls, drove the nine hours to Harare and then flipped on ZTV, a truly lamentable TV station. There on screen was Jonathan Moyo, the firebrand minister of information, giving a half-hour talk – about me. He had discovered that all of Zimbabwe's woes were traceable to RW Johnson. This imperialist spy was not only responsible for the series of opinion surveys that had given such encouragement to the gullible MDC – who would apparently never have mounted a challenge to Zanu-PF but for his efforts – but on top of that Johnson was responsible for the dreadful, lying reports in the London *Sunday Times*. Moyo concluded that should I dare show my face in Zimbabwe I would be severely dealt with. It was eerie, chilling stuff.

I phoned the *Sunday Times* and said what had happened. The foreign editor was ecstatic: 'You must write that up,' he said. 'Hang on,' I said, 'they'll get any article that I write faxed right back to them and that will tip them off that I'm in the country. They'll go mad – and come looking for me.' But the foreign desk was insistent and in the end I agreed. At which point I realised I had better change my local address, so I turned to my friend Don Heath. Don was a man of parts, a former game ranger with a PhD in zoology, an excellent shot and now the editor of *The African Hunter*. Don lived in a compound with other people I knew. It was as good a bet as I had.

I started writing the article but was interrupted by *The Sunday Times* picture desk. They had discovered that they had no picture of me. I explained that, amazingly, the Moyo broadcast had shown no photograph of me, which presumably meant the CIO also lacked one. The last thing I wanted was a mug shot of myself to appear over the article, for that too would get faxed back to Harare and then be used to track me down. The picture desk said the editor was absolutely insistent: they had to have a photo. 'Well,' I said, 'at least no mug shot of me over the article?' 'We promise,' they said. 'No mug shot.'

This meant I had to hire a photographer. He took hours photographing me from every conceivable angle. The foreign desk rang, wanting to know where my article was. I explained, with some irritation, that the photographer had delayed me. 'Oh good,' the desk said, 'we have to have a photo of you.' 'But dammit,' I said, 'you cannot put my mug shot over the article.' They promised not to. 'So why do you need a photo, then?' I asked. 'Oh,' they said, 'it's for your obituary.' It turned out that the editorial meeting had discussed the possibilities that I might be jailed, tortured or killed. In any of those cases they had to have a photo under the headline 'Mugabe's Terrible Vengeance Against Our Man in Harare'.

I had to laugh, for *The Sunday Times* was aggressive in their search for hot news and was forever suggesting near-impossible assignments. They were conscious of being Britain's (and perhaps the world's) top Sunday paper and they were determined to blow the opposition away every week. If I ever queried whether a certain assignment might be too risky I was immediately reminded of Marie Colvin, the paper's legendary war correspondent, who routinely took almost suicidal risks, one of which resulted in the loss of an eye. Marie was extremely brave and she produced great journalism. Like everyone else, I was shocked and saddened when she was killed in 2012 at Homs in Syria. Marie was apparently murdered on the express orders of the Assad government, which had forbidden her to be there. When, as per normal, she sneaked in anyway, they took their revenge. The Syrian artillery used the signals from her satellite phone to get a fix on the media centre where she was and then poured in the artillery fire that killed her.

Being at Don's was a different experience. Cartridges and gun parts lay around everywhere. Most days Don returned home from practising at the shooting range, bringing his fellow gun enthusiasts with him. They were all very tough guys and fine shots. Some had been Selous Scouts (Rhodesian Army Special Forces), others had been in the British South Africa Police, others were game rangers or hunters. They all had their own favourite guns and were horrified that I was not 'carrying', as they called it. I listened to the torrent of advice and then asked what would be the heaviest-duty weapon I could get. They looked at one another and then said that there was a nearby arms cache left over from the counterinsurgency war that included a SAM-6 missile. I said I would take a rain check.

I got to know and like these men. Typically they were passionate about wildlife and saw poachers as the enemy – several of them had been in firefights with elephant or rhino poachers. Any such encounter was a kill-or-be-killed situation. When Don did his morning exercises out on the lawn you could see the big white scar where an AK-47 round had gone into his shoulder. One of Don's friends had been with him that day and had instantly killed Don's attacker. Listening to these men was to hear of an Old Africa that one might have thought had disappeared. Don told me how he had taken a party of private hunters into the Congo. At one point they had come across a small village with a primitive butcher's shop selling quite recognisable human body parts. 'The scary thing about that,' Don said, 'was not so much the persistence of cannibalism – after all, we knew that was there. It was that there was no law and order at all. Anything might happen.'

Don also told me of an anti-poaching mission he had been part of in the Hwange National Park. Although he and his friends had a helicopter, they simply could not find the poachers. Instead they repeatedly came across elephant or rhino carcasses and, nearby, the still-warm ashes of what had been a barbecue fire, always under a large tree. From counting the impala bones strewn around, they were able to deduce that there must be a dozen or so poachers. They were being careful to have fires only at night, making the smoke invisible, and under covering trees that prevented anyone seeing the fire from a distance. It was a well-planned and effective strategy. Don and his three friends were on the top of a high ridge overlooking a vast plain below. They knew the poachers had to be down there somewhere – but simply could not find them. However one of the rangers, a former Selous Scout, remembered that there had been an arms cache not far away. The others pointed out that any arms still there would be rusty and useless. He agreed but said he remembered that there had been a consignment of infrared rifles developed by the Americans for night fighting in Vietnam.

Not too long after, he returned with just such a rifle. It was clearly unusable. But, he pointed out, the infrared scope still worked. They then constructed a primitive tripod and waited till evening. Placing the scope on the tripod, they moved it along the ridge, taking sightings. Sure enough they detected a heat source down on the plain, which they then triangulated to get an exact fix. They spent the night turning their helicopter into a makeshift gunship. At dawn they swooped in on the heat source, all guns blazing. They killed or captured all the poachers. It was a typical Zimbabwean story, using make-do and patched-up old technology to serve modern purposes.

Ian Smith still lived in Harare, next door to the Cuban embassy. In old age he had become a popular figure among young blacks because of his fearless criticism of the Mugabe regime, which he referred to merely as 'the bandits'. A local Zimbabwean journalist, Michael Hartnack, explained the phenomenon. 'They see him as a sort of white tribal chief,' he said, 'a wise and unafraid old man, commanding respect. To understand, you have to think of early-20th-century Americans gawping at Geronimo in his Model T Ford.'

When I interviewed Smith, it was rather touching. He lived on his own, his wife dead, his daughter far away in Cape Town. I remember his immensely knobbled hands and the veins standing out on his arms. He laughed at the Cuban flag flying next door – he saw the irony. He related how, when Mugabe won the 1980 election, he had offered his help, which Mugabe eagerly accepted. For many months they sat in the presidential office every morning while Smith went through the business of the day, explaining how everything worked. But when Mugabe decided to nationalise a slew of industries, Smith could not agree. Mugabe angrily ended the relationship.

Smith blamed the British government for failing to stand up for 'civilised values' in Rhodesia. Given that he still bore the scars of a wartime RAF fighter pilot, this was a deeply personal matter for him. But he told me he had recently visited Britain and attended the Last Night of the Proms. I could imagine easily enough how he would have been drawn to the passionate singing of 'Land of Hope and Glory' and the antics that customarily attend it. Sure enough, it had given him fresh faith. 'There were some young people there who really made me believe in the future of Britain again,' he said.

...

The land invasions continued and with them the destruction of Zimbabwe's economy. Crucially, President Mbeki supported Mugabe. No sooner had Mugabe lost the referendum in 2000 than Mbeki had summoned a secret meeting in Johannesburg of the southern African liberation movements (defined as those who had fought armed struggles against colonialism/apartheid) – Frelimo, the MPLA, Zanu-PF, Swapo and the ANC. The referendum loss was explained as the result of an imperialist offensive aimed at bringing down first Zanu-PF and then all the other liberation movements in turn. They must therefore all rally behind Mugabe. It was classic Mbeki paranoia. When the Southern African Development Community (SADC) met, all the other states were confronted by this powerful and united bloc, so they all rallied behind Mugabe.

I was in Harare for one SADC meeting. It was bizarre to hear the declarations of support for Mugabe's land seizures made by the SADC states while, simultaneously, the *Zimbabwe Herald* ran adverts placed by the self-same countries trying to encourage fleeing white Zimbabwean farmers to settle there, for such productive farmers were highly valued.

As the 2002 presidential election neared, I was tasked by an international donor to carry out opinion polling for Tsvangirai. This was strictly illegal: Mugabe had passed a law forbidding Zimbabwean parties from accepting support from foreign sources, though he, of course, happily accepted large donations from the Gaddafi regime in Libya. The donor insisted that his support depended on Tsvangirai's writing a letter to him expressing confidence in me, which Morgan happily did. I commissioned the Gallup interviewers by email from South Africa, sent them the questionnaire, and then sneaked into Zimbabwe by my usual back route and lay low. Once I had analysed the data, I had to give my presentation of the results to Morgan and his team in a secret venue at night.

It was all very cloak and dagger. It was also rather disappointing. I greatly admired Morgan's courage but he was a poorly educated man of the people, much more given to gregarious chatting with his friends than to listening to anything I could tell him. I ended up by telling him that modern politicians paid extravagant heed to what their pollsters had to tell them and that he would do well to listen. He took this in good part, but it was difficult to feel that the result was worth all the risks.

I made many friends in the MDC – most notably Fletcher Dulini Ncube, the party's treasurer. Fletcher was an individual of the utmost probity, a calm, older man who had fought in the liberation war and been badly tortured by Smith's forces. But as Mugabe's rule had worsened he had taken up the struggle against that regime too. During that 2002 campaign he was arrested by the Zanu-PF forces, who declared that they intended to force him to disclose the sources of MDC funding, using whatever means were necessary. According to another MDC activist arrested together with Fletcher, he was shackled and had as many as 12 interrogators at a time shouting at, beating and torturing him. Fletcher told them that Smith's men had failed to get anything out of him and he was quite certain that they would not succeed where Smith's men had failed. (He had told me: 'You are more likely to get pregnant than I am to give away any secrets.')

Nonetheless, I was scared when Fletcher was taken in because, of course, he knew everything about the polling assistance I had given Morgan and that it had been funded by an (illegal) foreign donor. I knew that Fletcher had bad problems with his eyes and that he needed special medicaments to put on them. We quickly heard that his interrogators had forbidden him all such 'luxuries', which meant he would go blind. I dreaded the possibility that Fletcher might crack under the unbearable pressure he would be subjected to, in which case I would no doubt be arrested in my turn – and Zanu-PF had many grudges to settle with me. But I had nothing to fear. Fletcher suffered dreadfully and lost an eye but he never talked. I cannot adequately express the gratitude and admiration that I felt for him. He died in 2014, sadly too soon to see the end of Mugabe's reign.

Inevitably, the 2002 election was rigged and was denounced as neither free nor fair by the Commonwealth, but was awarded an opposite verdict by the African Union, which, under Mbeki's guidance, supported Mugabe. The two South African judges sent as election monitors, Dikgang Moseneke and Sisi Khampepe, also concluded that the elections had not been free or fair, but Mbeki refused to release their report. One realised that Zimbabwe's future was settled largely by the question of whose sphere of influence it fell under. After Rhodesia's Unilateral Declaration of Independence (UDI) in 1965, the country left Britain's sphere and came instead under South African protection, which is why UDI lasted as long as it did. Zimbabwe has remained under South Africa's spell, which has doomed it to a long agony of disaster and decline. This situation continues today, with Cyril Ramaphosa pleading the Zanu-PF case to an unimpressed Western world.

But the chief blame lies with Mbeki: Mandela was revolted by the means Mugabe used to stay in power and would not have supported him. All told, many scores of thousands of people were killed, tortured or died through forcible neglect under Mugabe. In the end, Mbeki may be responsible for as great a loss of life in Zimbabwe as he was in South Africa through his refusal to allow Aids victims their necessary drugs.

For a while I served on the board of a charity helping Zimbabwean torture victims, as a result of which I saw many poor people with grisly wounds. I particularly remember one young man who had been stripped naked and forced to sit down on top of a (burning) paraffin stove. My great friends the Immermans decided, very sadly, that they had to leave for Australia. I was staying with them as they packed up and remember lying in bed among the packing cases wondering whether all whites who stayed in Africa long enough would ultimately leave as refugees.

My swan song in Zimbabwe came with the 2008 presidential election. The run-up to the election was exceptionally violent, for Tsvangirai had more support than ever and Mugabe was in a paranoid mood. I knew that reporting on the election for *The Sunday Times* would be risky.

I explained my concerns to Don Heath, who helpfully provided me with papers showing that I was in Zimbabwe as a big-game hunter, together with reservations at a private game farm and a certain amount of literature about hunting rifles. The Immermans had left, Don and Sheila Heath had two small babies to look after, Norma Kitson had died, and Dave had gone to live in an old-age home in Johannesburg, so I booked myself into a bed-and-breakfast lodge some way out of Harare. The first round of the election was followed by an eerie silence: no results were declared, and it seemed clear that Tsvangirai had won and that Mugabe and the army were considering their options.

The MDC held a victorious press conference at the Meikles Hotel in central Harare where their spokesman, Tendai Biti, put up figures showing a clear victory for Tsvangirai. (In typically shambolic MDC fashion, the figures did not add up.) The atmosphere of the conference was excited and almost ecstatic: this, surely, was the end of Mugabe? I found myself sitting amid a happy group of journalists – the *New York Times* man was next to me. He had apparently come all the way from New York to cheer this wondrous event.

I stepped out of the Meikles, leaving behind an exuberant crowd. I walked down to MDC headquarters at Harvest House, which was surrounded by a large and enthusiastic gathering. I can't explain this rationally but I suddenly had an overwhelming feeling that something was not right. I decided that I did not want to be anywhere near Harvest House, let alone back with that too-happy crowd at the Meikles. I got into my car and drove quickly back to my B & B. Just minutes later, as I later learnt, the police raided Harvest House, taking away everything and everyone they could find there. They also pounced on the journalists standing around outside Meikles, arresting anyone who did not have official government permission to be there. Among those arrested was the *New York Times* reporter.

Unaware of this, I sat down at the B & B to write my story for *The*

Sunday Times. Later that evening, I heard a commotion outside. Glancing through the window, I saw several policemen. I quickly stowed away my laptop and notes and went outside. There parked in the drive was an open lorry with at least 20 very frightened-looking people in it. Some of them seemed to be handcuffed or tied up. The owner of the B & B explained to me that the police were rounding up 'unauthorised foreign journalists' together with the owners of the lodges where they had been staying. I dived back into my room and came out with the papers proving I was a big-game hunter.

The police scrutinised these very suspiciously – I was worried they would ask to see my guns, for I didn't have any – but after a while they handed my papers back. I saw a look of immense relief cross the face of the lady who owned the B & B. I don't doubt that she knew I was not a hunter and was herself trembling at the thought of arrest. I shall never forget the looks of fear and misery on the faces of the prisoners as the police and the lorry drove off. They were all held for up to a week – a long time to be in a Zimbabwean jail – and no election results were published for over a month. Meanwhile a terrifying campaign of violence was launched against any real or suspected MDC voters. In the end Morgan withdrew from the election, saying it was a farce and that he would at least spare his supporters further persecution.

Zimbabwe's travail has continued. Mugabe has gone but this has made little difference. The economy has been wrecked beyond repair, and there is again hyperinflation. The Zanu-PF leadership have dug their country into a hole from which Zimbabweans cannot climb out on their own. At the time of writing, the successor Mnangagwa regime is appealing far and wide for help while continuing to behave in such a way as to ensure that it does not receive it.

CHAPTER FOURTEEN

How to Be Unpopular

In South Africa the years 1999–2007 were the years of Thabo Mbeki's untrammelled power. He was a ruler in the image of the philosopher kings of the independence generation elsewhere in Africa, with the same ambition to shape the intellectual climate. There was no shortage of sycophants, both black and white, to assert that Mbeki was a man of brilliant mind. This was absurd. Those who had studied alongside him at Sussex University laughed at the notion. He had been a poor student, they said, often copying other people's work, always late and behind. His girlfriend of the time, Philippa Ingram, attended a Marxist study group with him, which, she told me, was dominated by an extremely clever specialist in English literature. He had invariably opened his remarks with a wonderfully apposite quotation from a poet or dramatist. Mbeki was greatly impressed and thereafter sought to copy this style. His South African admirers failed to realise that what they were getting was a rather pale carbon copy of the real thing, for Mbeki's knowledge of literature was fragmentary at best. Similarly, Philippa was amused to hear Mbeki described as an economist: 'If you had any idea of what went into a degree in development studies in the Sussex University of that period, you would realise how funny that is.'

But he was the man in power and his ego was large, as was his paranoia. In addition, he had had a long career as a ladies' man. All these things came together over the problem of Aids. South Africa had the world's worst incidence of HIV/Aids, and although it was politically unsayable, the disease had a very marked racial incidence. Among Asians the disease was almost non-existent, among whites a little more present, and among coloureds even more. In all those communities the disease was still pretty much confined to the homosexual community. But the really enormous rates of infection – up to 35 per cent or even 40 per cent of the adult population in some locales[29] – were among Africans, where the disease had long since burst into the heterosexual population as well. These figures could only be explained by the fact that African sexual mores were very different from those of these other groups, with both more unprotected sex and multiple partners. This seemed to challenge Mbeki on every front. He did not want to accept that this huge disaster was largely caused by people being unwilling to change their sexual habits. And he was highly sensitive about the stereotypical image held by whites of the irresponsible and promiscuous African male.

Mbeki thus found it impossible to accept the orthodox explanations of the phenomenon. And, given his sense of intellectual grandiosity, he thought nothing of setting aside the views of experts and developing his own theory of Aids. For him it was axiomatically true that all disasters that befell Africans were the work of whites and Western imperialism. So he not only denied that HIV and Aids were connected but decided that the real villains were the big Western pharmaceutical companies that stood to profit from selling the antiretroviral drugs (ARVs) that could prevent HIV from developing into full-blown Aids. Accordingly, Mbeki forbade the provision of ARVs to the legions of the infected –

---

29   Such figures do not denote the rate of infection in the population as a whole but reflect that among young mothers and their children because they constituted the only group that was more or less obliged to frequent clinics and hospitals. This fact rather inflates the figures because young, sexually active women were always most at risk of infection by HIV/Aids, with their male partners suffering a rather lower rate of infection. The highest rates were in KwaZulu-Natal, especially in such African settlements as Mtubatuba, Gingindlovu and Hlabisa.

which meant gays, of course, but also, far more, young African mothers, condemning them and their babies to a dreadful death.

It is often said that Mbeki's ban on ARVs killed many times more Africans than apartheid ever did. This may well be true but it is a difficult estimation. Dr Pride Chigwedere, a Zimbabwean physician working at the Harvard School of Public Health, studied the matter and came up with a precise estimate that Mbeki's policies had cost the lives of over 330 000 people denied appropriate treatment between 2000 and 2005 and of a further 35 000 babies born with a (preventable) Aids infection. Despite the fact that Aids activists were calling for Mbeki to be put on trial for his deliberate prevention of proper treatment for the HIV-positive, he refused to comment on the paper but did not deny its findings. Commenting on the paper's methodology for *The New York Times*, Professor James Chin, an epidemiologist at Berkeley, called Chigwedere's numbers 'conservative' and 'quite reasonable'.[30] So the cost of Mbeki's denialism was close to half the number killed in the Rwandan genocide of 1994. Counting the costs of apartheid is far harder. Even if one adds to the victims of Sharpeville and the armed struggle the casualties of the Inkatha versus UDF/ANC war in Natal, one comes up with less than 20 000. But the pass laws and forced removals had the effect of dumping large numbers of Africans into desolate rural areas where, fairly certainly, they suffered higher mortality rates than they might have. We have no estimate of those deaths.

To watch this Aids genocide in action was a terrible thing. Moreover, the ANC tamely went along with it. The many commentators who wrote extensively about this in those years (of whom I was one) and the Aids activists of the Treatment Action Campaign were unappreciated by Mbeki. On every trip abroad he was surrounded by incredulous foreign

---

30   Harvard TH Chan School of Public Health, 'The cost of South Africa's misguided Aids policies' (Spring 2009).

journalists, wanting only to discuss his Aids denialism, to the exclusion of anything else. It was thus a huge disaster not only for the victims but also for Mbeki himself. It convinced Bill Clinton, Tony Blair and other world leaders that he was crazy and not to be trusted, and this in turn doomed all his ideas about an African Renaissance. Moreover, his paranoia also led him, as we have seen, into an unconditional support for Robert Mugabe, despite the latter's murders, torture and denial of democracy. Mandela had been very remiss in the way he had initially ignored Aids because he had been told such talk was unpopular with Africans. Mandela, however, compensated for this in his later years, and he also became a strong critic of Mugabe, showing just how much South Africa had lost in the transition to Mbeki.

While the economic boom occasioned by the commodity supercycle continued, it was nonetheless difficult inside South Africa to criticise Mbeki. His crony, Essop Pahad, a powerful minister in the presidency, was a bully, and the press was frightened of both him and Mbeki. My own situation was ironic. I was by this time pretty well used to being unpopular among the determined 'progressives' of Johannesburg's plush northern suburbs. Such folk displayed a sort of ironclad political correctness, though they were also quietly smuggling money out of the country and, often, followed their money abroad. The situation was contradictory. Though determinedly onside with the new men of power, they were voting with their feet against the country, while I, who was committed to staying, had clearly incurred the displeasure of both the Mugabe regime in Zimbabwe and of Mbeki and Pahad in South Africa. Sometimes, indeed, I was told that my criticisms of African nationalism showed that I was an embittered white racist.

There was no point in attempting to answer such charges. My extended family includes a number of black and mixed-race relatives, as well as Jewish, Asian, French, German, Russian and American members. It is a little United Nations all in itself. I am used to living with difference.

I also had a long career as a Labour voter in England and had friends in the French Communist Party. But there was no point making a song and a dance about that. The only thing to do was to carry on writing what I thought was true and let other people make up their own minds. And there were one or two bright spots. Helen Suzman had been deeply appreciative of my work in Zimbabwe and we had become very good friends. (She died in 2009.) More surprisingly, not long before his death in 2004 Anthony Sampson had written a very generous review of one of my books, causing me to wonder whether he had changed his views somewhat.

Nonetheless, in the strange (and strained) political climate of South Africa I continued to attract hostility from some quarters. Even in 2019, in an otherwise favourable review of one of my books, Judge Johann Kriegler noted that 'the very name of Johnson causes an uproar in some circles'.[31] I suspect that this situation derives largely from the widespread phenomenon of white guilt. Even if one agrees that collective guilt can never properly exist, many whites do feel historically guilty about apartheid. And, of course, there were many inexcusable evils in the past and there were also many individuals who behaved very badly indeed. But from this grew the expectation that all whites should behave as if they were guilty and should strongly restrict the things they were willing to say or even think. In addition, the notion that one can get on well with people of different opinions is not widespread in South Africa. Political difference is often treated as enmity.

There is certainly no good reason to give offence if it can be avoided. But there is also no good reason not to speak the truth, though one must always remember that one sees truth through one's own prism. This is where the dividing of the ways takes place and it is undoubtedly my willingness to describe and analyse things as realistically as I can (after

---

31 *Rapport*, 12 May 2019.

all, that was why I returned to South Africa) that has got me into trouble.

I remember in particular a conversation with John Battersby, then a correspondent for *The Christian Science Monitor*. John was a good chap and a good journalist, albeit of a very politically correct kind. He was so inclined to insist that whites were all terribly guilty that colleagues like Rian Malan would refer to him as John Batter-Me. One day John was talking passionately in this vein when I volunteered that I didn't feel guilty at all. As a young man I had done my pathetic little best against apartheid. I had then left the country for many years – and how could I feel guilty about things happening in South Africa when I was 6 000 miles away? And I had, very deliberately, come back to live in South Africa when – and indeed, *because* – apartheid was over. I volunteered to work for free to do what I could to help, though this offer was rejected. I believe in complete racial equality and try to practise it. So why should I feel guilty?

This was like a red rag to a bull, producing an explosion from John about universal white guilt. After a while I interjected: 'John, guilt has to be individual. There can be no collective guilt. I feel no individual guilt but you clearly do. I can't really argue. Perhaps you did cruel and unfair things to African people. I have no knowledge of that but if you did behave badly then indeed you should feel guilty and seek to make atonement.' Inevitably, John protested that he had always behaved impeccably. I said that I believed him – in which case, there was no need for guilt. Over the years I repeated very much this conversation with a number of 'guilty whites'. Invariably they insisted that they had done whatever they could to alleviate the cruelties of apartheid. But it was always clear that my own failure to feel guilt was my greatest sin. John Battersby, by the way, is another who has ended up living in London.

. . .

Things in South Africa began to change in 2005 after Mbeki dismissed Jacob Zuma from the deputy presidency. This split the ANC into Mbeki and Zuma factions. Almost overnight the South African press woke up from its long sycophantic slumber: there were now, so to speak, two ANCs, which, in turn, meant that it was no longer obligatory to be an Mbeki admirer. I was torn. I was well aware of Mbeki's demerits but I had few illusions about Zuma. He was clearly quite unsuited to exercising power in a modern state and I knew he was not to be trusted with money.

I met twice with Zuma in 2006 and 2007 when he was, effectively, running against Mbeki, and I was impressed by his natural warmth. He was adamant that Mbeki had made a great deal of money from the arms deal and that it was thus a cheek for him to accuse anyone of corruption. He was excited when I told him that I had been close to Rowley Arenstein – 'But he was our leader!' – and keen to introduce me to his sons. Rather tentatively, I said that I had the impression that Mbeki might have psychological problems. 'Oh yes,' he answered, 'and for a long time now.' It was refreshingly unguarded.

As the battle between Mbeki and Zuma heated up, Mbeki became increasingly edgy: he may have felt power ebbing away. He gave several strange, almost demented public performances and began to shower his biographer, Mark Gevisser, with crazy documents about Aids and to admit that he had been the real author of several notorious documents that had been passed off as the work of others or produced anonymously. Worryingly, he mused publicly that perhaps he should have taken 'the Jacobin option', which is to say a really sharp crackdown on his political opponents and on the press. (For Mbeki was sufficiently well-read in Marxism to know that it was under Jacobin rule that Robespierre held sway.) One of his particular dislikes was Mondli Makhanya, then the editor of the Johannesburg *Sunday Times* (not connected to London's *The Sunday Times*).

There were rumours that Mondli might be arrested, so I went to interview him. It was clear that he was indeed living with the real possibility of being detained. He seemed to have good contacts all the way into the president's office, knew the risks he was taking, and was showing great courage in the face of this threat. The scene inside the presidential office must have been very strained by this time: it was known that Pahad and other advisers had more or less forbidden Mbeki to talk any more about Aids. There were doubtless many arguments and distressed confidences, perhaps even explicit warnings, given to Makhanya in an effort to stave off a confrontation. There were rumours about warrants being issued for Mondli's arrest but then not being executed.

I told Mondli that I was convinced that the Zuma forces were going to win at the ANC's national conference, to be held in Polokwane in December 2007 – which would, at long last, bring Mbeki's rule to an end. Mondli and I were both Durban boys and were accordingly aware of the gathering weight of the Zuma coalition in a way that eluded many observers. Tony Leon told me how, on the eve of Polokwane, he had shared a flight from Durban to Cape Town with Alec Erwin, then an ANC minister. Alec had poured scorn on the thought that Mbeki could lose, declaring, 'That just shows how you haven't begun to understand the way the ANC works.' But, by then, a general air of delusion enveloped the Mbeki regime – a classic *fin de règne* sign. Alec too was a Durban boy and should have known better: Zuma had put together a coalition of the SACP and Cosatu, buttressed by the ANC Youth League and substantial Zulu ethnic support. This was a formidable bloc, though the media did not seem to understand that – and had no wish to upset Mbeki by suggesting that he might lose.

I remember Mondli grimacing and acknowledging, 'Well, you're probably right about Polokwane but that still means we have some difficult months to live through.' True enough. What had particularly enraged Mbeki was a recent (Joburg) *Sunday Times* lead story about the minister of health, Manto Tshabalala-Msimang, an Mbeki favourite who had loyally carried out his Aids denialist policies. The *Sunday Times* had found documentary evidence that the minister, a known alcoholic, had recently been lucky enough to find a donor for a liver transplant. She had been jumped to the head of the queue for such transplants, which, it was hinted, might have been due to political favouritism. But, the *Sunday Times* alleged, even in hospital she had created a scene, demanding wine and whisky. In addition, there was evidence that the minister was a kleptomaniac and had stolen watches off patients in hospitals. Mondli's headline had referred to the minister as 'a drunk and a thief'.

This meshed with another story. The deputy minister of health, Nozizwe Madlala-Routledge, had been sacked partly for her anti-denialist views on Aids but also because of a controversy over Frere Hospital in East London. The local press had revealed shocking instances of neglect and maltreatment at the hospital, flatly denied by both Mbeki and Tshabalala-Msimang. Madlala-Routledge had visited the hospital, however, and declared it 'a national disaster'. Mbeki had been furious, had sacked Madlala-Routledge, and had demanded that she repay a very large sum to compensate for her expenses during her years in office. This clearly vindictive action had also been covered by Mondli, much to Mbeki's embarrassment.

Some years before, I remembered, I had interviewed Bobby Godsell, the boss of AngloGold, who had said quite matter-of-factly that he could not see Mbeki getting through two terms, that he was just too fragile (read: damaged) a personality. Bobby, I could see, was assessing Mbeki as one CEO to another. He knew just how crushing the pressures of such a position could be and understood that you had to be a psychologically healthy individual to get through them. And, quite clearly, he didn't rate Mbeki. He was the only person I knew who called that so perfectly.

I sent off my article to *The Sunday Times* in London, reporting that it appeared that Mbeki had ordered Mondli's arrest but the warrant had not been executed – yet. I knew of course that this was bound to be denied. Mbeki always seemed to believe that he was so much cleverer than everyone else and that his hidden back-stabbing really was hidden. I also knew that British editors were extremely sensitive on the subject of press freedom, so the article would get space and run. Which it did. The resulting row had the happy effect that Mondli was left alone.

This was in the spring of 2007, when the Rugby World Cup was coming to a climax in Paris. South Africa had a wonderful team and cantered almost effortlessly to victory. Mbeki had flown to Paris to bask in reflected glory. In a final demented tableau the tiny Mbeki was carried shoulder high by several enormous Afrikaners, like a sort of mascot. It was a weird image. Mbeki had never in his life paid the slightest attention to sport, let alone the white man's game of rugby. To see him tossed around by these giants, grinning because he had reached the stage where he needed to feed off winning of any kind, was surreal.

A thought then occurred to me. Mbeki would obviously spend the night in Paris after the game, and on Sunday morning, not speaking French, he would want an English-language paper. As I well knew from the time I used to teach at the Sorbonne, the only such Sunday paper easily available on the streets of Paris is *The Sunday Times*. So by noon the next day Mbeki would be reading the article I had just written. I prepared myself for the inevitable blast. It came in the form of a long, paranoid and rambling letter, almost hysterical with rage, allegedly penned by the South African High Commissioner in London, Lindiwe Mabuza – but the prose was recognisably Mbeki's, doubtless dictated by phone from Paris.

'For many years,' the letter read, 'RW Johnson has waged a media campaign against our government, presenting himself as the great defender of democracy in our country, whereas we, who sacrificed everything to bring about that democracy, threaten the very democracy we fought for. Johnson is at liberty to continue along his merry way, masquerading as an expert on South Africa. But not even he should be allowed to propagate blatant lies about our country …'

The letter went on to enumerate 15 separate lies I was supposed to have told. Some of these were almost funny: for example, I had written that the South African Broadcasting Corporation (SABC) was 'as obedient to government fiat now as it was under apartheid' (this was not even very controversial); that the SABC had criticised the rest of the media for not being sufficiently pro-Mbeki (I had heard that many a time for myself); that there was a nationwide security crackdown under way with journalists and political activists being spied on (I had interviewed one of Mbeki's intelligence operatives whose job it was to tap phones and he had told me that the volume of tapping was quite unprecedented, and had even demonstrated to me the Chinese technology used to tap cellphones), and that this was creating a climate of fear and suspicion (even ANC politicians took the batteries out of their cellphones before they would have certain conversations). And so on and on. My article was described as 'a bundle of lies' and 'a veritable and highly toxic witches' brew of deliberate falsifications'.

The Sunday Times, on receiving this letter in London, passed it to me for comment. I said I did not wish to reply but merely stood by what I had written. So the letter, supposedly from Lindiwe Mabuza, was not published. Mbeki was, however, very insistent, so Ms Mabuza had to deliver a series of further letters to *The Sunday Times*, all demanding that the original letter be published. In the end she phoned the paper and was told that her letter had been sent on to me, and that, in the paper's view, this was sufficient. Naturally, Mbeki was not willing to let matters rest there – and by now my article had been reprinted in Australia, Canada and elsewhere – so a further document was prepared headed 'London *Sunday Times* censors South African High Commissioner', which then included the whole of Mabuza's letter as well. This document, which ran to three pages, was then read out on air by the SABC as a news item (no prizes for guessing how that piece of news selection worked) and was reprinted in many South African newspapers as a paid-by-government ad entitled 'The Government on RW Johnson'. I decided to ignore this.

I was left bemused by how faithfully Mbeki had followed the model established by the old apartheid government. His first mistake was that the Mabuza letter was far longer than my original article. Space in *The Sunday Times* is precious. A short, crisp reply would probably have been printed. Second, Mbeki should have realised that any newspaper of the stature of *The Sunday Times* is used to getting overlong letters from autocrats who do not much believe in press freedom. Third, the final move of giving their statement blanket coverage in the South African media was a parochial mistake frequently made by both the ANC government and its Nat predecessor. Finding that the rest of the civilised world regarded them as obnoxious and/or loopy, they responded by buying space in the South African press – where, by definition, they could not refute an international newspaper.

Only a month or two later came Polokwane and the entire Mbeki team – Essop, Erwin and many other unlovely folk – were booted out and in came another lot of, well, far from lovely folk, it has to be admitted.

As the years went by, the terrible depredations of the Zuma government made some people almost nostalgic for Mbeki, a mood encouraged, of course by such Mbeki courtiers as the Reverend Frank Chikane. Personally, I could never take Chikane seriously after he had attacked South African clerics who protested against the use of torture by Zanu-PF: what sort of clergyman is that? Nor could I share the nostalgia for Mbeki. Mandela had the grace to apologise for his early neglect of the Aids issue but there was never a word of apology from Mbeki for his record on Aids and Zimbabwe.

This lack of apology applies more generally. At the height of Mbeki's Aids denialism a special award for leadership was given to Mbeki by the University of Cape Town. If UCT had any sense of shame, an apology for this might be in order too. Sadly, Africa is not short of *génocidaires* and many of them go unpunished. But there is no need to go beyond that to flatter them as well.

...

In 2008 the world financial crisis broke and in 2009 President Zuma took office. The combination of hard times and the overwhelming corruption and incompetence of the Zuma regime produced a sharp change of mood. The fact was that whites, Indians and coloureds had been relatively untouched by the Aids pandemic. The black elite, though far more affected by it, felt ashamed of it and tried to pass over it in silence. While they were all making money, both blacks and whites were cheerful and what was happening to gays and to poor black women and children did not greatly disturb them. But now everything was different: times were hard and they could see their taxes being stolen. They were angry, critical and almost despairing of the state of the country.

This had odd results for me, for my critique of the regime was suddenly more widely shared. Indeed, things now worked the other way round. When I had noticed things going badly wrong in the Mandela and Mbeki periods, I had said so and been castigated as a result. Now, however, people would often turn to me to tell me how thoroughly disillusioned they were and to seek confirmation for their own dismal take on life. This I could not really provide, for I was much less depressed than they were and still happy to go on living in South Africa (while many of them were emigrating). The point was that I had always expected things to go pretty much as they had, so I couldn't really say I was disillusioned or disappointed. The only exception – also an oddity – was the small group of old white 'progressives' who had so bitterly condemned me in the past. Now, when I met such people, I would find that their view of the situation and mine were much the same but that they still insisted I was beyond the pale, though they couldn't explain quite why this was. I didn't really mind: as the old Yorkshire saying goes, 'There's nowt so queer as folk.' An old friend put it to me this way: 'People often get fed up with you when they think you're wrong, but they find it much harder to forgive you if it turns out you were right.'

When Helen Zille succeeded Tony Leon as leader of the DA in 2007, I offered her my assistance in the same role of informal adviser (doubtless one of many) that I had played with Tony. Unsurprisingly, she declined – politicians taking on a new job usually like to appoint a new set of advisers. I was happy enough, for I had plenty else to do. However, as time went by Helen began to steer the DA closer to the ANC and also, against much advice, brought – or tried to bring – into the party leadership Patricia de Lille, Lindiwe Mazibuko, Mamphela Ramphele and Mmusi Maimane. These were catastrophic choices: De Lille ultimately split the DA badly in its Cape Town base, and she, Ramphele and Maimane all ended up running their own rival parties against the DA, while Mazibuko became an equally envenomed enemy of the DA. Moreover, in Maimane's brief period as DA leader, he managed to alienate Afrikaans-speaking voters, thus undoing one of Tony Leon's greatest achievements.

I was appalled as I saw these developments unfolding. My desire to help the liberal cause in South Africa had been one of the major reasons for my return to the country, and I felt a sense of almost personal loss as I saw the DA drift away from its liberal principles. Moreover, the damage done in these years threatened to compound far into the future. I wrote a number of critical articles, analysing these developments and setting out my concerns. To my astonishment, Helen Zille claimed that my criticism was based purely on my being piqued that she had not allowed me to become her *éminence grise*. I decided to make no reply to this absurd claim but marvelled that my unpopularity extended not just from Thabo Mbeki and Essop Pahad to Robert Mugabe (and various other ANC and Zanu-PF leaders) but now to the DA leader as well.

Later, after Helen had surrendered the DA leadership and was, indeed, in the doghouse with Maimane and his advisers, we became friendly again, though I was careful to point out that I had not approached her until she no longer had patronage in her gift. She, for her part, acknowledged her past mistakes with such frankness that it was impossible to remain too critical.

. . .

In 2009 I stubbed my toe while swimming in a lagoon on the KwaZulu-Natal South Coast. The water turned out to be badly polluted and I contracted necrotising fasciitis, which kills some 89 per cent of its victims, usually within a week or so. I was lucky enough to survive, though I lost my left leg. This necessitated some changes in my life. I continued to roam around Africa for a while but it was a lot more difficult and laborious than before. Gradually, I accepted that the logic of my new situation was simply to concentrate on my writing, which is what I wanted to do anyway, and what I have done. It has, indeed, been quite a fecund period and this is my fifth book since the accident.

Given that I was as critical as many others of the excesses of the Zuma period, I thought I would probably remain as unpopular as before, but I am not sure this is true. The lists published of those who were spied upon by the intelligence services under Zuma do not (so far) include my name. I suspect that the different attitude derived from the fact that, in contrast to Mbeki, Zuma had no real ambition to shape the political or cultural environment. Mbeki wanted to establish his own intellectual hegemony and was accordingly much concerned with what writers and journalists said, but Zuma could not care about such things. He was simply uninterested in Mbeki projects such as the African Renaissance. Nor could he be bothered with such Mbeki-ite institutional initiatives as the Pan-African Parliament, Non-Aligned Movement summits or world conferences against racism. What Zuma wanted was power and money – much more traditional objectives in Africa – and he was only concerned to spy upon those who threatened him in that regard. Unfortunately, perhaps, nothing I wrote could have much effect upon that. It is still a little early to know what the Ramaphosa period will bring in this respect, but I shall be careful not to get my hopes up.

There are few prizes in Africa for those who speak out in an independent-minded way, let alone for those who advocate liberal principles. Something that Afrikaner nationalists, African nationalists and communists all heartily agree upon is their execration of liberals and liberalism. Moreover, in a political culture based either on ideological rectitude or on deference to chiefs (or both), there is a great deal of sycophancy and camp-following. The civic culture of a questioning and self-assertive citizenry is largely absent.

An additional problem of my own was that in Oxford it was normal to discuss matters with people of every conceivable shade of opinion. The only thing that mattered was whether they were interesting and intelligent. Africa's habits are much more communal and tribal. People of a particular political viewpoint not only consort together but also tend to avoid social contact with those who disagree with them. They will, indeed, often express personal dislike for those whose opinions they do not share, regarding such people as virtual enemies. Such habits derive from living in small communities that are ethnically, linguistically or religiously homogeneous.

It is hard, finally, to strike the right emotional balance between optimism and pessimism in Africa. Those who are full of optimism generally become disappointed, if not disillusioned, and then often emigrate. Those who are pessimists are liable to have at least occasional pleasant surprises that seem to negate their gloomy view. However, the New South Africa regards any sort of negative judgement about Africa as an ideological sin, as Afro-pessimism. So optimism is not only desired but also required. This makes the situation impossible for anyone trying to work out a fully realistic view of the situation, which, the world being what it is, is bound to be constituted of both positive and negative elements. That, then, is the secret of unpopularity. If you persist in taking a realistic view, no matter how good or bad that is in understanding or predicting events, you have failed the optimism test and are bound to be unpopular. I would recommend it to anyone.

CHAPTER FIFTEEN

Harold and Tom

In Durban I had become friendly with Harold Strachan, a fabled hero of the struggle. Visiting Harold's house was an experience: there on the kitchen woodwork were the bullet holes left by an assassin who had tried to kill Harold during the house arrest that followed his jail sentences. Harold was a painter of considerable talent who made his living as a picture restorer. Like everything to do with Harold, even this activity generated funny stories.

Inevitably, Harold was often brought dreadful pictures that their fond but ignorant owners wanted to be restored. Harold winced at such chocolate-box monstrosities but decided that the worth of all paintings lay in the love people had for them, so he would restore them.

One day a customer brought him a lamentably executed and sentimental picture of a cottage set among the Drakensberg mountains. Grimly, Harold cleaned it up and did what he could. His customer was ecstatic at the result and asked Harold to accompany him to an art gallery to show it to the proprietor. Harold quailed at the thought: the gallery in question was run by a German Jewish man of taste and sophistication who, Harold knew, would loathe the picture and have few reservations about saying so. But the customer insisted.

When they arrived, the customer proudly unfurled his picture. Harold saw a look of overwhelming scorn cross the gallery owner's face.

All he said, however, was 'Hah!' The customer, quite unabashed, continued to ramble on about his love for the picture. This brought forth another 'Hah!' even more withering than the first. The customer, oblivious to this, continued happily to explain that the picture had been painted by his uncle, whose Drakensberg cottage it was. At this the gallery owner remarked: 'Hah! At least it is someverr (somewhere).'

Harold had a sharp eye for the ridiculous and a similarly sharp ear for all the creole richness of South African accents and turns of phrase. He was equally happy with Zulu, Afrikaans and the Durban Indian vernacular. He enjoyed the way that many Zulu nouns began with 'i' and how this led to all manner of linguistic compromises as English became ever more dominant. He was thrilled when his architect friend Dennis Claude returned mystified from a trip to Zululand, where he had found that all the talk was of the popular demand for 'ifokona' (pronounced 'eefokona'). Harold, with much amusement, pointed out that what it meant was that Zulu country people no longer wanted their traditional round huts but modern buildings – 'i-four corner'.

There seemed to be a *Goon Show* element in Harold's family. His father had retired on grounds of ill-health in his early sixties and had then lived to be 95. What on earth did he do, I asked, in those intervening 30 years? 'He sat round and suspected people,' said Harold. He was loath to put any money into a bank but was finally pressured to do so. Never quite trusting the bank, he would then appear at intervals and demand to see his money. The bank would explain that his money was just an entry in the accounts now. This would not do: he would demand to see the exact amount in notes and coins counted out on the desk in front of him and would then object that these were not exactly the same notes and coins he had paid in (for he had recorded the numbers of the notes and the dates of the coins).

Harold greatly enjoyed the nuances of the Durban Indian community, their way of speaking, their quickness and unfailing commercial sense.

Indeed, with the collapse of apartheid he once again had Indian neighbours. Their back gardens were separated by a white wicker fence, and on Harold's side of the fence there grew a large and luscious paw-paw tree. Sitting out on his back verandah one day, Harold noticed a pair of brown legs moving intently along the other side of the fence – their owner was clearly bent double, keeping his head and torso out of view. The legs approached a spot where a particularly large paw-paw lay on the fence. With fascination Harold watched a brown arm snake out, grasp the paw-paw and begin to pull it. Harold called out, 'So how are you, Mahommed?' Mahommed – for indeed it was he – bobbed up, asking as he did so: 'So how much your paw-paw then?'

A bomber pilot during the war, Harold had an intricate knowledge of aviation. He once told me how, during his lengthy solitary confinements in jail, he had lain on his bed, working out in his mind exactly how to construct a Tiger Moth biplane, strut by strut, screw by screw, until it was complete, a mental exercise taking days. By such stratagems Harold contrived never to let his isolation overwhelm him. He told me too of the days when a prisoner was to be hanged, the unearthly chanting, singing and chants of solidarity with the condemned man as every prisoner protested against the awful ritual being performed in front of them.

After the war Harold travelled in Germany, keen to meet the men he had been fighting. He fell in with the rugged veterans of the Eastern Front and U-boat sailors. One of the submariners asked Harold where he was from. When he replied 'Durban', the man laughed and said 'Hotel Edward', referring to a stately old hotel on the Durban seafront. Amazed, Harold asked how he knew about the Edward. 'Every morning I see it through my periscope,' the man replied, for his U-boat had hunted Allied shipping off the Natal coast with fearsome success.

Keen to launch MK's armed struggle, Harold set off for what he called 'the cauldron' of Port Elizabeth politics, the real seedbed of the

ANC and SACP. He became a close comrade of Govan Mbeki (father of Thabo) and Raymond Mhlaba. Harold often said that nothing he saw in jail ever frightened him half as much as did Raymond Mhlaba, good friends though they were. Mbeki asked Harold how to make bombs. Harold said he had no idea; he had merely dropped them, not made them. But, with the aid of school chemistry books and a little general knowledge, he became a bomb-maker.

Govan served 24 years in jail with Mandela and did not see Harold again until he came up to Durban for the ANC conference in 1991. They talked about old times. 'You know, Govan,' said Harold, 'we were bloody brave.' Govan, almost crying, Harold told me, replied, 'Yes, Harold, we were bloody brave, we really were.' After two terms in jail Harold had a hard life: he was banned, under house arrest and the target of assassins, and he had little money.

But, despite his being a true hero of the struggle, once apartheid ended Harold played no role at all in ANC or SACP politics, and nor did the movement give him any recognition or job. Characteristically, Harold had been a member of both the Liberal and Communist parties simultaneously. However, during the struggle he had become aware of the immense will to power of many communists and how often revolutionary ideology masked strong personal ambition and other qualities that Harold found repellent. Harold was too good a student of George Orwell, too honest and too quick to see the funny side of things ever to become a reliable apparatchik.

As the election of 1994 neared, the Vicars of Bray – born-again ANC zealots – were everywhere, creating a difficult atmosphere for anyone who remembered how few people had been willing to stand up against apartheid at its height. It required nerve to keep one's balance in the face of the tidal wave of ANC hegemony. Moreover, some of the ANC ideologues seemed almost mad, living in a world of their own. For example, Harry Gwala, one of the ANC leaders in Natal, was a homicidal maniac; I interviewed one man who had run away from his job at the ANC office in Maritzburg because Gwala had already killed several ANC activists, and this man thought he might be next. Later, the SACP suspended Gwala for trying to kill Jacob Zuma and other ANC notables. There was great political excitement in the air but also uncertainty and fear.

It is not easy now to conjure back up that strange mix of paranoia and revolutionary euphoria, even though it lasted for years. I got a clear insight into it when, a few years later, I visited Barry Higgs's old friend Billy Nair, who had emerged from jail to become an ANC MP. I asked Billy how he felt about his years in Parliament. He sighed and said that had the ANC tried to legislate socialism in the way he had wished, they would have had to face US Marines storming every beach. I tried to explain how absurd such a fear was. Bill Clinton had been the US president at the time. He had relied heavily on the black vote and had assiduously courted Mandela. Moreover, many American soldiers were black. No American president could possibly want to bring down a black South African government, let alone do so. But it was no good. Men like Billy lived in an alternative universe.

As the great day of 27 April 1994 neared – the first of two election days – Harold suggested we use that day to see Peter Brown outside Pietermaritzburg. In the whole country only Rowley Arenstein had been banned longer than Brown, a former Liberal Party chairman. Through all that, Brown's gentle liberalism had been quite unswerving and he was regarded by many as almost a saint. 'We can always vote on April 28,' Harold pointed out.

So we drove up to the Browns' farm. We hardly talked about the election despite the fact that we had spent most of our lives wanting to see universal suffrage in South Africa. I think we were somewhat put off by all the fuss and razzmatazz. It turned out that the Browns hadn't voted that day either. I remember Peter and his wife, Phoebe, looking out over the kitchen sink at a piece of ground not far away and Peter saying, 'That's where I'll be. It's where I belong.' It was a small family graveyard where the Browns had always been buried. (He died ten years later and was indeed buried there.) We had a lovely lazy day at the Browns. As we drove back, Harold, who had felt the disaffection in the air, said, 'You know, I think I'll vote for Inkatha. Just to be otherwise.' My own vote was long promised to the (liberal) DP, which barely survived the election. It was all slightly quixotic.

. . .

Harold's wild sense of humour had long since brought him together with Tom Sharpe, who had arrived in Pietermaritzburg in 1951 at the age of 23, a recent Cambridge graduate. Tom had a passion for photography; in later years, when he allowed me to wander through his photographic collection, I was awestruck. It was a treasure house.[32] But Tom was also of a literary bent, with a sharp, ironic take on the lunacies of apartheid. There was no situation, no matter how dire, in which he could not see the funny side.

Tom and Harold were both contrarians. This was quite a bond – for a while. In 1961, however, Tom's satirical play, *The South African*, was performed in London, thus bringing to the attention of the authorities what a radical dissident they had allowed into their midst. He was arrested and deported. He was placed aboard a Southampton-bound Union-Castle ship in Durban, accompanied by a policeman who had to ensure that Tom did not hop ship in Cape Town but continued all the way to Britain. This was one Konstabel Els and Tom decided to make him the central figure in the satirical novel he was already plotting, *Riotous Assembly*. He was attracted by Els's complete lack of any sense of

---

32   The collection is housed today at the Tom Sharpe Foundation at the University of Barcelona.

irony or of the ridiculous and felt that this brutishness of character was perfectly reflected in his monosyllabic name. The book, an enormous best-seller, was translated into many languages. It also set Tom on the road to fame and fortune. He became easily the biggest-selling satirical writer of the age.

However, back in Durban, whenever Tom's name came up, Harold would curse him. Tom might have the knack of making people laugh, but he was, Harold insisted, fundamentally a cruel, unpleasant man. How could he be otherwise? After all, his father had been a Nazi and Tom had been brought up as a Nazi. It was clear that the friendship between Harold and Tom had gone badly wrong somewhere.

I gradually got the story out of Harold. Tom had become estranged from his young French wife, Criquette, and while Tom remained in Maritzburg, he rented a flat for Criquette not far off Point Road in Durban. Point Road – the road to the docks – had always been famous for its brothels and general sleaziness, but it was not without a certain charm. One day, Harold had started back home from the beach (where he had been fishing), laden with the shad that he had caught. Striding along Point Road, he heard a woman call and, looking up, saw Criquette waving from an apartment balcony. Harold ascended the stairs, they had a fine meal of fresh fish together, and Harold stayed there for the next six weeks. He was idyllically happy, for he had fallen in love with Criquette and was thrilled when she told him she was pregnant.

News of this development brought Tom down from Maritzburg, and when Harold next returned to the flat Tom and Criquette told him that they had decided to get back together again. Harold was shattered, wandered out and stayed drunk for the next several weeks. He finally woke up in a life-savers' hut on South Beach with no idea how he had got there. He stayed well clear of Criquette and Tom after that.

Harold later learnt that the rapprochement between Tom and Criquette had not lasted long – he wasn't sure it had ever really been genuine – and that Criquette, still pregnant, had returned to France. Later still he heard through the grapevine that Criquette had had a son – his son. He repeatedly asked Tom for Criquette's address in France, but this, to Harold's undying resentment, Tom refused to supply. Criquette later married a very wealthy man, and a mutual friend, while on a visit to Europe, reported that he had seen her wearing a fur coat as she descended from a Rolls-Royce. But she had disappeared forever from Harold's life. His old friendship with Tom curdled into the purest gall.

All this and more I heard on the many occasions that Harold came down to the South Coast of KwaZulu-Natal (as Natal became after 1994) with me and Irina Filatova, whom I had married in 2002. Irina had been a professor of African history at Moscow State University and then at the University of Durban-Westville. She and I owned a holiday house down at Trafalgar on the South Coast and Harold would visit from time to time. He died in February 2020.

I did not become acquainted with Tom until the early 1990s when he revisited South Africa. He and Harold took good care not to meet up with one another. I liked Tom but I had to tread carefully to maintain my friendships with the two of them. Tom was then living in Cambridge and, as I related in my Oxford memoir,[33] he seemed to get some of his ideas for *Porterhouse Blue*, one of his most successful satires, from a visit he made at my invitation to Magdalen College, where I was then teaching. We got on famously and he invited me back to his large and lovely house in Cambridge.

No sooner had I arrived there than Tom told me that he'd picked up some old German gramophone records at a sale in Royston. 'Must have been some old fascist living there,' Tom said. 'Just listen.' There came blasting forth 'Lili Marlene', the 'Horst Wessel Song' and a series of other Nazi marching songs. The music was both eerie and stirring.

---

33   See *Look Back in Laughter*, pp 190–191.

Tom knew the German words for each of the songs and marched up and down the living room, singing lustily, adding at one moment, 'Of course, Mr Cohen next door doesn't like it when I play this, but bugger that,' or 'The Shapiros next door don't like listening to this,' and finally, 'Mr Finklestein over the road does not appreciate this, of course.' Long before the end my belief that Tom had any Jewish neighbours at all had evaporated along with my belief in the Royston fascist. The performance climaxed with the most alarming piece of music I have ever heard, the 'SS March', in which the beat is provided not by drums but by the rhythmic crash of a thousand jackboots.

At the end of this bizarre performance Tom exclaimed, 'Ha! Why should the devil have all the best tunes, hey?' 'But your father was a Nazi, wasn't he, Tom?' I asked. 'How did you know that?' he demanded. 'Harold,' I said. 'Oh yes, Harold,' said Tom ruminatively. He then searched his shelves and flung down a printed pamphlet, 'See if that doesn't knock you off your chair,' he said. It was a sermon by Tom's father, the Reverend George Coverdale Sharpe, given in 1920 or 1921. And Tom wasn't joking, it was the most powerful and impressive sermon I have ever read.

Reverend Sharpe had a wonderful command of the English language, but surpassed that with his passionate honesty, speaking a raft of truths that must have been deeply unpopular so soon after the First World War. He began by reciting the comforting myths: how a war had been fought to end all wars; that no Allied soldier had died in vain; that their deaths were glorious and would forever be remembered; that those who survived would receive 'homes fit for heroes'; and that Germany had been rightly punished by the imposition of heavy reparations, which would prevent it from ever threatening peace again. Every single one of these statements was a lie, the reverend said. Most German 'atrocities' had never occurred; millions had died in vain and most would soon be forgotten; those that survived would never receive 'homes fit for heroes'.

Worse, not only could Germany never pay the absurd reparations laid upon her by the Versailles Treaty and enforced by foreign occupation, but the vengeful and unfair nature of that treaty made another war inevitable. Lloyd George and Clemenceau were a pair of dishonest scoundrels and Woodrow Wilson had been naive, arrogant and ineffectual. There was a lot more in that vein. One could easily imagine the indignation that would have greeted it. It was magnificently brave and entirely true.

Tom's father had travelled frequently in Weimar Germany and felt a tremendous sympathy for the Germans as they suffered civil unrest, foreign occupation and national humiliation. All life was sucked out of their economy by reparations – an appalling fate for Europe's most cultured nation. The Reverend dreamed of the day when the Germans would stand up again and shake off all this misery. When the Nazis came to power he felt that at last the hoped-for resurrection had begun and he uncritically embraced Hitler's 'national revolution'. Tom, who was five years old when Hitler came to power, was taken by his father on many trips to Germany – the Nazis were eager to cultivate such sympathisers – and they attended several Nuremberg rallies. No wonder Tom knew the words of those German marching songs.

So the Reverend Sharpe became a member of the pro-Nazi association The Link, and when war broke out in 1939 he feared that he would be rounded up like other fascist sympathisers and interned on the Isle of Man. Accordingly, the Sharpes repeatedly moved house, hoping that the authorities would never quite catch up with them. It was a narrow squeak but it worked.

Tom's father had died not long before the end of the war. 'It was a great mercy,' said Tom. 'Only a few months later the Allied armies overran the concentration camps and suddenly we all saw the dreadful pictures from Belsen, Auschwitz and so on. These were pictures of pure evil. It would have broken my father's heart because it would have made it obvious that he had been completely wrong about Nazism from the start. He was a deeply moral man and he would have found it unbearable to realise he had been working for such a wicked cause.' And the Reverend Sharpe really had gone the whole hog, even declaring that he hated Jews 'in the sense that I hate all corruption'.

One hesitates to accept that a 'deeply moral man' could have been an anti-Semite right through the terrors of Kristallnacht. It would be fairer, I think, to say that, like not a few other people, the Reverend Sharpe was carried away by the original righteousness of his cause and then made a fatal error of judgement. We have seen this many times. FW Deakin, in *The Brutal Friendship: Mussolini, Hitler and the Fall of Italian Fascism*, instances left-wing Italian socialists who were members of the Comintern and who, as the Poles advanced upon Moscow in 1920, stood next to Lenin while the Bolsheviks burnt all their documents. The same men ended up as Fascists and stood next to Mussolini in 1945 when his government in turn burnt its documents as the partisans advanced upon it. No doubt they had begun with a righteous concern for the plight of Italian workers and peasants.

Similarly, in contemporary South Africa one can find many people who took the side of the ANC, infused with a righteous hatred of apartheid, and then gradually found they were supporting a party so riddled by corruption as to be little better than a criminal organisation. In all such careers it is only fair to concede that the initial beliefs were indeed fully righteous. But what creates disaster is the blind, unquestioning belief and partisanship that this leads on to. There must have been many moments in the 1930s when Reverend Sharpe could and should have re-examined his choices and premises. Just because he had seen through some fake atrocities in the First World War didn't mean that the Nazis could not commit real atrocities. It shouldn't have needed the horrors of Belsen or Auschwitz to effect a change of heart.

Later, I asked Tom about Harold and Criquette. 'Oh well, you know Harold,' was about all he would say. He gave the general impression that

Harold was too feckless and unlikely to support Criquette. He pointed to the fact that when Harold had later married and become a father, he had almost immediately gone to jail for sabotage – 'and where did that leave his wife and child?' I was not sure that this was fair, though I could hardly deny that Harold would have been unlikely to provide Criquette with fur coats and a Rolls-Royce.

What was not in doubt was that Tom was a good friend to me. When he heard that I had lost my leg, he besieged me with telephone calls from Spain, where he had taken up residence. These calls, which generally came through in the evening, were fairly tipsy (for Tom started his drinking early in the day) and always very warm. Tom kept insisting that Spanish medical care was wonderful and that I should come to Spain to acquire a really good prosthetic leg. Ultimately, Irina and I accepted Tom's kind offer and flew to Barcelona where Tom's lady friend, Montserrat (Montsie) Verdaguer collected us and drove us to Tom's house at Llafranc, near Girona.

Tom's arrangements were unorthodox. He lived in Spain – the only place, he said, in which he could write – while his wife, Nancy, stayed in Cambridge. Occasionally Nancy visited but the rest of the time Montsie stayed at Tom's. Tom strongly denied that he and Montsie were romantically involved but there was no doubting the affection they had for one another. Montsie, a doctor herself, had secured the services of a top prosthetist for me.

It was all rather wonderful. We stayed with Tom and Montsie for two weeks while I was fitted out with a very advanced prosthesis with a computer in it and Irina and I toured around the Catalan countryside. Tom was the soul of hospitality and always amusing. Affecting a Churchillian air, he would surface around eleven in the morning, settling down with a large cigar and a larger whisky (which he pronounced medicinal). As he moved round the house he would softly sing the old South African anthem, 'Die Stem' ('Ons vir jou, Suid-Afrika'), with a look of malign amusement on his face. Montsie told us that Tom's books had sold prodigiously in both Spanish and Catalan, and even more enormously in Germany, but Tom seemed to have little regard for his writing. 'You can't call them books. What I write are amusements,' he said dismissively, while pressing on me various books by other people, all of which he declared to be superior to his own.

Tom was, at that stage, 83. He complained that he had lost the muse, that he had tried to write but that nothing would come. I think, looking back, that he had also given up trying to write. He was having difficulty walking but his attitude towards almost everything was amused, benevolent and ironic. He was particularly taken with Irina, whom he christened 'Blossom', and gave her several photos of himself, one as an earnest young man. We flew back to Cape Town greatly in his debt.

A few days later, I was making toast for myself in our kitchen and realised I needed the butter and marmalade, which were on the other side of the room. The thought suddenly seized me that perhaps, with my new prosthesis, I might manage to cross the kitchen without crutches. And so I did, unsteadily. I called Irina and demonstrated again how I could do it. We both cried. After two terribly hard years of prostheses that didn't work, of crutches that broke my shoulder, and of many, many falls, I could walk again. I have never once used crutches again or even a stick. Freed from the tyranny of crutches, I was able to go to the gym, put on a bit of muscle and, at last, begin writing again in earnest. Tom died two years later. He may have given up the writing himself, but he had given it back to me.

CHAPTER SIXTEEN

In Search of a Conclusion

It now seems almost funny that my original abhorrence of apartheid led me into a fairly uncritical support for African nationalism. For the main thing to grasp about African nationalism is that it is the opposite of what it seems and promises to be. Although African nationalist politicians frequently advocate socialism, in practice they are key actors in the primary accumulation of capital. The result, everywhere in Africa, has been a huge increase in inequality, one that goes far beyond anything seen in pre-colonial African society or even in colonial society. The wealth gap between a Zulu chief and his subjects, for example, was relatively narrow. The gap between white and black in colonial Africa was much wider. But, even so, none of the white prime ministers and presidents of South Africa and Southern Rhodesia became wealthy men. Contrast that with the huge looting by Jacob Zuma or Robert Mugabe or the fact that Cyril Ramaphosa has a fortune of almost half a billion dollars. This pattern of rule by a country's richest men is seen in many other African states. The richest black man in South Africa is Patrice Motsepe – Ramaphosa's brother-in-law. The richest black woman in South Africa is Bridgette Radebe, the wife of the longest-serving ANC minister, Jeff Radebe, and she is Ramaphosa's sister-in-law. Thus under the banner of socialism one builds a plutocracy.

Moreover, colonial rule often brought quite rapid economic growth, while in South Africa ANC rule has seen slow growth and a trebling of unemployment. Naturally, the black elite likes to depict inequality as the result of the apartheid inheritance but this does not explain why inequality has mushroomed under black rule. Indeed, the point of bringing the discussion back to the apartheid inheritance is to deflect attention from the social processes actually going on.

As Keynes pointed out, when facts change it is only reasonable that one's ideas change too. The worrying thing is when ideas fail to develop and change. I got this feeling sometimes when I talked to Tariq Ali, an old Oxford student friend who turned protest politics into a sort of permanent career. Fifty years later all his beliefs seemed to be exactly the same as when I first met him. It was rather the same with Ronnie Kasrils. Ronnie still believes in the revolution but feels it has been betrayed. Yet if one looks at what African nationalism has produced in the rest of Africa, how can one feel that the outcome in southern Africa is a betrayal? It is just more of the same. The real question is how anyone could work most of their life for the ANC and expect a different result.

Barry Higgs once told me how Joe Slovo and Ronnie had visited him in Devon to try to persuade him to go and help MK in Angola. They offered lengthy explanations couched in the phraseology of Marxism-Leninism. Barry, whose family duties precluded him from going, remarked that their words were exactly the same as when he had first met them over 20 years before. 'Yes,' they replied, 'because it all remains just as true.' Barry observed that all other branches of knowledge changed and developed over 20 years. If Marxism-Leninism was immune to change, it must be a religion.

The ANC argues that there is a qualitative difference between 'liberation movements' that had to fight an armed struggle and those that didn't have to fight. True, movements that succeeded through armed struggle tended be more ruthless and more ideological. But that was insufficient to guarantee the survival of the PAIGC in Guinea-Bissau, while both the FLN in Algeria and Zanu-PF in Zimbabwe decayed long ago into military dictatorships. In southern Africa, Frelimo, the MPLA and the ANC have all become deeply corrupt. In power, they differ little from other regimes in Africa.

A better question is how far such movements are nationalist. The sense of national community is weak or absent from most African states – loyalty is more often felt towards one's clan or ethnic group. Moreover, once Africans were emancipated from colonialism there was no obvious target for nationalist mobilisation. Many of the states are in any case war-torn, weak or failing. What is more distinctive about these movements and parties is their African-ness, not their nationalism.

Cultural habits of mind tend to get embedded in popular consciousness over a period of many hundreds of years and are thenceforth very hard to budge. Take France, for example. Although it is a country of revolutions and republics, France had Europe's first centralised kingdom, which for centuries remained Europe's most powerful and absolute monarchy. Thus, at a fundamental level France remains a deeply monarchical country. De Gaulle recognised this when he installed a strong executive presidency, seven-year terms and no limit on the number of terms a president may serve. This is also what accounts for France's pervasive *étatisme*: French people are long used to a central power that involves itself in every aspect of social and economic life. What would be abhorrent to, say, Americans, seems natural to them. This is how a political culture is formed and persists.

The analogous institution in Africa is the chieftaincy or clan leadership. Many – though not all – Africans became habituated to the rule of a strong man. The chief's status meant that he possessed many wives, which in turn produced huge extended families or clans, a form of social organisation that became the model for the whole society. All land and other resources came ultimately from the chief, thus embedding a very strong set of patron-client relationships. Hence patronage politics is the norm throughout Africa. It is this that produces the phenomenon, ubiquitous in Africa, of the 'big man' with his own distinctive style of authority. This is distinctly pre-modern: typically, the big man does not examine files, consult advisers or even consider precedent or possible consequences very much. He simply announces his decisions as so many ukases. It is a style of authority disastrously ill-suited to complex societies.

This underlying political culture – generally referred to as neo-patrimonialism – has many consequences. It seemed quite natural that Mandela had praise-singers from the start, and nobody queried too closely how he came by his money and houses, for these were the normal attributes of the big man. It seemed natural to Jacob Zuma that he should build himself a sort of royal kraal, that he should have multiple wives and as many children as possible, and that he should amass as much wealth as he could lay his hands on. These were, after all, the normal attributes of the 'big man'. When challenged about his obvious corruption, Zuma would adopt an air of injured innocence, for he regarded all that he did as natural. Moreover, this spilled over into a general sense of immunity, for if X or Y had accumulated great wealth by illicit means, wouldn't everybody have done the same if they could?

When I began to study African politics properly at Oxford, the field was dominated by development economists. The job in hand was modernisation and the economists were powerful because they had aid agencies at their backs. In their view, politics didn't much matter and nor did corruption – it was just another way of distributing resources. Before setting off on their missions to this or that African country, they would ask their political science colleagues what sort of government that state had. They had in mind a simple quadripartite model. So a government might be bad but strong, or occasionally weak but good. The rare ideal, of course, was good and strong. Political scientists would argue in vain that everything depended on governance. If that was not right, no amount of aid would help.

Only very gradually, after hundreds of billions of dollars in aid had been wasted, was this lesson learnt. By the end of the 20th century the chorus became overwhelming: everything depended on good governance. This was why Thabo Mbeki, in his pursuit of the New Partnership for Africa's Development (Nepad), introduced the African Peer Review Mechanism, the idea being that only Africans were fit to assess one another's governance. The mechanism could not possibly work and, indeed, when South Africa was peer-reviewed and certain criticisms were made, Mbeki was furious and shouted defiance at the critics. With that the mechanism effectively died. The incident illustrated why this is such a difficult problem to tackle.

Living in Africa has made me re-examine a number of my own assumptions about governance. When I was in Oxford I used to teach Western comparative government, chiefly involving the USA, Britain, France, Italy and Germany. Over time this could make one rather complacent. These countries had very different political systems, and there was always a certain amount of patronage and corruption everywhere, but almost everywhere things got done (Italy was the outlier). Infrastructure got built and was maintained, economies grew, and law and order was respected. After more than 20 years of teaching about these countries, I thought governance seemed not too difficult. Different countries had different ways of going about things but they all, roughly speaking, got there in the end, even the Italians.

Africa shook up such assumptions. Failures of governance were everywhere and there was absolutely no feeling that all these countries would 'get there in the end'. The beginning of wisdom, I realised, was to accept that governance was intrinsically difficult. After all, of all of earth's creatures, man alone has developed and experimented with different forms of government, whereas a pride of lions or a herd of elephants has the same sort of rudimentary governance structure that it has always had. Generally speaking, animals organise themselves around a few simple principles: the existence of an alpha male or males, protection from predators, the survival of the species and thus the primal importance of producing and rearing the young. Man alone has developed from the simple model of the alpha male/chieftain to monarchy and feudalism, and thence to bureaucracies, parliaments, elections, republics and democracy.

As this evolution took place human systems of governance became increasingly complex. Power, once vested in the alpha male, was now divided into many parts (Max Weber's 'specialisation of function') with rules providing for the relative autonomy of each part. This complexity rested on a recognition of how difficult good governance was. When governance was chiefly or monarchical, the chief naturally used his power to amass wealth, allowed no other institutions independent of himself, and handed out jobs and resources to his family. But, since such a style of governance had numerous weaknesses, over the years in the West it was displaced by new rules and institutions. Each of these rules tried to curb what had hitherto always been regarded as natural behaviour. What was more natural than the self-gratification of amassing wealth, or having as many wives as one wished, or giving jobs to one's sons and nephews? Or, once one had achieved power, just keeping it? These instincts still exist in most men. After all, we were cave-dwellers for hundreds of thousands of years, and that is when our instincts were formed.

Only in the past few hundred years have these more sophisticated forms of governance been developed, and only in some parts of the world. Which is to say, 'good governance' is a difficult and ambitious enterprise. It is not surprising that most of the world still languishes under dictatorships or corrupt and undemocratic rule. Francis Fukuyama once prematurely celebrated the inevitable and worldwide triumph of liberal democracy as the single model to which all countries would evolve. Leaving aside the other problems of 'the end of history', this was also a gross underestimate of the difficulties involved in achieving a liberal democracy.

It is difficult to talk about my hopes for South Africa because I realised from the outset that the chances of the ANC succeeding as a government were very poor. The fact that a quarter of a century later this failure is complete has given me no pleasure. However, given the poorly educated state of most of the African population, a successful transition from white rule depended heavily on whether the ANC would use the skills of the better-educated section of society, irrespective of its colour. Simultaneously there had to be a massive educational effort, ensuring that soon there would be enough Africans able to do any and every job. This was not politically risky in that African majority government was now installed for the indefinite future: nothing could change that. This was the most fundamental policy choice that had to be made by Mandela and Mbeki.

Sadly, such a rational solution never came close to happening. The ANC wanted the jobs in the public service for its own cadres and replaced the skilled with the less skilled or the unskilled. It bothered little about the education system and allowed it to deteriorate steeply. The country has paid a dreadful price for these choices and the damage to the entire public sector seems, at this point, to be irrecoverable. By 2020 the results included a bankrupt national airline, the railway system under administration, frequent power cuts and water shortages. Meanwhile unemployment and inequality have both soared. At the time of writing average per capita incomes have fallen for five consecutive years, with a sixth in prospect.

The results are sad. If you to talk to ordinary black people they are demoralised and bewildered that they were promised so much yet find themselves worse off than before. This was sad too for the many whites (including me) who had hoped their skills would be of use to the new regime. I felt a particular pang at the ruination of the University of KwaZulu-Natal. It was my alma mater, and I had even been approached to apply for the vice chancellorship myself in the 1980s. I was desperately sorry to see its despoliation and glad I had not been there to see it up close.

However, South Africa has advantages. Compare Zimbabwe. It too has dug itself into a deep hole from which it cannot climb out. It desperately needs (and begs for) World Bank and IMF help but cannot get it both because of its debts and because of its denial of democracy. So it struggles desperately but hopelessly, its economy fallen apart, its population fleeing. South Africa, on the other hand, still has the attention of the Bretton Woods institutions both because of the size of its economy and because of its symbolic importance – largely due to Mandela.

In addition, South Africa enjoyed a tutorship in democracy. I saw this in Senegal too. There, under colonialism, the four communes of Senegal elected deputies to the French National Assembly from the 19th century on. The rest of Senegal sat transfixed as it watched the hurly-burly of these elections. Gradually, even down in the rural Casamance or up on the borders of the Sahara, the Senegalese learnt the rules of the democratic game and, like spectators at a tennis match, yearned only to be part of the game themselves. This has had a lasting effect. The Senegalese have consistently avoided the danger of single-partyism, ultimately voting one leader out of power democratically and installing the opposition.

South Africa is similar. There a whites-only democracy existed for many decades before 1994. Africans watched it and learnt to understand the game and internalise its norms. This has been of fundamental importance to the development of multiparty democracy in South Africa since 1994.

The key point is this. In 2000 Mugabe set Zimbabwe on the course to destruction. Had democracy prevailed he would have been thrown out in 2000, 2002 or at least 2008, and some of that damage would have been repaired. But Zimbabwe had been a de facto one-party state since 1980, so the route to democratic change was closed off. This, however, has not happened in South Africa. Slowly, the ANC has been socialised into accepting democratic alternation – so that in 2016 it could even see (and accept) that Johannesburg, Pretoria and Port Elizabeth had been won by the opposition. This is not to say that there might not be cheating in some future election, but it seems unlikely that the electorate, the media and the courts would accept it. This is a very fundamental difference, for it leaves the road open to democratic change in South Africa.

. . .

Living in Africa means that you never get fully used to it. Things can always happen that shock or surprise you. For some years Irina and I owned a beach cottage down on the South Coast of KwaZulu-Natal. There was a thin coastal strip of mainly white settlement and then a vast Zulu hinterland across the main road where there was almost 90 per cent unemployment, a very high rate of HIV/Aids and considerable crime rates. We employed an older African woman to clean our house. She lived in the nearby location (as she called it) in a hut without electricity, a bed or any bedding. One daughter was a prostitute in Durban; her other children were jobless and lived off their mother's wages.

I always gave this lady a lift back to the location – and it seemed churlish not to pick up her friends too, so the car would fill up with middle-aged Zulu women. I soon learnt that their alacrity in accepting lifts was not just about avoiding a long walk. It had to do with the fact that their path back to the location was known as a hunting ground for *muti* murderers – killers who sell body parts to sangomas for use as part of 'traditional' spells and witchcraft. In fact one of the women, a mother of two, was later burnt alive as a witch. The murder of such innocent women as 'witches' is still not uncommon in some parts of the South African countryside. Research by Childline, an NGO, shows that at least

22 per cent of the rural South African population have had first-hand experience of the trafficking of body parts, though Childline warned that many were frightened to speak and that the practice 'was getting out of hand'.[34] Even though you know such things are there, each time you encounter them it comes as a shock.

Life in Africa has its own rhythm, and it is slower than in Europe or America. This is where man began, where he learnt to walk on only two legs. Life is still ruthless here: there is a lot of war, social unrest and grotesque looting, lots of crime and cruelty. But there is also a timelessness, the wonderful beauty of the African environment and a wildlife that has been annihilated almost everywhere else on earth.

Africa has been good to me. It has given me many fascinating experiences and I have never ceased to enjoy its natural beauties. Moreover, I returned to Africa with a sense of purpose about what I wanted to study and write, and I have largely been able to fulfil that purpose. But Africa, especially South Africa, is often so disturbing, so saddening, so gladdening and just plain interesting that once you've lived there long enough, it's hard to live anywhere else. Harold Strachan once went to visit friends in Australia. On his return he told me what a nice place it was, 'but, finally, rather bland', he said. 'It was a relief to get back to abnormality.'

Most of all there are the friendships and, usually, the stories that stem from them. Just after the 1994 election I was staying with Lawrie Schlemmer in Johannesburg when a group of youths from the ANC Youth League marched down the road singing freedom songs and chanting. On the grass verges of the suburb sat a number of Zimbabwean and Malawian gardeners. They began laughing and jeering, 'You'll soon learn better! Your songs will seem like a joke. Just wait and see.' This produced a collective punch-up. Lawrie rolled his eyes and said: 'These

---

34   *Independent Online*, 15 January 2010.

guys are too smart to be gardeners. They should give them government jobs.'

Another friend's daughter, Margie, was threatened by a rapist. She hired a security guard to watch her house by night – a pleasant young Afrikaner called Jannie. After three weeks Jannie reported having several times heard rustlings in the garden bushes by night – but that was all. Margie then told Jannie she could not afford to continue to employ him. Jannie was much concerned for Margie's safety and came up with a proposal that they use the court record to discover her assailant's address. He, Jannie, would then go round there and kill the man for a payment of R5 000 ($290). Margie said she didn't have R5 000, so Jannie suggested they work out an instalment plan.

Margie, still feeling unsure, consulted her father. A very bad idea, he said. This sort of job had to be carried out by an experienced hit man. Jannie had no experience of this sort of work and would probably muck it up one way or another. He'd leave clues, talk about what he'd done, or fail to kill the bad guy. So her father settled on her verandah with a variety of guns, blasting away at any nocturnal rustlings in the bushes. Once this produced a sharp human cry and the sound of someone running away. With this the problem appeared to vanish. The details that mark this as an authentic story of the New South Africa are the idea of killing on an instalment plan, the rejection of a hit-man solution purely on the grounds of inexperience and the DIY approach to law and order. For South Africa once emerged from being a sort of Wild West frontier society, left that world behind, and has now again become a lawless frontier.

That frontier world has its allure and produces a 'can do' attitude to life. I had a friend, Stuart (Stu), who had been a farmer in Zimbabwe but in the 1990s decided to sell up so that he could go into fish farming in Mozambique. The problem was the stringent exchange controls, which prevented his taking money out of the country. Stu reconnoitred the situation, made a number of trips down to Johannesburg, and then used his contacts in the Zimbabwean gold-mining industry to exchange the proceeds from his farm sale for a number of gold bars. He then acquired a strong suitcase into which he packed the gold bars and spent much time practising how to walk with it in such a way as to conceal how heavy it was. But, of course, if the suitcase was weighed at the airport, the truth would out.

Stu then bought an air ticket to Johannesburg and, on the allotted day, went to Harare airport with his case and locked himself in a toilet. He allowed the first, second and third calls for his flight to pass. Finally, he burst out of the toilets, racing towards the customs and immigration desk, shouting wildly that he was late and had a plane to catch. Stu, a well-known figure at the airport – a small and folksy affair – was familiar with most of the officials who, as he had counted on, allowed him to burst through their line unhindered. Once in Johannesburg, Stu exchanged his gold bars for dollars, which he then used to buy his fish farm plus a refrigerated light plane. He then established a successful fish farm with an airstrip, flying out his fresh fish from his remote Mozambique fastness to their ultimate destination in high-class Johannesburg shops and restaurants. One cannot imagine a British or French farmer even thinking out such an audacious scheme.

Other stories crowd in. Omry Makgoale has been a friend from whom I have learnt much. Like many an ex-MK combatant, he has terrible tales to tell of the beatings and torture he endured in the MK camps. Even after he was released, Omry was endlessly snubbed by the ANC; when other ANC members elected him to represent them, he was never allowed to do so. In Johannesburg, Omry would sometimes meet in the street members of the ANC security department who had been responsible for his maltreatment in the camps. They would greet him and insist on having a drink as old comrades, a rather grisly, almost surreal gathering. Omry knew that although the party's security department was supposed no longer to exist, the ANC had quietly kept it in existence and that his old torturers were still members of it. So he would put a good face on it and agree to join them – but was careful never actually to drink for fear of poisoning. Omry, who has rejoined the ANC, has since campaigned very bravely and with growing impact for reform of the electoral system. Despite all the corruption, there are still some fine people like Omry in the ANC.

Many of the stories depend for their power on the existence of a frontier society. This is a state that South Africa seems unable to escape, making the past seem nearer than it is. Harold Strachan once told me how back in the 1940s he had friends who were game rangers in Mfolozi Game Reserve in Zululand. Mfolozi is the world's most important reserve for white rhinos and also had a fine assortment of buck, giraffes, zebras and so forth, but in those days it had no lions. Two of the rangers decided to visit some of their friends in the Kruger National Park where, around the barbecue, they were asked about life in Mfolozi. They said it was fine – but a pity to have no lions. Their friends immediately volunteered to give them some lion cubs rescued the previous week after their mother had drowned. The cubs, still small, were being bottle-fed with milk. The two rangers happily put them into a cardboard box, which they carried back to Mfolozi in their pick-up truck. They fed the cubs until they were big enough to forage for themselves, when they simply let them loose into the bush. Without telling anyone.

A while later one of the rangers got divorced and remarried. Unable to afford an expensive honeymoon, he suggested to his bride that they live for two weeks in a remote rangers' cottage at the far end of the reserve, a beautiful spot where they would have complete privacy. This she happily accepted. The cottage was a simple Parks Board building, encircled by a stockade and with all the rooms branching off a corridor that ran the whole length of the house. All went well until about three o'clock one morning when they heard a loud crash. They sat up in bed, much surprised but puzzled. It was one of the cubs, now a fully grown lion. It was hungry, could smell humans and their cooking, and had just smashed down the stockade gate with one mighty paw. The door was open and it walked into the house, looking for food.

Naturally the lion first made for the kitchen, which exuded attractive cooking smells. Hence the young couple, sitting up in bed with their bedroom door open, witnessed the surreal sight of a fully grown lion padding down the corridor past their door. The lion, finding nothing to eat in the kitchen, padded into the next room, where it chewed up the ranger's mackintosh because it smelt of him. This provided little sustenance, so next it came into their bedroom to eat them. By this time the ranger was sitting up in bed with his shotgun, loaded with LG (large game) cartridges, and shot the lion through the head. A regular pantomime followed in which the rangers had somehow to explain the presence of full-grown lions in Mfolozi, inventing various stories of how they must have escaped from another reserve, wandered in from elsewhere and so forth.

Someone else from whom I learnt much was Judith Todd in Zimbabwe. She too had funny stories to tell me, but she had also struggled over the years against Ian Smith's UDI and then against Mugabe. What I treasure most is the memory of meeting her father, the former prime minister of Southern Rhodesia, Sir Garfield Todd, a fabled figure for liberals in southern Africa. Todd was one of those rare wholly good men who worked unceasingly for African betterment. His efforts to coax his white electorate into seeing the wisdom of extending the franchise to Africans brought about his downfall, but he never gave up. He was placed under house arrest and was then detained and exiled by Smith. Later he was stripped of his nationality by Mugabe, whom he also came to oppose. Sir Garfield was in his nineties when I met him at Judith's house in Bulawayo, but he was still spry, his wits about him and with a ready smile. After his death, aged 94, Judith gave me an engraved silver cigarette case, a gift to Todd from his grateful constituents in the 1950s. It is a period piece and one of my most precious possessions.

Occasionally, there are moments that seem to sum everything up. I remember as a teenager, though as if it was yesterday, stepping out into the garden of our old verandah house in Durban, the sun warm, the sky blue. All around me were the subtropical blooms of a Durban summer – the yellow and white frangipani, the bright red poinsettia, the purple bougainvillea, the delicate mauve of yesterday, today and tomorrow and the pink hibiscus. Overhead I could hear doves cooing in the trees. The thought came to me very powerfully: this is paradise.

That thought returned to me in 1995 when Breyten Breytenbach, after his long years in exile, came back to South Africa and published *Return to Paradise*. But Breyten had developed strong roots in Europe and kept disappearing back there (he now lives in Spain). And his absences grew longer as his irritation, indeed his indignation, with the ANC grew. His friend Van Zyl Slabbert, observing this, issued a word of warning: 'Hey, Breyten. You know there's only so many times you can return to paradise before the guy on the gate starts asking you about the sins you've committed. It could get embarrassing.' Lovely place, lovely friends, lovely times.

Index